Praise for
Your Million Dollar L

"Every so often a book comes along that you know will add a huge amount of value to the lives of many people. This is that book. All budding entrepreneurs who truly desire to be successful and make money their way—as well as those who are already established business owners and simply want a new and improved way to live a happy and profitable life—have an opportunity before them to learn from one of the best. Buy one copy for yourself and give one as gifts to all the others you care about who have their own value to add to the world."

Bob Burg, author of *Endless Referrals*
and coauthor of *The Go-Giver* and *Go-Givers Sell More*

"Tamara Monosoff is an inspiring dream catcher. Her book, *Your Million Dollar Dream*, is a heart-pounding read for entrepreneurs who want to make money their way. She answers all those nagging questions that might keep us from our destiny. Read it and fly."

Nell Merlino, creator of Take Our Daughters to Work Day,
leader of Make Mine a Million $ Business,
and author of *Stepping Out of Line: Lessons for Women Who Want It
Their Way in Life, in Love, and at Work*

"Get ready to let your dreams take flight! From start to success Tamara Monosoff shares her step-by-step plan to reach Your Million Dollar Dream. Packed with helpful resources and time saving shortcuts, you'll find yourself reaching for this book over and over again. Tamara taught me things I wish I'd known years ago; it would have saved me a lot of time and money."

Jamie Novak, The World's Most Relatable Organizer,
founder of BiteSizeLiving.com,
and author of *Stop Throwing Money Away*
and *The Get Organized Answer Book*

Also by
Tamara Monosoff

Secrets of Millionaire Moms: Learn How They Turned Great Ideas into Booming Businesses

The Mom Inventors Handbook: How to Turn Your Great Idea into the Next Big Thing

The One Page Business Plan for Women in Business (with Jim Horan)

YOUR
MILLION DOLLAR
DREAM

TAMARA
MONOSOFF

Mc
Graw
Hill

New York   Chicago   San Francisco   Lisbon   London   Madrid
Mexico City   Milan   New Delhi   San Juan   Seoul
Singapore   Sydney   Toronto

ISBN: 978-0-07-162943-0
MHID: 0-07-162943-2

McGraw-Hill books are available at special quantity discounts to use as premiums and sales promotions or for use in corporate training programs. To contact a representative, please e-mail us at bulksales@mcgraw-hill.com.

This book is printed on acid-free paper.

To my precious daughters,
Sophia and Kiara

Contents

Acknowledgments

This book is written for you, and I have written it for a reason. Over the past six years, I have been struck by the countless smart, creative, and talented people I have met from every type of background. Again and again, I hear people struggling, questioning, and searching for how to approach their next steps to create better lives for themselves and their families. I've met senior executives of major corporations, mothers who have dedicated years to raising their children and are now ready to reenter the workforce in some way, others who have built their own businesses and are making great efforts to find new ways to grow, and many others who are struggling for survival. Thank you to each of you for sharing your stories; you have touched my heart and were the impetus for writing this book.

There are few words that adequately describe my gratitude, appreciation, and love for my husband, Brad Kofoed, who spent endless hours listening, brainstorming, reading drafts, editing, and supporting this project, as well as sharing the care for our daughters.

I wish to also acknowledge my precious daughters for their patience and willingness to share their mother with the other heartfelt project in the house (this book). Even at their young age, they supported my writing, and I greatly appreciated their sweetness and lively cheers each time I finished a chapter.

Once again, my family has proved to be an unceasing, continuous resource of love and support. My mother and father, Geraldine and Harris Monosoff, continue to be my inspiration and guiding angels. All of my siblings—Scott Monosoff, Dana Dworin, Lance Monosoff, and Tia Monosoff—have instantly stepped forward when I needed them the most, and words fail to describe what they mean to me. I am especially grateful to my brother-in-law Christopher Dworin, whose detailed comments improved every chapter of this book.

My husband's parents, David and Ginny Kofoed, who after 24

years as my in-laws, feel like my parents too, have always made themselves available with their love, support, and frequent child care.

I wish to express my deepest appreciation for my treasured editor, Jennifer Rung, who not only is phenomenal at improving the words of everything she touches but now feels like a member of my family. This is our third book together.

I wish to acknowledge Jessica Faust, my literary agent, for believing in this book from the start and for her ongoing commitment to me and my books.

I am grateful to Francine Kizner, who guided me with her knowledge and expertise in technology and social networks as well as provided outstanding research and information for this book. In addition, she personally coached me as I learned the ins and outs of how to use social networks myself and patiently answered my endless questions.

I wish to express my appreciation for Ann Noder; she is not only an extraordinary public relations expert, but she has become a trusted friend.

Special heartfelt thanks to Jim Horan, founder of the One Page Business Plan Company, for granting me permission to share his business planning method with each of you.

A warm thank you to Bob Burg, author of *Endless Referrals* and coauthor of *The Go-Giver*; Jamie Novak, author of *Stop Throwing Money Away*; Nell Merlino, author of *Stepping Out of Line*; and Jenna McCarthy, author of *The Parent Trip*, for their friendship, feedback, and contributions to this book.

No entrepreneur is successful alone, and I am no exception. I am fortunate to have continuously received guidance and support as I have navigated my way down the winding path of building and growing my own business. It is not possible to list all of those who have offered wise counsel and support through many twists and turns, but I would like to express my gratitude to Helen Harmon, David Zimmerman, Bill and Theresa Armour, Kevin Fisher, Jayne

Spiegelman, Barbara Friedman, Dusty Eber, Enoch Poon, Stuart West, Mike Prozan, Maxine Clark, and Herb Briggs and his talented team.

The week this book was due, my hard drive crashed, and everything on my computer froze. I must thank my tech guy, Dave Hunt, who retrieved every word of this book!

I am grateful for the talented team at McGraw-Hill for their support and belief in the value of this book. I especially want to express my gratitude to Donya Dickerson, Joseph Berkowitz, and Jane Palmieri for their superior editorial guidance.

A Note from the Author

Dear Reader,

In 2005, McGraw-Hill published my first book, *The Mom Inventors Handbook*, based on the many lessons I learned as I launched my first invention, the TP Saver, a product that prevents kids and pets from unraveling the toilet paper. I subsequently licensed, produced, and marketed other inventions from mothers under our trademarked Mom Invented® brand. The response I received exceeded all my expectations. In my second book, *Secrets of Millionaire Moms*, I offered more general business information and a dose of inspiration shared by some of our nation's most successful women in business.

The writing of this book has taken place immediately following an incredibly rewarding joint project with my friend Jim Horan, author and creator of *The One Page Business Plan*, which I will touch on in Chapter 13 on business planning.

As I write this book, we appear to be beginning the long climb out of what has been the worst global economic recession since the Great Depression. I know the fear, and I wear scars left by an economy that turned upside down without regard for those of us who have already paid our toll. While some businesses have not survived this storm, others have learned critical lessons that could not be found in any MBA curriculum or self-help program. If I have learned anything from observing and experiencing the last 24 months, it is that we cannot take anything for granted.

As I wrote this book, two things came to mind. First, the timing of this and the One Page Business Plan project were at once horrid and marvelous. I was writing business books at a time when I was personally facing some of the greatest business challenges of my career. However, I was also focusing on "business planning" and thinking every day about "making money my way" while being in service to others. In fact, I would go so far as to say that my business and I are the first beneficiaries of what is written in this book.

I did not ask for the "opportunity" provided by these economic circumstances—or for the financial wounds I am now licking—but looking at it now, it clearly was just that: an opportunity. No other force could have persuaded me to look so closely at my business and to make such fundamental changes to virtually every aspect of my company over just a few months' time.

As I have continued my dialogue with women and men over the past few years, I have increasingly heard comments about the need to earn money—but with a reluctance to do so within the constraints of what they have done in the past. In many cases, the people I have spoken with would not describe themselves as entrepreneurs, or even "prospective entrepreneurs." That is fine. However, when I have changed the language of our dialogue and spoken about "making money *your* way," they are right there—that language feels right to them.

My goal for this book is to help as many men and women as possible find and create the financial lives that work for them. This will break, or at least rupture, a few firmly held viewpoints and old methods of justifying unsatisfying choices. But this is the road less traveled and, in my view, the one each of us is capable of and deserves.

You are about to change your life. That's awesome. Now since you are taking this stand for yourself, there's one point that I need to make right now before you read any further.

Make no mistake, if the title *Your Million Dollar Dream* gave you the impression that this process would be all about squeezing in a couple hours of work between lattes, yoga, and making bank deposits, I am sorry to say that it isn't.

Your Million Dollar Dream is really about making money *your* way. And making money *your* way is about taking control of your finances in a way that benefits every aspect of your life. This is big. Changing your life in a profound way will require profound effort. But if you're passionate about those efforts, it will feel less like work and more like a calling. This book will provide you with information, exercises, and resources to lead you in this pursuit.

Your Million Dollar Dream is about taking responsibility for your current situation, learning about and committing to your dreams, studying the opportunities before you, and then working to execute a plan.

So there you have it. The process you are about to embark on, or perhaps are in the midst of, will be scintillating, exciting, and fun. At times, it can also be challenging. But the nature of the change you intend to make for the rest of your life is profound, and it is worth it. You will not have a boss to report to, you will set your own schedule, and your income will be dictated not by an annual "performance review" but by your own passion, creativity, and effort.

I have always loved Robert Frost's oft-quoted poem "The Road Not Taken." It is so relevant to the moment and to the choices you will make as you travel through the coming chapters, I encourage you to read and reread the poem, which ends:

> Two roads diverged in the wood, and I—
> I took the one less traveled by,
> And that has made all the difference.

Onward!

Tamara

I continue to be inspired by a poem called "What Is Success?" often attributed to Ralph Waldo Emerson, and I wanted to share it with you.

To laugh often and much;
to win the respect of intelligent
people and the affection of
children;
to earn the appreciation
of honest critics and endure the
betrayal of false friends;
to appreciate beauty;
to find the best in others;
to leave the world a bit better,
whether by a healthy child,
a garden patch or a
redeemed social condition;
to know even one life has
breathed easier
because you have lived.
This is to have succeeded.

Introduction

Your Million Dollar Dream Means Making Money Your Way and Creating Your "Someday" Life Today.

When one door closes another opens; but we so often look so long and so regretfully upon the closed door, that we do not see the ones which open for us.
—*Alexander Graham Bell*

Emily D. is a mother of two who recently made partner at her law firm. Those around her consider her very successful—she makes a six figure income, and she is her family's primary breadwinner. But she dislikes her job and the long hours, and for years has longed to do something creative, on her own terms. Yet she also wonders how she could ever leave such a high-paying position she's worked so hard to achieve. She's making money—but *not* her way.

Daniel R. fell into real estate sales in his early twenties and never left. Though the money was often good, he always felt less than inspired by the job. But since the real estate market has deflated, he's not even reaping the financial rewards he once did, so he's even less enthusiastic about his work. At age 40, however, he thinks it may be too late to start something new. He's still making money—but *not* his way.

Jen D. worked at an ad agency as a graphic designer until her son was born five years ago. She wanted to stay home with him, but she also wanted to continue making money. So she started a line of custom cards and stationery, selling them online. Although she's had opportunities to expand, she turned them down, because she knew it would mean going from part-time to full-time work—taking time away from her son. Jen's making money—and she's doing it *her* way.

You picked up this book, which leads me to believe you must be thinking about ways in which you can make money—on your own terms. Perhaps you're a professional looking for a new direction, or you've been recently laid off; a worker who needs more income or a flexible schedule; a stay-at-home mom who wants to help support her family by making extra income; or a college student looking for a way to pay back school loans after graduation. Or you may be in circumstances similar to Emily D.'s or Daniel R.'s: you are "successful" but unfulfilled. It doesn't really matter where you are or where you've been. What matters is where you want to go and how you'll go about getting there.

Fortunately, the timing for this book has never been better—yes, even when the economy is less than stellar. That's because in the past 10 years, there has been a movement away from the traditional idea of a "career" and toward work that supports our lives as a complement to—not in toleration of—our families and our desired lifestyles. Many post–World War II and baby boom workers stayed in one career, and even at one company, for most of their lives. Today's work patterns have shifted and continue to shift.

Many factors have contributed to that shift: the change in traditional family structure from one-parent incomes to two-parent incomes through the eighties and nineties; the recent trend of mothers "off-ramping" to take care of young kids; and dads wanting more time for family life. Part of the shift results from the elimination of job security, pensions, and lifetime health benefits for both white collar and blue collar workers.

These factors have created a fertile landscape for a new way of thinking about work, making money, and what we want out of life. It's opened up the possibilities for people to start making money *their* way. For some, it's about making a lot of money; for others, it's about having more time. For still others, it's about embracing a completely new field or industry they've always dreamed about; using the skills they've already developed in a new, more meaningful way; or fulfilling a desire to "give back." Regardless of one's primary motivation, for most it's about gaining a newfound sense of freedom, flexibility, creativity, and self-reliance that many people crave but haven't known how to achieve.

Some of us have stepped out of the rat race in search of "balance" but find ourselves at a crossroads, trying to figure out what we want to do next in our lives, knowing that we ache to find the right fit yet struggling to know how to start the new journey.

At the same time, others of us are striving to make money as fast as possible, often in jobs in which we are unhappy, in an effort to create comfort and satisfaction in our lives. But satisfaction remains out of reach. That is because there is something we miss in this approach. We can't really recognize what would bring satisfaction without pausing long enough to listen. Instead, we tend to just go even faster in the same job and say to ourselves, "A dream is nice, but I don't have time to dream—I have a mortgage to pay." So we simply concede that this is as good as it can get for us, finding ways to switch off.

I have experienced both circumstances. However, I have learned that taking enough time to explore, learn, and plan are going to provide you with a new foundation from which to start and to thrive. In essence, I am asking you to suspend the rationale you have used in the past and take that time now.

This book provides the path to get you where you want to go, no matter what your specific goals or desires—so you can start making money *your* way. It will help you choose or create work that is satisfying and that supports what you want to achieve in your life. Success will look different for every person. You might want to make millions by building a business you can pass on for generations. You may want to create a business that brings in the same income you're making right now. Or, you may want to create side work that will make you an extra $20,000 per year, doing something you love. There are countless variations, but all of them will lead to one result: making money your way.

No matter what your goals, entrepreneurship is the key to getting there—that's why, ultimately, this is a book about entrepreneurship. It will help match your individual personality, skills, goals, dreams, and even risk tolerance to the exact *right* kind of business for you. And no matter what that ultimately turns out to be, this book will offer detailed information, support, inspiration, and concrete opportunities so you can breathe power into your ideas, take action, and create what is truly possible, right now: the life you have long dreamt about having and the ability to make money your way.

THE TIME IS NOW: TODAY IS YOUR "SOMEDAY"
How many times have you said or thought that "someday" you'd do this, or someday you'd become that? Now's the time to start down the path to fulfilling your future as an entrepreneur. This book is all about turning "someday" into "today."

Of course, starting a business—with all the risk that entails—is easier said than done, right? Yes, and no. If you've been plagued by doubt—or just uncertainty as to what path you want to take—this book will shift your thinking, no matter what's transpired in your life, financially or emotionally. You will have to give up the viewpoint that there is something wrong with you or your life and discover how the ups and downs and turmoil you've faced may contain hidden gifts. If, for example, you've already been scraping by financially for many months or even years, you actually may be better equipped to handle these rough economic times than many others who have been taken by surprise. If you suddenly find yourself facing financial challenges you've never imagined, take heart. Recognize that you now actually have more control over your future than you ever had before.

To do this and move forward to build a plan to make money *your* way, it is essential to recognize that your power and creativity are based solely on the "now." Instead of focusing on what you've lost, focus on what you've gained—a chance to build a new life. But to make "someday" today, you must take focused action.

This requires information. In other words, it's time to gain as much knowledge as possible. If you are interested in being an entrepreneur and you know exactly what type of business attracts you the most, learn all that you can about that topic. Or, if you are grappling for direction and haven't yet found clarity, then it's time to explore, search, and investigate different options until you find one that feels right for you. This book will help you do that. It will provide you with the pathway and will open up the doors to new thinking—and to new opportunities. The more you uncover and discover, the more choices will become available, and the more you'll be able to take focused action to start making money *your* way.

Turning "someday" into "today" can be relevant for any aspect of your life: your relationship with your partner or your kids, the pursuit of your art, education, or a new job. However, this book is about entrepreneurship, and I will focus the balance of this book on making your million dollar dream come true through becoming an entrepreneur. What's magical about pursuing this route is that many of the other aspects of your life—like those mentioned above—subsequently fall into place as a result!

In the first chapter, you will discover the three most common options most entrepreneurs take when starting a business. To help you narrow your options so you can begin pursuing your ultimate focus, Chapter 2 will help you understand the role your personality plays in your entrepreneurial choices and then help you formulate and commit to your dream. In Chapter 3, we'll delve into the nitty-gritty, so you can make an honest assessment of your current financial picture and establish a foundation for achieving your next steps. Chapter 4 provides many valuable resources for getting the money you need to start turning your dream into a reality.

In Chapter 5, I will share the importance of marketing, and Chapters 6 and 7 cover sales strategies and how to bring people to you through the power of the Internet. In Chapter 8, we'll delve further into the awesome possibilities of the Internet, including innovative Internet marketing strategies and how they can help you achieve sales.

In Chapters 9, 10, and 11, you'll learn how social networks like Facebook and Twitter have revolutionized communications and marketing—and how they are absolutely critical to today's business success. And finally, in Chapters 12 and 13, we'll get into the nuts and bolts of running your business, from incorporating social consciousness and efficiency into your strategies to the practical task of building and writing your business plan. I share all these topics so you can begin rethinking and redesigning your future with valuable tools and resources that help you every step of the way.

By deciding that "today" is "someday," you are joining an elite group of people who have created extraordinary lives and in many cases also found ways to give to others. For an entrepreneur, anything is possible. Your creativity can flourish with results that go beyond your dreams. So let's get started!

PART 1

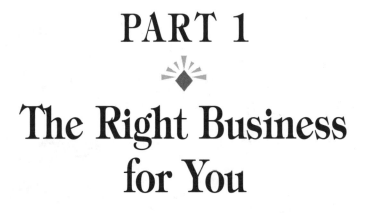

The Right Business for You

What Business Fits *Your* Million Dollar Dream?

Money will come when you are doing the right thing.
—Mike Phillips

Before you take on any project—whether it's renovating your home, planning a family vacation, or making a big purchase—a key first step is exploration. What's out there? What are your options? What are the latest and greatest ideas? By exploring the choices, you open your mind and heart to exciting possibilities you may have never considered.

This is especially true when you're starting a business. There is no single path, and you can change your life right now. You have complete freedom to choose what you want to do, how hard you want to work, and how much money you want to make, which can be liberating and daunting at the very same time.

If you have already determined exactly what that path is and the type of business you wish to launch, great! Use the information in this chapter to gain insights into how you might adapt your approach to your business, customers, and employees.

However, if you like the idea of choosing your future but have not come up with a path that fits, then you are at the right place. The focus of this chapter is to help those whose direction is not yet clear. If that's your situation, you will want to engage deeply with the materials in this chapter and with the associated resources and exercises, which will help get your creative thoughts and ideas percolating and get you on the path to reaching your ultimate goal.

This section is intended to get your mental wheels turning and your inspiration firing by offering you insights on identifying the business that works best for you and how to approach it in a way that maximizes the likelihood of success.

THE THREE ENTREPRENEURIAL APPROACHES

You've probably never thought about it before—I know I hadn't when I first started my business—but there are three distinct approaches to choosing a new business. While there are variations that may incorporate more than one of these in combination, here are the three general routes most entrepreneurs take when starting up a business:

1. Do what you know.
2. Do what others do.
3. Solve a problem.

Let's start with a detailed understanding of each approach, explore some pros and cons of each, and then look at examples of how each type of approach can lead to fulfilling, successful businesses.

THE FIRST APPROACH TO ENTREPRENEURSHIP:
DO WHAT YOU KNOW

Maybe you've worked in a particular industry for another company, and you have acquired skills and knowledge over time in that industry. Perhaps you grew up learning a specific skill from your family. Or maybe you've devoted time and energy to a hobby that could become a profitable business. If so, starting your own company in the same field may make sense. For instance, a bartender or waitress may decide to open a restaurant; a woodworking hobbyist may become a full-time carpenter; a staff graphic designer may start his own Web design company; or a corporate accountant may open her own firm. All these are examples of doing what you know in order to make money your way.

Of course, there are pros and cons to every approach.

"Do What You Know" Snapshot: Dooce

Heather B. Armstrong, a graphic designer, was working full time when she started her blog/Web site, Dooce.com, in 2001 on the side. In the early days of blogging, Heather established herself by writing a personal and irreverent chronicle of her life. She documented life as a single woman in Los Angeles, getting married and having children in Utah, and everything in between, gaining a huge following along the way. Her hobby eventually turned into a full-time job that generated advertising, and today the site and her business support her whole family (her husband quit his job to be a stay-at-home dad). She's also written two books.

DO WHAT YOU KNOW: THE PROS
Your Risk Is Lower
The advantage of starting a business based on the experience you've attained, whether working for someone else or on the side as a hobby, is that you already possess the knowledge you need to move forward. Unlike starting a business in a brand-new industry (a teacher who wants to open a gift shop or a lawyer who decides to open a bed and breakfast), you are essentially selling the skills, expertise, and knowledge you've already developed. Of the three approaches discussed in this chapter, this is likely the fastest way to start a business. And since

you already possess the knowledge, the venture is less risky; you are not starting from square one, and you know the nuances of both your skill set and the industry in general.

The risks in this approach, although somewhat minimized, lay in the specific areas of the business you have not had to deal with when working for someone else. That could include any area outside your specific area of expertise. If you were in sales, bookkeeping may be new. If you were in production, sales and finance may be areas you will need to learn. The best way to mitigate these risks is to identify and acknowledge them immediately and compensate for them in your business planning process. You may hire qualified people, get training in these areas, or adapt your model to better fit your strengths.

You Can Leverage Your Existing Clientele

We all know the power of the Rolodex (or your BlackBerry's contact list)! Having an existing network of contacts and clients—people with whom you've already cultivated strong relationships—can give you the leading edge you need to launch powerfully into business. If you have created strong bonds and worked to build trust with your clients, it is likely that they will follow you when you create your own venture.

"Do What You Know" Snapshot: Saybr Contractors

Karen Say started working in the construction industry as a receptionist at age 19. By the age of 29, after having been exposed to every aspect of the construction business, she founded her own construction company, Saybr Contractors, Inc. (www.saybr.com). Now 12 years old, Saybr is the first public-private natural gas fueling facility at Seattle-Tacoma Airport, with revenues of over $25 million!

Your Learning Curve Is Short

There are still things you will need to learn quickly if you take this approach to being an entrepreneur. You may need to learn to set up a business structure and build or sell your products or services, but you will be doing so with an enormous advantage: your knowledge of the industry. That knowledge affords you a significant time and learning advantage. With other approaches, entrepreneurs start out with a lot more to learn and a much greater degree of uncertainty.

"Do What You Know" Snapshot: Sweet Sally's Bakeshop

Sometimes what seems like a worst-case scenario pushes us to confront and pursue our dreams. When Lehman Brothers went bankrupt in its much-publicized collapse, Sally Saltzbart Minier, the vice president of dining services there, suddenly found herself unemployed. She had been responsible for keeping 27,000 employees fed at Lehman locations throughout the world. Now she decided to venture out on her own and put her skills to work. With all her experience—and recipes passed down from her Jewish mother and grandmother—she launched her own bakery, Sweet Sally's Bakeshop (www.sweetsallys.com). Until that point, she said, she had always been afraid to take that leap.

You Understand the Challenges of the Industry

If you're a copywriter for an advertising agency who wants to start freelancing or a sales representative for a medical company who plans to start up a distributorship, you already understand the industry and the challenges that are associated with it. This gives you an enormous advantage over the entrepreneur who starts without any industry knowledge and who might require years to gain it, often by "learning the hard way," figuring things out, and making mistakes. How many failed restaurants were started by individuals who thought that since they ate out often, they knew enough to open and run a restaurant?

"Do What You Know" Snapshot:
Pitch Public Relations

Ann Noder, CEO of Pitch Public Relations (www.pitchpublicrela
tions.com), represents another terrific example of "doing what you
know." After working as a television news anchor, Ann decided to
move to the other side of the camera. She went to work for a PR firm
pitching client stories to the news media. She climbed the ladder
quickly to become president of a 25-person, rapidly growing PR firm.
At some point she realized that she could go out on her own and call
her own shots. Her ramp-up time was measured in days, rather than
the typical months or years many entrepreneurs experience.

DO WHAT YOU KNOW: THE CONS
It May Not Excite You
One business colleague recently shared with me his feelings about working in his industry. "Stay out of the corporate world!" he told me. "I would
rather mow lawns five days a week if I could earn the same money."

If you've been working in the same industry for the past 10 years,
you may want out because you're bored or you want to try something
new. Perhaps you crave entrepreneurship because it will give you a
chance to do something entirely different from what you're doing now.
Clearly, then, doing what you know may not be the right approach for
you. If you're a staff mental health counselor who's burned out, for
example, starting a private practice may not change things enough. If,
however, you love the work or field but not the circumstances (e.g.,
low pay, having a boss, the work hours, the commute, poor working
conditions, or challenging office politics), the reverse may be true.

You May Not End Up Doing What You Love
No matter what your knowledge or skill set, becoming an entrepreneur
may actually take time away from what you ultimately feel passionate

about. For example, if you're a top pastry chef at a large hotel and you love making pastries, starting your own bakery will inevitably take time away from the part you love—the baking. You will need to spend a tremendous percentage of your time marketing, managing people, dealing with finances, doing paperwork, and making sales. In other words, you may end up doing "business" rather than what you love best. On the other hand, if you go into it with this knowledge ahead of time, you have the opportunity to structure the business in a way that supports what you want and love to do; you can temper the issue by hiring people to do the tasks that you like least or that you're least equipped to perform. If you don't like sales and accounting, for instance, then hire a commissioned salesperson and outsource an accountant. Many of these issues can be overcome with careful business planning (see Chapter 13).

"Do What You Know" Snapshot: Innovation Protocol

When Sasha Strauss, who worked in developing brand strategy at corporate firms, found his evenings and weekends inundated with freelance branding projects, he knew it was time to launch his own company. To remain part of the creative process, he structured the company uniquely: instead of making himself the head of the company, he decided to treat himself as more of an employee, fostering a collaborative approach with his 15+ person firm. The focus is on getting results, building creative and memorable strategies, and creating top-quality brands. His firm, Innovation Protocol (innovationprotocol. com), has since worked for clients such as Johnson & Johnson and Sanrio.

THE SECOND APPROACH TO ENTREPRENEURSHIP: DO WHAT OTHERS DO

Experience isn't always necessary to build a business, and this second approach to entrepreneurship enables you to move forward in entirely new directions—directions that are supported by research and analysis of the market. With the "do what others do" approach, you'll research the marketplace (or rely on current research), analyze your opportunity, and move forward with the "right" business for you, your marketplace, and your potential customers.

In the first approach, risk was reduced by "doing what you know." This section presumes that your desire is to do something completely new to you. When entering a brand-new field, risk is a major issue to consider. For this reason and others, research is even more critical to this approach. First, you will want to be certain that the reality of your new endeavor will match your perception of what the business is like. Second, the better you analyze opportunities, the more you will be able to recognize and avoid the risk factors.

"Do What Others Do" Snapshot: Saturday Morning Success, Inc.

Kristi Frank had a background in real estate and went from being fired in the first season of Donald Trump's *The Apprentice* to being inspired in her personal and professional life. Later, as a new mom, she became active online and soon grew intrigued by the power of online marketing. She saw what other online marketers were able to achieve. She attended conference after conference to learn the trade. She began to understand how to build online marketing lists and put what she was learning to the test. Finally, she launched her own Web site, www.saturdaymorningsuccess .com. Today, just two years later, she can be seen as a regular panelist and speaker at online marketing conferences.

Not only will it be important to understand the available market you wish to serve but also any necessary training, certifications, and other things you will need to address.

As you can see, this area is vast. Many of these businesses will fall under the following categories, with some examples of each:

- Consultancies (computer, software, business)
- Agencies (independent insurance, distributorships and manufacturers representatives, real estate brokerages)
- Independent tradespeople (plumbers, heating and AC companies, painters, repair people)
- Hospitality (restaurant, hotel/motel, entertainment)
- Self-employed professionals (accountants, attorneys, freelance journalists)
- Network marketing (health supplements, lotions, kitchen gadgets, telephone systems, pet products, jewelry, cosmetics)
- Franchises (all of the above)

As you explore, choose the opportunity carefully, and make sure that you connect with the culture of that industry.

DO WHAT OTHERS DO: THE PROS

First, you will want to determine, with a considerable degree of confidence, if there is a market for your business. There already may be a solid amount of data enabling you to question and validate the market for the business. Second, the availability of training and certifications for virtually any subject through local community colleges, vocational programs, online programs, and various government and nonprofit organizations has never been better. Third, you can choose something that both feels right to you and meets your initial investment capabilities. Fourth, you are your own boss—you can use your own creativity and work ethic to build exactly the type of business with the type of culture you want.

DO WHAT OTHERS DO: THE CONS

These can be very competitive businesses. Because the existing market is so apparent, many people are trying to serve it. For example, think of the dozens of restaurants competing for diners. There is a dry cleaner in practically every strip mall, and almost everyone has a friend who is in real estate.

Differentiating yourself from others can be difficult and expensive. You will need to find ways through the quality of your service, pricing, and branding to address these challenges. Finally, depending on the nature of your business, creating the infrastructure and tools can be costly. Software programs for billing, reservations, customer management, telephone systems, inventory tracking, vehicles, and design are only a few of the potential challenges for a new company.

Think Creatively to Differentiate Yourself

At its core, this approach definitely relies on research and analysis of the marketplace to uncover opportunity. But there's no reason it can't also fulfill your personal interests or passions. Unlike the first approach, "Doing What You Know," this second approach really enables you to consider a world of options and to do something related to what you've always dreamed of doing. So what is it that you love? When you're working your day job, what work do you daydream about? Do you have a knack for cars (auto business)? Are you devoted to art (interior design business)? Do you love computers (tech support company)? Do you have a passion for animals (pet care business)? Do you love to cook (catering)? Tapping into that thing that you already love—the thing you talk to your friends about, dedicate your weekends to, or spend time thinking about—is a good place to begin researching new opportunities.

If you think you want to pursue this path but are not certain what you want to do or are frustrated because nothing seems to grab you, find a comfortable chair, get a flip chart or notepad, and start brainstorming!

First, write down the work or skills in which you have competence, even if you've never been paid. For example, are you organized, communicative, a good writer, good with math, computer savvy, etc.?

Write down businesses you have seen that are interesting to you. If you need a jump start, grab the yellow pages, open coupon mailers, read the classified ads in the back of business publications, visit online school programs for possible curriculum and certification programs, and look at franchise directories (such as the one suggested in the next section).

Each time you see something that seems interesting, add it to your list.

After you have come up with a good list, take time to think about your strengths, challenges, and preferences. Consider what you have already learned about your personality. Are you extroverted, or do you prefer to work alone? Are you comfortable with technology? Are you mobile, or do you prefer to stay in an office?

Now match these personal preferences and attributes with your initial list of business types that interest you. Circle the top three that feel the most "right" to you at this moment.

"Do What Others Do" Snapshot: Seattle Chocolates

Jean Thompson was a former Microsoft employee and a mother of two when she took over the helm of a chocolate company in which she had been a silent investor. While she knew she loved fine chocolate, she confesses to having started with virtually no knowledge of financial statements. Despite this initial lack of necessary skills, she helped Seattle Chocolates (www.seattlechocolates.com) to become one of the nation's top-selling premium chocolates.

DO WHAT OTHERS DO: POINTS TO CONSIDER

Franchises

When you're choosing a business based on research and data, buying a franchise can be an advantageous approach. First, a definition: a franchise is a company you buy into that offers a predesigned system for business. You commonly get to use the company's trademarked brands and other proprietary materials, and you benefit from its marketing programs, systems of doing business, and ongoing support. In return for all these systems and expertise, you usually pay an initial franchise fee followed by ongoing royalties to the franchisor. Franchisors are licensed and regulated, so there's some degree of oversight as to how they do business.

There are additional reasons to look into franchising. First, by looking into the various franchises available (and there are thousands), you can get many ideas for businesses in proven markets, whether you choose to do it on your own or buy into a franchise. Second, while a franchise business has its own set of cons, by opening a franchise, you will instantly overcome many of these challenges. For instance, anyone could open his or her own housekeeping service. However, they would do so without the benefit of an established brand, pricing, or any ready-made marketing materials. On the other hand, by buying and opening a Merry Maids franchise, you can present the impression of being part of a large, well-established, and trusted business, which could be important for a service that involves strangers roaming around customers' homes.

CONSIDERING A FRANCHISE

Obvious examples of franchises are companies like McDonald's and Subway, but there are many lesser-known franchises in countless product or service areas that may interest you. These include everything from cleaning services to staffing firms to retail stores. You'll also find franchises in hundreds of other categories, including health care, construction, maintenance, and tutoring.

For a list of franchise categories, visit the International Franchise Association site at franchise.org/franchisecategories.aspx.

There are franchises you can start from home too. One note of caution: many home-based "business opportunities" may sound like franchises, but are actually network marketing companies. There are a number of ways to tell the difference. Having been presented with many of these "opportunities" myself, the most obvious hint to me is that, after listening to a pitch for a fair amount of time, I have heard more about the "opportunity" to make money—and how others have made money—than I have about the product or service itself. You see, the success of people in network marketing businesses is generally dependent on getting other people to buy an "opportunity" from you to sell the "opportunity to sell" to others, and so on. The surest way to confirm you are discussing a franchise opportunity versus a network marketing "opportunity" is by simply asking to see the FDD (Franchise Disclosure Document, formerly known as the UFOC). If they don't have one, it is not a franchise. Note: a network marketing opportunity may also work for you as long as you know that that is what you are getting.

"Do What Others Do" Snapshot: Fetch! Pet Care Franchisee Kelly Strowd

After 10 years in law enforcement, Kelly Strowd was burned out. One day her curiosity was piqued by a magazine article about the pet-sitting industry. An animal lover with five dachshunds of her own, Strowd thought a pet-sitting business sounded great—but risky. That's why when she opened her first Fetch! Pet Care franchise (www.fetchpetcare.com) in Chapel Hill, North Carolina, she kept her day job as a detective, working nights and weekends with a team of six pet-sitters. But soon demand increased, and her team grew to 48. She purchased two more territories, which allowed her to approach the business full-time. Although she's in a totally new field, she does use the skills she learned as a detective to hire people her clients can trust with their pets and homes. Clearly, it's working: she had sales of $225,000 in 2008 after just two years in business.

STARTING A FRANCHISE: THE PROS

It's All Been Figured Out

Instead of starting your business from scratch, opening a franchise allows you to look at many existing models in other territories, and to see precisely the risks and rewards. One of the strongest advantages that a franchise offers is an established business model and training. As I have alluded to earlier in this chapter, creating a brand that consumers know, trust, and recognize is an uphill, expensive task. Therefore, starting with a well-known brand can be a major advantage when starting a business; for example, compare starting your own ice cream shop to opening a Ben & Jerry's franchise. Most people recognize and think favorably of Ben & Jerry's based on years of branding, retailing, and advertising, so the moment you hang your shingle you'll have loyal customers who already know which of your flavors they love. Compare this to years of marketing and building a business for a new, more unfamiliar venture.

Your Competition Is Controlled

With franchises, another advantage is that competition within your franchise is controlled (in theory). It's in the best interest of the franchise owners to help you succeed. For this reason, the corporate office will often limit the number of branches in each territory so that you are not competing directly with another franchisee. Their growth will be greater by having one successful franchisee in a territory than by having two struggling franchisees in the same territory. It should be mentioned that this is worth careful analysis when considering a particular franchise.

The Business Model Is Proven

Part of the challenge of starting your own business is establishing not only your brand but your method of doing business. For example, if you're selling jewelry, you need to decide whether you'll sell to retailers or directly to consumers; whether you'll sell via the Web, open a store, or work through other existing sales channels; and how you'll handle additional issues such as pricing, distribution, marketing, and fulfillment. Plus, before selling you a franchise, the franchisor will typically do market research to ensure your area has sufficient demand for its product/service. The franchisor will offer ongoing support including national/regional advertising, which can drive more customers to your business. You also get resources from the franchisor for your own local marketing campaigns.

In addition, for many businesses, technology is important. Often franchisors will provide a custom software package specially designed to support the nuances of the business. This alone could make the difference between success or failure. With franchises, you get all of this in a model that's already been proven in other markets. That means much of the work and many of the decisions that can feel overwhelming on your own have already been researched, tested, and proven elsewhere.

STARTING A FRANCHISE: THE CONS
It Can Be Costly
Buying a franchise can be a daunting experience. The barriers to entry tend to be high, with buy-ins ranging from several thousand dollars to more than a hundred thousand dollars. The up-front capital costs will vary depending on the franchise you choose, but expect to invest money at the outset to purchase the rights to become part of just about any franchise. While you'd need to invest money in any start-up, if you go it alone, there is the option to grow organically and at your own financial pace. When it's a franchise, there are set fees, up-front investments, and capital reserve requirements you are obligated to meet right away.

Your Turf May Be Limited
When you buy into a franchise, you are generally given an existing territory in which to operate and market your product or services. You can't reach out beyond your defined territory (other than by buying additional franchises, if allowed), even if you see a great opportunity. This can be very frustrating.

It is important to have a clear understanding of the extent of your territory, the rules of competition between fellow franchisees, and your franchisor's level of commitment to limiting the number of potential new franchisees in or near your territory.

The Rules of Engagement Are Firm

With franchises, the rules are the rules, and there is little flexibility within the franchise structure. The franchisor has established a model for success and does not want you to change the formula. Therefore, creativity is often discouraged or even forbidden. Even if you have great ideas and an ability to see new opportunities, the franchisor is invested in building the brand their way, and they will not encourage individuality. If you view entrepreneurship as a way to set free your creativity in how you do things, where you do them, and how much money you can make, a franchise may not be right for you. Likewise, if you find that you like a particular market and a particular business model but don't like the constraints of a franchise, you can always open a business in the same industry that competes with a franchise. You will have some initial disadvantages, which are outlined above, but you will also have some advantages, including flexibility in your approach, unlimited territory, and freedom from fees or commissions to the franchisor.

Your Income May Be Limited

In some cases there is a cap on how much money a single franchise can earn within a limited territory. Make sure that you know the full extent of your revenue potential (and any potential cap) before you invest in a franchise. You'll want to make sure that the financial cap is consistent with the money you expect to make and that that number fits with your personal financial goals. For more information, interview current and past owners of the particular franchise that interests you.

There's Competition at Your Back

Franchises often grow within competitive fields and new, hotter franchises can come along to compete with you. With limited flexibility to be creative due to franchise rules, dealing with outside competition can be challenging, unless, of course, you *are* the "new competition."

BUYER BEWARE

If you're researching and considering buying a particular franchise, there are some warning signs to look for. Not every company presenting itself as a franchisor is legitimate, honest, or as successful as they'd like you to think. The following are red flags you should look out for when dealing with franchisors:

- Reluctance to give names of current franchisees
- Promises you'll get rich quick with a limited investment
- Request for deposits to "hold" a franchise unit
- A pushiness to close the deal quickly
- A lack of clarity when answering questions
- As in any business situation, be cautious before you commit to any agreement!

HOW TO FIND A FRANCHISE THAT FITS

Buying a franchise requires lots of research. First, you'll want to choose a brand you feel good about and an industry that fits with your interests and personality (there are at least 80 industries, so chances are good there's a field you'll be drawn to). It doesn't need to be a big franchise to be worthwhile, and there are many options that enable even cash-strapped entrepreneurs to enter the marketplace.

A good place to start researching all franchise opportunities is the International Franchise Association (www.franchise.org). Other independent franchise lists are available on sites like Entrepreneur.com (www.entrepreneur.com/franchises/franchise500/index.html),

Franchise Direct (www.franchisedirect.com), Franchise.com (www.franchise.com), or Franchise Gator (www.franchisegator.com).

Once you've targeted your options, more research is crucial, from reading the FDD (franchise disclosure document) to brushing up on your business basics so you can manage your new venture properly. Look for a franchise that offers substantial training so you're comfortable from day one, and make sure you'll get the support you need from the franchisor, whether it's setting up your store, training your first-time staff, or having the proper tools to manage your finances. It's also a good idea to contact current franchisees and those who have recently left the system to learn about their experiences.

QUESTIONS TO HELP EVALUATE IF A FRANCHISE IS A GOOD FIT FOR YOU

Note that once you get deeper into the process, franchisors will also be interviewing you. Most likely you will meet personally with a franchise representative, at which time you'll both have the opportunity to evaluate the facts and determine if it's the right fit on both sides. This could take anywhere from a few hours to a full day, and you may wish to have an attorney present to help you. Be sure to ask as many questions as possible so you are aware of all the details involved. Also, do not feel intimidated; few people have an innate understanding of the franchise process. Here are some questions you may want to ask your potential franchisor:

- What are the pretax net profits of existing operations?
- What is included in the training process, store design, site selection, and/or facility construction?
- What type of working capital is required after the initial fee and investment?
- What is the typical financial performance of a franchise?
- What is the market for reselling successful franchises?

- What are the territorial restrictions and protections?
- What is the primary competition?
- What are the company's expansion plans in your region and elsewhere?
- What type of business and marketing support is offered once the franchise is off the ground and open for business?
- Have any franchises failed or gone bankrupt?
- How will potential disputes be settled?

Also, be sure to ask for a current list of franchisees, and then visit or talk to as many franchise owners as you can. Ask about their typical day, current challenges, their working relationship with the franchise company, sales patterns, and if the experience has met their expectations (and if not, why). Talking to current franchise owners will give you a picture that goes beyond economics; it will provide a view into the day-to-day lifestyle and responsibilities the business entails, so you know if it will fit your goals and your expectations.

THE THIRD APPROACH TO ENTREPRENEURSHIP: SOLVE A PROBLEM

Life is either a daring adventure or nothing.
—Helen Keller

It's something you probably say to yourself regularly: "If only a product or service existed that would solve problem X." Usually this type of thought comes naturally within the course of a day—while you're cooking, cleaning, driving, taking care of the kids, golfing. Whatever your activity, opportunities to solve challenges regularly present themselves. If you're creative, you probably come up with new ideas frequently.

The third approach to entrepreneurship taps into this type of creativity, which aims to identify a problem and solve it. What could be improved or made more efficient? What is missing from the marketplace that could make life easier/better/more convenient? While the solution could be a product invention or a variation of an existing product, it might also be a service that could improve peoples' lives or address a specific need. In some cases, the "solution" is actually creating a new market. Even so, whether consumers were asking for it or not, a need exists and the solution gains demand.

This approach can represent both the greatest monetary risk and the greatest potential for creative and financial reward. Even if you have knowledge related to a new venture, because it is truly novel there are simply many unknowns. And, unlike the second approach, there is no proven market, so your sales forecasts are hypothetical, or, as an investor once said to me, "pure fiction."

The "solve a problem" approach requires the highest learning curve and can require significant investment. Also, it is not uncommon for powerful competitors to enter your space just as you begin to gain momentum.

Because the minority of people who attempt this approach overcome these barriers and achieve success, the rewards can be extraordinary. If successful, you can earn hundreds of thousands of dollars—perhaps millions. And these are the kinds of companies that can be sold to larger corporations for sizable sums. Further, there are few things more satisfying and fun than to see something you have conceived all the way through to fruition.

When it comes to this approach, I can speak from personal experience: I created my business in response to a market need I observed and then met. It began when my toddler-age daughter found great entertainment unraveling the roll of family toilet paper. Cute, yes— until she clogged the toilet. When I went to the store to purchase the gadget that would prevent this, it didn't exist, and there came my inspiration. I reached out to other parents to find out if this was a challenge for them too, and when I found out it was, I went through the process of inventing and launching the TP Saver® into the marketplace. Seven years later, it is being sold through retailers across the country.

Throughout the invention process, I met many people along the way who helped me, and I realized that after going through the process I was in a position to help others. That's when I conceived of my first business, Mom Inventors, Inc. Today, the company helps other moms bring their products to market by offering them information and support—and by licensing, manufacturing, distributing, and selling products invented by moms under my internationally trademarked Mom Invented® brand.

"Solving a Problem" Snapshot: Shutterfly®

If you have ever stored photos online, you have probably used a service like Shutterfly (www.shutterfly.com). Today Shutterfly is a publicly traded company with a market value that is near that of Kodak. What you may not know is that in 1999, Jayne Spiegelman, a former retail executive and mother, came up with an idea for using the Internet to create and store photo albums. She launched Shutterfly and grew it to a point where it went public in a $350 million offering in 2006.

SOLVE A PROBLEM: THE PROS
The Creativity Is Boundless
When you create a business that fills an existing gap in the marketplace, being creative is not just possible, it's essential. It is completely up to you to open up your creative channels and to take chances experimenting with your ideas. It requires a willingness to explore your options, read everything, look at the examples of others, and then

allow yourself to put your own twist on things. It relies heavily on trusting your intuition.

You May Have Little or No Competition

When you find a clear market opening, there may be little or no competition, at least in the beginning. This is an incredible opportunity to create a new space in the market. If your idea is a good one, competition will eventually come on your heels, but you will already have paved the way and still have the opportunity to lead or to sell your business to those who want to enter the market.

> ## "Solve a Problem" Snapshot: Young Chefs Academy
>
> Julie Fabing Burleson and Suzy Vinson Nettles had a strong desire to run their own business and had made several attempts before coming up with the idea for Young Chefs Academy (www.youngchefsacademy.com). Inspired by Burleson's four-year-old, who was trying to help in the kitchen with a catering project, they finally found a business that fit them perfectly: both loved to cook, and Nettles had 10 years of teaching experience. Today, Young Chefs Academy teaches cooking to kids ages 4 to 14 through classes, camps, and birthday parties. The classes teach kids kitchen safety, etiquette, table setting, and more. Although they began by offering only weekend classes, they quickly expanded, then began franchising a year later. By mid-2009, more than 50 Young Chefs Academy franchises had opened across the United States.

You Have No Rulebook

The best part of creating a business from scratch in a clear market space is that there is no prescribed corporate structure, process, or requirements. You make it up as you go. Although it can be a daunting task at times to create the system, at least it is your system, and you have complete freedom and flexibility to make the necessary adjustments as you move forward.

SOLVE A PROBLEM: THE CONS

You Have No Rulebook

It's both a pro and a con. You have to make up the rules as you go along, and you may travel down many blind alleys before you find the rules that lead to your success.

ADAPT OTHERS' EXAMPLES TO CREATE SOMETHING NEW

There are few models to emulate when you are creating something new. Yet research is still critical in the quest for success. Even if the businesses you're learning about don't do exactly what you are planning to do, see if there are aspects of those businesses that make sense to emulate. For example, I know of an entrepreneur who started a combination launderette/Internet café in a college town. While this combo did not exist in her market, she was able to research the two halves of it by looking at existing, stand-alone launderettes and coffee shops. This approach requires a willingness to observe others, use what you can, work hard, and make up the rest. It is also important to read, listen, and learn about business models that are not working, so that you can avoid pitfalls without having to actually experience the failure yourself.

Your Risk Is High and Unknown

Not only don't you have a rulebook, you don't have a road map either. Creating a brand-new product or service is not like buying a franchise, where a clear path and a support system are provided. Instead, you are on your own. You must rely on your own vision of the gap in the market and create the business out of thin air. There is no "right" way to do it. It's nice to have this freedom; however, the risks of failure are high. No matter how much you research the space and how hard you work, you are venturing into uncharted territory. You will earn the respect of some, but the passion and belief in your vision will need to come from you, especially when things don't go as you had planned.

You Have a Large Learning Curve

> *Learn from the mistakes of others. You can't live long*
> *enough to make them all yourself.*
> —Eleanor Roosevelt

When you start a new company from scratch, every aspect of your business needs to be created. This is an enormous task that requires a tremendous amount of learning, patience, and skill acquisition—or the knowledge to do what you know and outsource what you don't. You will make mistakes. It's inevitable. What's important is that you try to make as few of them as possible, and learn from the ones you do make.

Most Start-Up Businesses Fail

As you probably already know, most small businesses fail within the first three years. However, if entrepreneurs dwelled on this statistic, new businesses would never be created. Start by devoting substantial time and effort developing and critiquing your plan. Focus on what you *can* do and what *will* work. Let go of ideas that aren't working quickly. There is no place for an ego in this process. When I can see that an entrepreneur is so in love with his idea that he can't see the glaring warning signs before him or hear the messages that people are telling him, things will fall apart quickly. Be willing to let go and move on. I have seen many inventions that were fantastic in concept. However, that does not mean they should all be taken to market. The business case must be scrutinized.

"Solve a Problem" Snapshot: The Boogie Moms

During cold season, kids often get red, chapped noses. In 2007, Mindee Doney and Julie Pickens, now known as "The Boogie Moms," created Boogie Wipes® (www.boogiewipes.com), a new product to ease one of the worst and most obvious signs of a cold—a runny nose. Boogie Wipes are made with saline (saltwater) and offer an effective, gentle way to dissolve kids' mucus. They also help prevent chapping by releasing vitamin E and aloe into the skin, providing a "natural" solution for parents. Mindee and Julie saw a need in the market and solved a common, everyday problem. The Boogie Moms made more than $4.8 million in their first two years in business!

BUSINESS DEFINITIONS DEFINED

There are several ways people describe the type of business they are in, and in most cases more than one description will apply. While there are hundreds of categories that get very specific, for our purpose here, which is to help with the process of finding your niche, let's review the most popular categories:

Service business. A person (or more than one person) delivers a service, such as housecleaning, massage, or tax preparation.

Product business. The business is based on the offer of a specific product, such as a household gadget, software program, or children's toy.

Retail food service. A business that directly provides food products (e.g., a pizza parlor).

Food business. A business that offers a food product that is prepared for sale, direct to consumer or wholesale (e.g., your own jarred tomato sauce).

Professional. A firm that provides professional services (e.g., a law firm, accountancy firm, detective agency, or computer support company).

Technology. A company in the tech field, which can include anything from software development to the sale of mobile devices.

Media. A business that focuses on some aspect of media, such as publishing, content production, public relations, or advertising.

Other classifications are based on the target customer. Who is your customer?

B2B ("business-to-business"). A business that sells to other businesses. A printing company or medical device manufacturer are good examples.

B2C ("business-to-consumer"). A business that sells to end consumers. A retail shop or eBay PowerSeller are examples.

THE ADVANTAGE OF ADVISORS

Given the risks associated with starting something so new, it's important to get as much support as possible. When proceeding down this path, you need to pay special attention to your advisors. You need to make sure that your paid advisors, such as your attorney, accountant, and marketing consultants, have sufficient experience in this kind of endeavor. Then you need advice from other businesspeople, especially other entrepreneurs. You can create an informal or formal circle of advisors called an advisory board. Find people who have taken this kind of risk themselves or who have specific knowledge that is useful in your business area. They should also be people you can trust to give you honest feedback, even when they don't agree with your direction, and who will still stick with you even if you make choices contrary to their advice.

CONCLUSION

*Always leave enough time in your life to do something that
makes you happy, satisfied, even joyous. That has more of an
effect on economic well-being than any other single factor.*
—Paul Hawken

I hope this chapter has given you an idea of the incredible number of
options you have and approaches you can take to start making *your*
million dollar dream come true. This exploration was intended to open
your mind to the many possibilities so you can begin to set the stage
for a lifetime of fulfillment in every area of your life. In the next chapter, you will be taking an introspective look within to see which of
these possibilities might be the best fit for your life.

Your New Future
Starts with You

Every other chapter of this book shares specific information and resources to equip you for business. However, before we get down to "business," let's first put the emphasis on you. This approach, and this chapter, is very different than what you might see in a typical business book because it speaks directly to the most central element to your success—you. That's because you are central to creating your own fulfillment, and only you can define what will ultimately fulfill you. This chapter will enable you to look at your own personality and better understand the role this can and should play in helping choose your path. And then it will enable you to take complete ownership of your future by helping you to define your specific dream and commit to your ideal future once and for all!

WHAT ROLE DOES YOUR PERSONALITY PLAY?

There are many tools and assets we bring to the table when starting a business. None is more important than you. Each of us is wired differently, and to some extent this wiring will play a role in determining what we will be best at, enjoy most, and find most challenging. With that in mind, I want to share insights and research that will prove useful in understanding personality and what role it plays as you begin to formulate your business idea and, eventually, your plan. Turning inward for a little self-evaluation is the first step in making money your way.

YOUR DREAM AND YOUR PERSONALITY

Business experts have long known the importance personality plays in business success, which is why some of the world's biggest and most successful companies train their managers to do personality assessments for potential and current employees.

When starting your own business, you begin with a blank slate: you are free to design it to fit your needs, your lifestyle, and exactly who you are. But what specific impact does your personality type have on selecting the "right" business for you? And what role does your personality type play in your business success? In this section, we will explore several different kinds of personality tests and how they might affect your thinking about your prospective or current business. By examining your personality in depth, you will be able to answer questions like: What kind of business suits my personality? What type of role am I drawn to naturally? What traits do I need to compensate for? This knowledge can be a powerful tool. If you are like most people, certain tendencies and preferences may suddenly make more sense to you and quickly clarify the approach that is most likely to meet your needs and goals.

This knowledge can also lead to a deeper understanding of those around you, such as customers, clients, vendors, and potential partners, which can help you adjust your own communication to bring more positive results. I have taken many of these tests myself and can therefore verify that they're a terrific way to better understand yourself and how your personality relates to your own business. While we're all made up of many traits (some that may even appear to conflict), these personality assessments will help us gauge which traits are dominant, revealing both our strengths and those areas that require a bit more attention.

PERSONALITY AND ENTREPRENEURSHIP

Although there are proven personality tests that have been around for decades (which we'll discuss later in this section), Bill Wagner's book, *The Entrepreneur Next Door*, is a tremendous tool because it directly focuses on the relationship between personality and entrepreneurship. Wagner believes that personality does have a significant influence on how you perform as a business owner and that the secret to success is choosing a venture that fits one's entrepreneurial personality. In a recent article by Wagner entitled "What's Your Entrepreneurial Personality Type?" he explains:

> Successful entrepreneurs share a number of common personality traits, and these traits are the predominant indicators of their success—outweighing education, family ties, skills, and experience. Moreover, people who choose business ventures that are in sync with their true personalities tend to experience the greatest level of success and fulfillment.

Wagner identifies seven broad personality types. **Generalists**, who are more strategic or leadership-oriented, include the Trailblazer, the Go-Getter, the Manager, and the Motivator. There are also three **Specialist** personality types, who are more tactical in their behavior; these are the true "experts" who enjoy the details and are typically very good at them. He calls these three types the Authority, the Collaborator, and the Diplomat. For a brief summary of the seven types, visit his Web site, The Entrepreneur Next Door (www.theentre preneurnextdoor.com), to find out which best describes you.

There are other tests that can help inform you about how to approach business, how you process information, how you interact with others, and how you make decisions. One of these was developed by Dr. David W. Merrill and Roger Reid back in the 1960s and is still in use today for achieving success in sales and management careers. The Social Style Model divides people into four Styles: Driving, Expressive, Amiable, and Analytical.

WHAT'S YOUR ENTREPRENEURIAL PERSONALITY TYPE?

To discover more deeply the "real you," you can take Wagner's 60-question test, which is also available on his Web site (theen trepreneurnextdoor.com/tests/entrepreneurial_pers.html). I took the test myself, and I believe my test results accurately reflect my entrepreneurial approach. It costs $10, takes about 15 to 20 minutes, and provides a detailed report on your entrepreneurial style, including the aspects of your personality that are well suited to owning a business and those that could be problematic.

Driving Style. These people thrive on the thrill of the challenge and the internal motivation to succeed. Driving Style people are practical folks who focus on getting results. Words that describe them include action oriented, problem solving, direct, assertive, risk taking, and independent.

Expressive Style. These people are very outgoing and enthusiastic, with a high energy level. They are also great idea generators but usually do not have the ability to see the idea through to completion. Words that describe them include verbal, motivating, convincing, impulsive, influential, charming, and confident.

Amiable Style. They are dependable, loyal, and easygoing. They like things that are nonthreatening and friendly. Words that describe them include patient, loyal, sympathetic, team oriented, relaxed, and trusting.

Analytical Style. Analytical people are known for being systematic, well organized, and deliberate. Words that describe them include controlled, orderly, precise, disciplined, cautious, and logical.

See Figure 2.1 to see where you fit.

Knowing who *you* are in relation to others is important. If you are Driving (which I happen to be) and the person you are speaking with is Amiable, you need to alter your way of communicating or the two of you will most likely clash. The relaxed Amiable Style may be put off by your action-oriented Driving Style. You may be seen as demanding, impatient, and forceful, which would instantly conflict with his or her easygoing and patient Amiable Style. However, if you can quickly assess that this person approaches things from an Amiable Style, then you can tone down your focus on results and instead recognize that this communication would be much more effective if you adjust and connect in a more personal and nonthreatening way, allowing time for things to unfold. On the other hand, if an Amiable person wishes to connect with you, he or

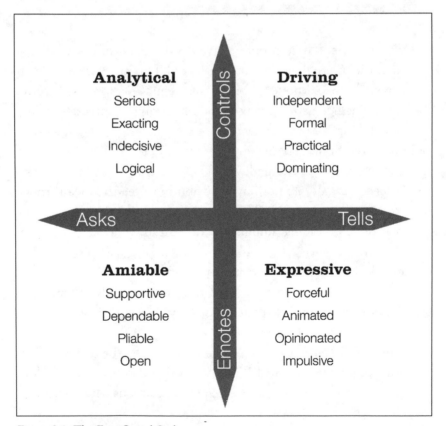

Figure 2.1: The Four Social Styles
Source: TRACOM Group

she will need to adjust his or her own behavior to get right to the point.

One mistake common among business owners is the expectation that everyone is—or should be—just like them, and that these people should accommodate the owner's communication needs, rather than the other way around. For example, I recently spoke with a business-woman (Amiable) who hired a financial planner (Analytical) to help her figure out her next steps. She said that although he is offering sound advice, she finds herself drained of energy in his presence and resistant to his recommendations—so much so that neither of them wants to continue working together. We had a brief discussion about Social Styles. As an Amiable person, she felt the need to make tough decisions in a relaxed, friendly environment, with time to process the informa-tion. As an Analytical Style, his approach is, "Here are the facts, now make your decision." However, armed with this new recognition, she realized how the two could work together and that she could, in fact, get her needs met. She came to understand that she does need his expertise and that she cannot take his style personally. She has adjusted how she interacts with him so that she now takes the information he provides home, which gives her ample time to digest it and make criti-cal business decisions on her own terms and in her own time.

You can determine where your personality fits in this framework through books, career coaches, or Internet sites, but the originator is the TRACOM Group, which offers a variety of Social Style tests and books at www.socialstyle.com. The advantage of going directly to the source is that they provide comprehensive results that can clearly articulate your findings.

A DEEPER LOOK AT WHO YOU ARE: MYERS-BRIGGS

Another of today's most respected and well-known personality tests is called the Myers-Briggs Type Indicator assessment. Developed in the 1940s by Isabel Myers and her mother, Katharine Cook Briggs, the test is continually updated, and more than 2 million people take it every year.

The Myers & Briggs Foundation (www.myersbriggs.org) instructs people interested in taking the test to find a certified career or counseling center so that a certified administrator can give you the test and review the results with you.

In the meantime, however, the following is an overview of what the test will identify, mainly the dominant factors in your personality, your natural tendencies, and how you process information and make decisions. These are all aspects of our personality that emerge on a daily basis in business.

WHAT'S AGE GOT TO DO WITH IT?

Does your age matter when starting a business? Yes! You will find successful entrepreneurs in every age group, but when starting out and choosing your business, it is essential to examine where you are now. Twenty-somethings (Gen Y) may have less money but be willing to take more risks. People in their thirties and early forties (Gen X) may be right in the middle, with a little money saved and a willingness to take moderate risks, recognizing that building financial wealth is essential in this next phase of their lives.

Baby boomers in their late forties to early sixties, on the other hand, may have more disposable income (and time) to invest in a new business. However, given the recent economic downturn, many of them are finding themselves back at square one again, having lost their fortunes and retirement funds and looking for new ways to create wealth. Finally, if you're in your sixties to early seventies, you may need to find a business that presents less risk to protect your financial security.

The bottom line is that regardless of age, it's never too early or too late to think about ways in which to creatively generate income.

- What is your age, and where do you fall on this continuum?
- What is your tolerance for risk?
- Do you have savings, investments, and retirement funds?
- Are you looking to supplement your existing income, or do you need to create a full-time source of income for your survival?

Definitions of Personality

In the four pairings below, you will find descriptions from Wikipedia of two opposing personality traits. Each of us favors one over the other in each pairing, and the test reveals which of the two suits you more.

The **extrovert's** flow of energy is directed outward toward people and objects, and the **introvert's** is directed inward toward concepts and ideas. **Extroverts** are action-oriented and desire breadth, while **introverts** are thought-oriented and seek depth.

Sensing and **intuition** are the information-gathering functions. Individuals who prefer *sensing* are more likely to trust information that is tangible and concrete. They prefer to look for details and facts. On the other hand, those who prefer *intuition* tend to trust information that is more abstract—those flashes of insight that seem to bubble up from the unconscious.

Thinking and **feeling** are the decision-making functions. The thinking and feeling functions are both used to make rational decisions. Those who prefer *thinking* tend to decide things from a more detached standpoint, measuring the decision by what seems reasonable, logical, consistent, and matches a given set of rules. Those who prefer *feeling* tend to come to decisions by associating or empathizing with the situation, looking at it from another angle, and weighing the situation to achieve the greatest harmony, considering the needs of the people involved.

Judging (thinking or feeling) or **perceiving** (sensing or intuition) functions describe how we relate to the outside world. People who are "judging" types prefer to "have matters settled," and those who are "perceiving" types prefer to "keep decisions open."

So what does all this mean? Do you have to take any of these tests in order to start a business?

Not necessarily. However, among my goals for this book is helping entrepreneurs increase their chances of success. Risks must be considered when you're deciding whether to launch a business and what type to launch. While there are numerous considerations to take into account in making these decisions, identifying a business and role for oneself that is compatible with one's personality can only enhance your chances of success and satisfaction. Further, this awareness can increase the likelihood of your success in the ongoing management of the company. This knowledge is a hidden and powerful opportunity, one that will serve you well both in choosing a business that fits your style and building a business that works for you.

DEFINING YOUR DREAM

In this section, you can use the insights you've gained about your personality to define your dream and commit to your future. If you are like most people, there have been times you have dreamt about what you want. Often these dreams get dismissed or tabled until "someday." Notice how easily all the "reasons" and "obstacles" roll off your tongue. I am convinced that you—and only you—have the power to make today that someday. To do this, your dream must become as real, automatic, and comfortable to voice as the excuses, reasons, and explanations why you cannot live your dream.

> *If you can dream it, you can do it.*
> —*Walt Disney*

Dream, *noun:*
1. An aspiration; goal; aim
2. A condition or achievement that is longed for; an aspiration.

One of my fondest memories as a child is a tradition that my mom created. On every family member's birthday, my mother would light the birthday candles and say, "Now everyone close your eyes and take a quiet moment to think about a wish you would like to have come true." She established early on that these should be things that we really wanted, specific wishes and dreams, big or small. After about two or three minutes of silence, she would ask who wanted to share their dream first.

I realize now why she did this. Most kids, growing up, are told to keep their wishes "secret"; if we share them, they won't come true.

Virtually every person I have asked remembers this childhood myth. However, luminaries such as Oprah and Dr. Wayne Dyer say the opposite—that the only way for your dreams to come true is to speak about them with conviction, creating a shift to commitment, and taking the necessary actions to make those dreams a reality. Forty years ago, my mom was right! We often hear "Dream big!" or "Go after your dream!" By acknowledging what you **aim to achieve** (dream), you can make the commitment to begin a new journey—one filled with authenticity about who you are today (not who you were in the past) and what you intend to create in this next stage of your life, personally and financially. There are no boundaries with dreams. They can be shaped to fulfill needs, transform your life, and provide for your family or others.

WHAT MATTERS MOST TO YOU?

Some people recognize their dream fully; they may not have made the commitment to pursue it, but they know it nonetheless. For others, it's not quite that easy. Perhaps they've been shutting out these thoughts for so long they're buried. Or perhaps they've never allowed themselves to think past the reality of today. Coming to recognize your dream is a process, and hopefully the information in Chapter 1 helped open you up to new possibilities. Even if you think you know your dream, the exercise below will help confirm that you are on the right track.

Examining what matters most to you should take into account every aspect of your life, including your personality, your circumstances, your passions, and your goals. For example, if your children are small, you probably don't want a business that keeps you away from them 14 hours a day. If church or temple is a central part of your life, then choosing a business that gives you time to fully participate is something to consider. Is creativity important to you? Do you like things to change and evolve each day, or do you prefer things to stay somewhat the same? For me, running a business, writing books, and raising my daughters takes up most of my time. In addition to these three things, it is important to me to be in close touch with my parents. For now, PTA has taken a backseat. As part of defining your dream, take the time first to examine and think carefully about what's most important to you personally (not what others tell you is important) so that you can eventually consider these things when identifying the "right" business for you. Here are some areas in which to begin exploring. Write down your answers to the questions below.

Be careful not to base your answers on how you have felt in the past; instead, do your best to answer based on where you are today.

Adrenaline. How much do you enjoy a fast-paced, action-packed, travel-filled schedule? Do you love negotiating and creating new deals? Is media exposure exciting? Or do you prefer to work behind the scenes, or at a slower pace?

Teamwork. Do you want to build and lead a team? Is this camaraderie important to you? Or do you thrive while working on your own?

Creativity. Is being creative—whether in your craft or your thinking—a driving need for you? Do you crave creative outlets to be satisfied? Or do you prefer more practical pursuits, such as quantifiable goals and tasks?

Your Art. Do you want to "do the work" (e.g., be a baker) or build a business (e.g., be a CEO)? Say you love to refinish furniture, and your pieces are in high demand. If you decide to open a shop, your attentions will turn to other aspects of business, including manning the store, managing employees, marketing, and managing the accounts. If you'd rather spend all your time scouting old pieces and artfully refinishing them, know that the efforts required to grow the business will likely take away time and focus from what you love best.

Family. How much time do you want to dedicate to family? Do you have small children and thus require a flexible schedule, or are your kids in college, leaving you with more discretionary time? If on your own, are weekly, monthly, or annual visits with family enough?

Community/Religion. Are you involved in community projects? How frequently do you want to volunteer? Do you spend a lot of time at your place of worship? How much time do you need, and what flexibility do you need to continue participating? Are these events usually on the weekend, enabling you to attend without having it affect your business hours? How much time will satisfy you?

Friends. How much time do you typically spend each week/month with friends? Do you meet them during the day or evening? If you work during the day, are your evenings free for friends? How much time spent with friends would satisfy you?

Learning. Do you like to take classes or set aside time to learn something new? How much time do you need for this? Do you thrive on learning new crafts or skills or require time for reading about new topics or interests?

WHAT IS YOUR DREAM?

Hopefully, this last exercise in self-evaluation has enabled you to start thinking about the factors that will ultimately fuel your dream and commitment. As you move forward, keep the answers readily accessible. They will help you stay focused and avoid veering off into directions that may seem "right" but in reality aren't. If those directions do not fit into the criteria you established, you may find yourself in a place in which you are still not making money your way. I encourage you to refer back to these entries frequently.

> *Life shrinks or expands in proportion to one's courage.*
> *—Anaïs Nin*

With those answers at the top of your mind, I would like you to do something now without consideration for anyone else in your life—not your children, spouse, parents, not anyone. Ask yourself, "What is my deepest dream or wish for myself?" Do not edit or censor your voice. If negative thoughts or excuses begin to rise to the surface, acknowledge them, write them down—then stuff them in a drawer. And don't worry about the details or the "how" at this stage.

Write down something even if it seems like a stretch! It can be personal, about your business, or a combination of both. It doesn't need to be perfect. If you hear an internal critic tell you why you can't do it, flick him away. What's the first thing that comes to your mind?

What is your dream for yourself? Write it down here, on a separate piece of paper, or online at www.yourmilliondollardream.com/ mydream to share with others. It can have multiple parts or dimensions, or you may have more than one dream. When you think you're finished, write some more.

_____

_____

_____

_____

_____

Now it's time to visualize your dream.

First, describe success. What does it look like for you? What does it feel like? Describe in detail what your office, income, schedule, and day-to-day activities will look like. Provide as much detail as you can. Write down the color of the walls, what you'd like to be doing at 3 p.m., the make and model of car you'll be driving. Spare nothing! Use an entire notebook if necessary.

_____

_____

_____

_____

_____

Now, act "as if." What does "act as if" mean? Just what it says! _Act as if you already are._ **It means trying on a new role for size, embracing a new mindset, and acting on your intention "to become" with reinforcing behaviors.** Act as though you were living this dream today. The payoff for this role-play comes when you realize your acting is no longer acting and you've rightly grown into the new role, becoming what you wanted to become.

Next, examine the answers to these questions:

Why is it important to you to live this life?

_____

_____

_____

_____

_____

_____

What will following your dream do for others (e.g., family, community, customers) in this new life you are creating?

_____

_____

_____

_____

_____

_____

ASSESSING SKILLS AND GOALS

When you define your dream as it relates specifically to your business, you will at some point also need to acknowledge your personal skills. If you dream of being the next American Idol but can't carry a tune, you may need to reflect on this goal. Unfortunately, though, recognition of our barriers is seldom the problem. In fact, it tends to become the primary contributor to our "story" and the reason for remaining stuck and dissatisfied. While it's important to acknowledge limitations, don't stop there! Instead, look at them simply as a challenge that requires you to ramp up your efforts at finding useful information and solutions, not barriers.

You don't have to be a whiz at everything to be successful in business. After seven years of running my own company, for example, looking at financial spreadsheets still makes my head spin. They are the last things that I want to focus on. Realizing this was an area of weakness, I sought out a financial expert to help fill the gap, someone who can coach me through the numbers and help me strategize. Does this mean that I shouldn't be in business? Absolutely not. If you're "real" about what you need help with, you can find people with the appropriate skills to fill in the gaps.

You should also consider the following points when defining your dream of a new business:

Financial goals. Whether you want to make an extra $20,000 per year to supplement your income or have dreams of much higher numbers, the goal and the direction you choose need to be compatible. You need to think proactively about what appeals to you and what lifestyle you are seeking to create. It's good to know what you want to earn from the beginning. This way, if you are thinking about starting a franchise, for example, you can interview experienced franchisees to gain insight into the industry, challenges they face, marketing tactics that have worked, and get a realistic idea of the potential income.

Lifestyle goals. Many entrepreneurs choose to go into business because it gives them a more flexible work schedule. While being your own boss means you call the shots, you might be surprised that with this flexibility often comes longer work hours, including late nights and weekends. It's also difficult to take vacation time when you are the one running the show. Therefore, know in advance what you want, and interview others in similar businesses to find out if your goals are realistic. Most business owners you seek out welcome these questions because they remember what it was like to start out.

INTUITION: WHAT IS IT?

The more we learn to operate in the world based on
trust in our intuition, the stronger our channel will be
and the more money we will have.
—Shakti Gawain

It is necessary to dig deep and listen to your intuition. In brief flashes, many of us have experienced that "moment of truth" or "knowing"—that intuitive sense that tells us that we are or are not on track; a feeling that we should be doing something different; or a sense that something is not quite right. However, many of us tend to crush those moments. Why do we do that? Why is it that so often when we have those moments of clarity, we tell ourselves, "That's ridiculous, I could never do that" or "That's not practical or realistic" or "I don't have the time or money to make that happen" or "That's something I may do 'someday,' but not now."

It always comes back to the same necessity: go deep
enough and there is a bedrock of truth, however hard.
—May Sarton

When you ask yourself the following questions, what do your answers reveal? Are you doing the things that make you happy now? Are you being yourself, or are you acting? The question that next arises is: do you want to feel the same way five years from now?

By understanding and harnessing the power of our intuition, we can finally embrace what we know to be true and overcome the negative voices or "reasons" we automatically repeat in our heads that paralyze us and keep us from taking action.

Without consideration of anyone else in your life, answer the following questions on a separate piece of paper.

- When are you the happiest and worry-free?
- What do you want to be acknowledged or known for?

- What moves and inspires you? That is, what gives you energy even when you're tired?
- What are you grateful for?

This second exercise on intuition is intended to reveal what your intuition is telling you. Some describe this as a "gut" or "heartfelt" feeling; others have described it as a "moment of clarity" or "divine intervention." Write your thoughts down here, in a journal, or on a separate piece of paper. I have included some questions I would ask to help open your thinking ("as if" I was sitting with you over tea). Don't edit yourself as you write. Just keep writing. If you can't think of anything, write, "I can't think of anything to say." List the mundane, if necessary, just to break through any challenges. What is your intuition telling you? Here are some examples: A dance instructor "knows" that going to culinary school is the right thing to do. A stay-at-home mom "knows" that her friends always buy what she suggests—she loves to source stylish, inexpensive clothing and would like to start a business as a personal shopper. A schoolteacher has come up with a hot new gizmo to solve a problem in the pet market; he "knows" that he needs to unleash his creativity. General answers are okay, as the next chapter will help you narrow your thinking further.

> *Trust in yourself. Your perceptions are often far more*
> *accurate than you are willing to believe.*
> —Claudia Black

What would you secretly love to do? List more than one thing if you wish.

_____

_____

_____

_____

_____

_____

When you see yourself smile with satisfaction at your achievement, what are you doing? What do you "know" is true for you?

_____

_____

_____

_____

_____

Sometimes, we've buried our feelings for so long that it's difficult to immediately identify them or recognize them. More quiet contemplation may be required for your intuition to prevail and for you to get to what you "know." What's essential is that you wrestle with yourself. I've done this exercise many times. Sometimes I've written down what I think is holding me back only to realize what the "real" barrier is after more reflection. The hardest thing to come to terms with is the realization that you yourself are the only barrier that is in your way. It's so much easier to blame others or current circumstances.

An excellent resource that I love is a book called *The Artist's Way* by Julia Cameron. This book is packed with exercises that will help you get to the kernel of what your heart has been trying to tell you.

TAKE RESPONSIBILITY TODAY

If you've gone through the prior exercises, you have listened to your intuition and defined your dream. You know what matters most to you or are working toward this, and you've visualized what your ideal life looks like. Your next step—one that can be your greatest obstacle—is committing to that dream.

Verbalizing your dream is an essential step. But the real shift occurs when you commit yourself to "do" something. Anyone can talk about a dream. But without taking full responsibility and making a commitment, the "dream" is just a "fantasy." To be clear, one cannot achieve a dream without making a very clear decision and then committing to making it happen. Understand that if you don't commit, **you must also accept full responsibility for remaining stuck**. Your story will no longer excuse you.

I have said this elsewhere: these changes will be rewarding. But "rewarding" does not equate to "easy." It is "easy" to accept things as they are, to feel dissatisfied, to switch on the TV until everything starts over tomorrow. Making your million dollar dream come true will take tremendous effort, and you will need to achieve things you didn't know you could achieve.

We need not look far to see this approach work. One recent extraordinary example of this occurred in 2008, when a young American Olympic swimmer named Michael Phelps won eight gold medals. The more one considers the odds of this feat, the more extraordinary it becomes. To win a single gold medal, an athlete must defeat the best swimmers in a given stroke, in a given event, from America and every other country in the world. To do this eight times in multiple strokes, distances, and team relays is phenomenal. Considering the added personal challenges of growing up in a single parent home, it's no wonder Phelps's story captured our hearts and the media's attention so fully.

To Phelps, all that mattered was his dream, which had fully formed four years earlier. Every day he showed up at the pool to fulfill what was clearly in his mind. "Reasons" did not prevail over his dream. In every area, our world is full of inspiring role models like Phelps, who've achieved their dreams despite seemingly impossible odds. All their stories begin with taking responsibility for their future and making that first commitment to themselves.

There is a useful model of success that I will share here. The following is commonly how most people view success:

"Have" =   Our primary focus is on what we do or do not have (cars, house, clothes, money, etc.).

"Do"   =   We do what we can within these limitations.

"Be"   =   We are happy or sad as a result of what we have. For example, "If I 'have' a new house, I will 'be' happy." "If I 'have' a new car, I will 'be' happy." "If I 'have' a new husband, I will 'be' happy." "If I 'have' a new body from plastic surgery or dieting, I will 'be' happy."

But this model of success is upside down. Now read it this way:

"Be" = We are being our authentic selves. We are committed to being successful in whatever ventures we choose.

"Do" = We are doing what it takes to "be" this person.

"Have" = As a result, we will "have" abundance in our lives.

At this point, I am about to ask you to make the decision to make this shift in your thinking and approach. If you need to take some more time to formulate your dream, take it. But understand that from this first commitment will come other commitments. Note that I am not expecting you to have your plan or road map all worked out yet. That will come in later chapters. For now, **your commitment to commitment** is what matters.

> *Find out who you are and do it on purpose.*
> —*Dolly Parton*

Right now, your "commitment statement" doesn't have to be perfect. But your decision must be clear. At this moment, you may hear all those negative reasons—the ones you listed and stuffed in a drawer earlier in this chapter—starting to rattle their way out. They are not going anywhere, so leave them there. Then speak these three statements aloud and repeat them until you believe them:

- "The only person responsible for the direction of my life is me."
- "I am 'being' an authentic and successful person today."
- "I commit to do what it takes to realize my dream."

Fill in the blanks below. If your "story" or "reasons" attempt to prevent you from making these statements, take responsibility and put them back into the drawer.

I have decided to be _____ (e.g., financially secure, excited to work, unafraid, a leader, etc.)

I will give or permit myself _____ (e.g., the chance to let go of guilt, feel joy, to take time off, etc.) as a result of this achievement.

I will do something for others including _____ (e.g., put my nephew through college). List any that fit:

_____

_____

_____

_____

You can print out a commitment certificate online at www.yourmil liondollardream/commit. Feel free to tape it to the bathroom mirror, inside your closet door, or on the fridge so you are reminded daily of your commitment and your dream! And don't forget to say:

- "The only person responsible for the direction of my life is me."
- "I am 'being' an authentic and successful person today."
- "I commit to do what it takes to realize my dream today."

The process of creating your dream is about placing yourself, as you have just done, firmly in the future. Once there in your mind, work backward to identify what you must do and what must occur to get there. This process works because success is derived from committed focus. By working backward from your point of success, you can focus on what you need to do, rather than focusing on all the "why nots" in your drawer that normally demand—*and receive*—your devoted attention.

SAY IT WITHOUT APOLOGY

There is one final step to committing to your dream. While recogniz-ing, writing, and committing to your dream is important, speaking your dream with intention is just as critical. It will breathe power, life, and belief into your dream.

Here's a personal example: I remember the first time I sat in my new business office and company headquarters (a.k.a. my second daughter's bedroom) and answered the telephone, saying, "Mom

Inventors" for the first time. The first day or two, I did so with an element of disbelief. I questioned myself: "Who is going to believe it's a 'real' company?" But as I said it over and over again, I began to believe in it. And to my surprise, nobody calling ever questioned it. In fact, my belief created the images others had of a much bigger corporation than I had even envisioned. Practically nothing else really changed within this period of time, but by just saying it, it became "real."

Another way to verbalize your dream is by revealing it to others. People often say that their business became "real" to them as soon as they printed a business card. A client, a payment, a designated phone line—none of these things seem to matter as much as that name on a company card. By putting it in writing and then speaking about it to others as a real entity, you are truly committing yourself to your future.

But even before printing up business cards, simply tell people what your dream is. Telling other people your dream may feel embarrassing. Understand, though, that embarrassment is merely the anticipation of criticism (even from those who love you), and there *will* be criticism about your dream. Expect this—but do not let it interfere! The first stages of commitment are delicate, and criticism can be a killer of dreams. Do not let this happen. If you understand and observe how you feel at the moment the criticism is delivered, you will realize that the embarrassment isn't actually generated by the critic or the *criticism*. The embarrassment is a choice you have made. Again, it is generated by *you*. If you have taken responsibility for yourself as I have asked, you are also responsible for your anticipation and reaction to criticism—and for your next actions.

There are plenty of positive actions you can take in the face of criticism. Get comfortable and habitual about declaring your dreams. Talk to a trusted friend or family member and speak with intention and say your dream boldly, without apologies or explanations. Tell more than one person, if you wish. Just say, "I am building _____." As you share your dream again and again, you will gain power and conviction, you will become more confident, and miraculously it will become "real." Commit to it. Say it. Believe it. You will find that when you take these steps, not only are you changing the direction of your own life, but you will inspire everyone else around you. Take a stand for yourself. You don't have to accept that the life you want is only the privilege of others. It can be yours. It is your choice.

WHAT IF YOUR SIGNIFICANT OTHER DOESN'T SUPPORT YOUR DREAM?

Many women and men have told me about their spouses' lukewarm responses to their initial business ideas. As disappointing as this is, taken in context, it's not an unreasonable reaction. If you're focused on career or kids or other interests, your spouse may not consider your idea, at the very beginning stages, to be any more serious than, say, the thought that, "I would like to learn French." And you are likely to hear all the "why nots" that you initially heard from yourself too. Again, you are responsible.

Once you take action, however—fleshing out your ideas and moving through the first phase—you may find yourself astonished (like the majority of entrepreneurs I interviewed for this book) at the support and passion with which your spouse embraces the business and even becomes actively involved.

If you do not find support from your spouse, you have choices. You can either do it alone, or you can find a group of supportive people who believe in you and your idea. You are the one who is responsible for your success and happiness.

You have already made great strides. Knowing yourself more accurately, accepting responsibility, then defining and committing to your dream is essential to your success. Now it's on to "business."

The next chapter covers one of the most fundamental aspects of your start-up: how to prepare your personal finances to establish the very foundation for your business.

Get Money Smart: Laying the Financial Groundwork for Your Business-to-Be

There are few, if any, aspects of business more challenging and more important than financing your venture. There are thousands upon thousands of columns, blogs, articles, and seminars on this subject. I have a slightly different take on financing, however. Instead of telling you "about" getting money in a generalized way, I will begin by explaining what crucial choices you will need to make that will truly free you to finance your business. It's not just about getting this loan or that line of credit. Instead, the foundation for these choices is based on both your personal and business lives. Those two lives are inevitably interconnected when you choose the entrepreneurial life.

> *The veil that clouds your eyes shall be lifted by the*
> *hands that wove it.*
> —*Kahlil Gibran (1883–1931)*

The means for laying this financial groundwork cannot be found in a single Web site, loan program, or grant but instead through tremendous thought and effort, much of which will begin here. Then, in the next chapter, you will find some valuable resources that will help you build on that groundwork.

First things first. Before you can adequately and economically "finance" your business, you will need to figure out what your needs are, take responsibility for understanding your personal finances, give up avoiding or denying the reality of your situation, and be willing to struggle through these next steps. You need to be completely honest with yourself about your personal finances before you can even consider getting the money needed to "fuel" the business.

Also, despite the reassurances by many business gurus that "money is always available," in my experience, it is just not that easy. Although there are some valuable resources listed at the end of this chapter, they are of limited value until you first think through where you are financially, right now, and then identify exactly what you need to start and grow your business. This chapter will provide the framework to help you do just that, which, in turn, will prepare you to delve into all those resources armed with the right information.

There are four things you will achieve in this chapter. First, you will learn the importance of determining the money you have "in the bank" right now, so that you can know your starting point. Next, you will develop and evaluate your business model and how it relates to your financial needs. Once you've done that, you will have an opportunity to choose the category of business you are creating. That will finally lead you to understand the financial options that make the most sense, given the nature of your business.

THE HARD TRUTH: EXAMINING YOUR PERSONAL FINANCES RIGHT NOW

Taking control of your personal finances will give you a sense of both power and relief. Until you have a perfectly clear picture of your current debt, monthly expenses, and upcoming needs (college tuition, braces for the kids, etc.), it can be foolhardy to move forward with financing your business. If you have already done this evaluation, you can skip ahead. If not, however, this is a "must do" task before going into any type of business. This section will provide the structure for helping you evaluate exactly where you stand, right now.

STEP 1: EVALUATE YOUR DEBT

As many of us know, nothing feels more out of control, plaguing, and exhausting than the worry that comes with being in debt. Facing this challenge, however, is the first step in creating a healthy personal life that will lay the foundation for a strong business. Once you have an honest picture of your debt (Figure 3.1), then and only then can you come up with a plan to address it.

	$ Amount
Mortgage 1	
Mortgage 2	
Mortgage 3	
Subtotal	
Auto Loans	
Personal Loans	
Subtotal	
Credit Card 1	
Credit Card 2	
Credit Card 3	
Credit Card 4	
Credit Card 5	
Credit Card 6	
Subtotal	
Student Loans	
Spouse Student Loans	
Subtotal	
Past Due Service Providers	
Past Due Income Taxes	
Past Due Property Taxes	
Other Debts	
Other Debts	
Other Debts	
Other Debts	
Subtotal	
Grand Total	

Figure 3.1: Personal debt worksheet: how much money do you owe?

STEP 2: FIGURE OUT MONTHLY EXPENSES

In addition to knowing the details of your debt, it is essential to evaluate your monthly expenses accurately (Figure 3.2). How much are you spending on groceries, entertainment, eating out, dry cleaning, iTunes, toys, DVDs, clothes for the kids, health insurance, rent, mortgage, preschool, day care, etc.? It can feel like you've cut back, but until you really sit down and figure out where your money's going (the juice bar? the burger place? the movies? the salon?), you won't have a complete and clear picture of where your expenses lie.

It's also helpful to evaluate if you have—or anticipate—unusual expenses, such as those caused by an illness or health condition in the family. Do you have savings for unexpected situations? You can never anticipate when a large expense will come along. For example: our youngest daughter, the acrobat, has had two visits to the emergency room this year, and because our insurance deductible is high, we ended up with thousands of dollars in bills that were not anticipated in our personal budget.

To begin figuring out your monthly expenses, sit down with all your bills, your checkbook register, or your bank statements. Make a scheduled appointment with yourself, weekly if necessary, to go through these expenses, and don't put it off. Choose a time when you're alert, focused, and not distracted.

As you go through each item, put it in the proper category: debt or monthly expense (or both, such as a credit card).

> *The more you own the less money, time, energy, connection, and space you have.*
> *—Jamie Novak*

STEP 3: DOCUMENT YOUR CURRENT MONTHLY INCOME

Hopefully, money's coming in from somewhere. Now is the time to evaluate and document all sources of income (Figure 3.3). If you receive a monthly paycheck, what is the amount? Is a spouse, partner, or other family member helping to support you? Look at every stream

		Monthly Expenses	Annual Expenses
1	Housing		
	Rent/Mortgage 1		
	2nd Mortgage/equity line		
	Mortgage 3		
	Renters/homeowners insurance		
	Maintenance		
	Neighborhood Dues		
	Property Taxes		
Subtotal			
2	Credit		
	Credit Card 1		
	Credit Card 2		
	Credit Card 3		
	Credit Card 4		
Subtotal			
3	Transit		
	Car Payment 1		
	Car Payment 2		
	Auto Insurance		
	Registration		
	Repairs		
	Gas/Oil		
	Mass Transit/Parking		
Subtotal			
4	Child Care		
	Babysitting		
	Nanny		
	Tuition		
	Programs		
Subtotal			
5	Food		
	Groceries		
	Eating out		
Subtotal			
6	Insurance		
	Life Insurance		
	Health Insurance		
	Other		
Subtotal			
7	Medical Care		
	Noncovered medical		
	Dental		
	Vision		
	Other		
	Other		
Subtotal			
8	Utilities		
	Electric		
	Gas		
	Water/Sewer		
	Telephone		
	Cable		
	Internet		
	Trash		
	Cell Phone		
	Other		
Subtotal			
9	Income Tax Payments		
	Past		
	Estimated		
Subtotal			
10	Personal Care		
	Clothing		
	Hair		
	Other		
	Other		
Subtotal			
11	Entertainment		
	Travel		
	Movies		
	Books, etc.		
	Alcohol		
	Tobacco		
	Other		
	Other		
Subtotal			
12	Miscellaneous		
	Pet Care		
	Charity		
	Other		
	Other		
Subtotal			
	Total Expenses		

Figure 3.2: Personal monthly expenses worksheet: how much money is going out?

of income. Are you living on unemployment or disability? Are you living on savings? Did your former company give you a severance package? Are you earning dividends on investments or income from real

CLEAR CLUTTER TO SAVE CASH

In her new book, *Stop Throwing Money Away*, organization expert and author Jamie Novak makes it crystal clear that our financial health is tied to our organizational abilities. She calls it "the clutter cash connection" and asserts that the more stuff you can get rid of or simply not buy, the more cash you'll have on hand.

How can you start simplifying and saving?

- Know what you have on hand to avoid unnecessary purchases.
- Return items you're not going to use.
- Think about the hidden costs of items; buying even a simple skirt will take up space in your closet, cost money for dry cleaning or time for washing, and possibly require alterations or repairs.
- Use what you have creatively: can you use shoeboxes to organize small items instead of buying storage boxes?

GET MONEY-ORGANIZED!

Bills crumpled at the bottom of your purse? Receipts stuffed in the back pocket of your jeans? Mail hiding under stacks of magazines? It's time to set up a bill system that works! Choose one designated place for bills, your checkbook, stamps, and other supplies so that you have everything together. Get organizational supplies from an office supply store, or designate a drawer, bin, or basket you already have. Set up a file folder system, by category, to file bills away in an organized manner. By organizing your papers, you are taking control of your personal finances, which will inevitably lead to other benefits.

	$ Per Month	$ Per Year
Job		
Spouse Job		
Part-Time Job		
Property Rent		
Commissions		
Consulting Fees		
Investment Income		
Unemployment		
Pension		
Child Support		
Alimony		
Other		
Total Monthly Income		

Figure 3.3: Personal income worksheet: how much money is coming in?

estate? Regardless of your situation, it's important to know exactly what your monthly income is and what that looks like in relation to your debt and current monthly expenses.

Also be sure to include any impending changes in your overall financial picture. One change in my family, for instance, is that my youngest child has just completed preschool. Now, with both children entering public elementary school, we will personally save $800 per month. With the kids' after-school program, we can save even more. These are the kinds of considerations to think about. Are you aware of any changes that will occur in your life that will impact your income?

People react differently to gathering their financial information. For some, looking at personal finances is depressing and can cause stress and anxiety; for others, it provides clarity and a sense of relief and well-being. If the process is making you anxious, try to separate yourself from it emotionally. In this way you are merely looking at the facts that could just as easily apply to someone else. No matter what the circumstances, this exercise will benefit you. The only way to alter your future is to take conscious steps now, and you will have already begun the process. My hope is that you can view this as the starting point—and a step toward creating your new business and new life.

At this point, you should be able to state your current financial situation clearly in terms of (1) debt, (2) monthly expenses, and (3) monthly income.

A PERSONAL MONEY MANAGEMENT TOOL THAT WORKS

If you are a finance whiz, then perhaps software programs like Quicken and Excel are the right thing for you. However, if you're like me, you need a program that is so intuitive and simple that it doesn't even feel like a money management program.

The best free solution that I have found to date for managing personal finances is www.mint.com (Figure 3.4). Now that you have pulled together your debt, monthly income, and expenses from the sections above, it should be easy to take this information and open a free online account on Mint.com. This service helps manage all of your personal finances—bank account, credit card, and investment accounts—with a high level of security to protect your privacy and confidentiality. Plus, when you sign up, you remain anonymous.

Mint offers simple technology with helpful charts and graphs to assist you in creating a budget and sticking with it.

The best part is that Mint automatically updates all of your

Figure 3.4: Mint.com home page.

accounts every night, which means that you will not need to import data—ever. Mint does all of this for you, and it tracks all of your spending activities, even from multiple bank and credit card accounts. Finally, it will help you reduce debt. Once you have shared all of your debt information, Mint provides specific, individualized suggestions that can save you real money, such as lower interest credit cards, credit consolidation, and lower cost providers for your typical monthly bills.

BUSINESS START-UP COSTS: HOW MUCH DO YOU NEED, AND HOW WILL YOU PAY?

Once you've gotten your personal finances in order, the question becomes: how much money do you personally have available for your business that you could spend without putting you or your family in jeopardy? This money could be the portion of your income not needed for monthly expenses; your savings; equity in your home; bonuses from your current job; an inheritance; or money you can borrow from your life insurance or retirement plan. All of these different sources add up (Figure 3.5). Take a few moments and write down here, or on a separate piece of paper, details about the money you have access to right now:

_____

_____

_____

_____

	$ Amount
Checking Account Balance	
Savings Account Balance	
Investment Accounts	
Retirement Plans/401(k)	
Home Equity	
Available Credit Line	
Other	
Total	

Figure 3.5: Personal liquidity worksheet: what money do you have right now?

BORROWING FROM LIFE INSURANCE AND RETIREMENT: DOABLE BUT RISKY

Many financial experts worry that borrowing from your life insurance and retirement funds may jeopardize your family's future—and see this as a last resort. Some life insurance policies allow borrowing from death benefits and others only from cash value (money you've paid in premiums). However, Scott Ditman, a tax expert, says, "Tax-free loans from life insurance policies may be practical if they're used to produce income, but it's not good if you borrow the money to eat."

As for taking out a loan from your company retirement account—it can be tempting because it's seemingly uncomplicated, but be advised that it could end up chaining you to your job. These loans typically must be repaid within 30 to 60 days after leaving the company to avoid triggering federal and state income taxes, and that may include a 10 percent penalty for early withdrawal. Despite these risks, however, studies show it's becoming an increasingly common practice.

Each one of us needs to assess our own circumstances. Risk-taking choices have to fit with your comfort level. As an entrepreneur, you will face many tough decisions, and the most important thing is to make informed choices that feel right to you.

CONNECTING THE DOTS: HOW MUCH MONEY IS NEEDED FOR YOUR PARTICULAR BUSINESS?

This is one of the biggest questions that entrepreneurs need to answer, and it is not a simple one. A very popular rule of thumb is that you need six months of funds in the bank to cover all your personal and business expenses to support the launch of a new business. But what does that mean? And where do financial advisors get this number? This is your business and your life, so the answer to this is highly personal.

All of us have different amounts of funds and different types of businesses, and frankly, I don't recall ever having "six months of funds" in the bank when starting my business. Although I cannot answer this question for you, I have created a framework that I hope will enable you to answer the riddle for yourself.

When we think of "financing the business," we need to connect the dots between what you are building and how much money is needed. Now is the time to build the financial basis for your plan in order to make the right decisions and take steps toward financing the business.

It's hard to know what type of funding your business will need when you are first starting out, but it will help to understand the continuum of business types and their financing needs as a starting point. One end of this continuum is a "pay as you grow" type of business, where the initial costs and expenses are low. Immediate income is a priority, and as income is generated, it is used to finance expenses. This type of business presents the lowest risk. Some examples of "pay as you grow" type businesses are consultancies, small home-based businesses, some online businesses, manufacturers sales reps (reps who sell other peoples' products and get paid a percentage of sales that they generate), and sales agents. Start-up costs can range from a few hundred dollars (for business cards and a phone) to $50,000 for the first year of business.

At the opposite end of the continuum is a business with a high "burn" (spending more than bringing in) rate. These businesses have high initial costs and ongoing expenses, but they offer the greatest potential for achieving a large spike in future growth and a high valuation. Income and revenue are not priorities in the short term, and significant funding is often required to finance growth. These are the highest risk businesses. Examples include biotechnology companies, software companies, real estate development projects, and Web network applications, such as Facebook and Twitter. While some of these companies will start on a shoestring, companies in this category generally require substantial early stage funding in order to finance rapid growth before they generate profits and cash flow. For example, after raising millions of dollars in investment and being acquired by Google in 2006 for $1.65 billion, YouTube analysts estimated that YouTube would still lose hundreds of millions of dollars in 2009.

WHERE IS YOUR BUSINESS ON THE FINANCIAL CONTINUUM?

By the end of this next section, you will have a clear sense as to where your business falls on this continuum—and the associated costs. Evaluate each question carefully, jot down your answers, and you'll begin developing a more accurate picture of what type of financing you'll truly need. Once you go through this exercise, you will have a sense of (1) how much money you need to start, and (2) what your monthly cash flow will look like for the first six months of business.

Capital Expenses/Start-Up Costs

When starting a business, it is important to look at your capital expenses. This is the money you will need to set up your business initially. These are usually one-time costs like equipment purchases (computers, phone, fax, BlackBerry); legal setup (structuring your business as a sole proprietorship, limited liability corporation (LLC), C corp, partnership, or S corp); intellectual property (patents, trademarks, copyrights); design work (logo, brochures, letterhead, business cards); lease deposits; furniture (unless you are using a home office); purchase of Web site URLs and Web site development; and any other costs that are relevant to your particular business. Make a list here or on a separate sheet of paper. What are your one-time start-up costs? It may take a bit of research by Internet and word-of-mouth to give each line item an estimated cost.

Monthly Operating Expenses and Revenue
The next numbers to consider are your monthly operating expenses and revenue (i.e., money going out each month and money coming in each month). This is called your profit and loss (P&L) statement. The beauty (yes, beauty!) of creating the P&L is that in addition to providing a basic plan to work from, it will also give you the ability to determine the nature of your business. Monthly expenses include things like phone service, Internet service, rent, and inventory. Estimate what you believe each of these items will cost. This may take some legwork.

Now that you have written this information down, look at your revenue and your expenses and calculate how much you think you'll fall short each month. What will the costs be over the first 12 months? What are your ongoing costs after that? That will help you determine how much money you need to raise, or whether you need to modify your business plan. (See Chapter 13 for business planning.)

Next, take all of your expenses and revenue and put them into a budget worksheet. There are free templates available online at Score (www.score.org/index.html), a national association dedicated to helping small business owners. Or you can create your own using a program such as Excel. The last book that I coauthored, *The One Page Business Plan for Women in Business* (published by The One Page Business Plan Company, 2010), also comes with a CD developed by Jim Horan, founder of the One Page Business Plan Company, with sample budgets to help guide you. In this worksheet, you can plug in all of your revenues, expenses, and cost of goods sold (COGS), and it will automatically calculate the rest, providing numbers and charts that give you a financial picture of what your business will look like over a 12-month period. (For further explanation of terms like cost of goods sold, margins, and markups, see Appendix.)

Figure 3.6 is an example of a budget worksheet from a consulting services business. Take out your calculator so you can follow along!

Look at the chart. In the right hand column, you will see that her

	Month 1	Month 2	Month 3	Month 4	Month 5	Month 6	Month 7	Month 8	Month 9	Month 10	Month 11	Month 12	Total
Revenues	3,500	4,000	4,500	5,000	5,500	6,000	6,500	7,000	7,500	8,000	8,500	9,000	75,000
– Discounts													0
– Returns													0
Net Sales	3,500	4,000	4,500	5,000	5,500	6,000	6,500	7,000	7,500	8,000	8,500	9,000	75,000
Overhead Expenses													
– Salaries & Wages	1,800	1,800	1,800	2,500	2,750	2,750	3,000	3,500	3,500	4,500	4,500	4,500	36,900
– Overtime													0
– Employer Taxes	180	180	180	250	275	275	300	350	350	450	450	450	3,690
– Employee Benefits	350	350	350	350	350	350	350	350	350	350	350	350	4,200
Staff Expenses	2,330	2,330	2,330	3,100	3,375	3,375	3,650	4,200	4,200	5,300	5,300	5,300	44,790
Staffing Percent	*66.6%*	*58.3%*	*51.8%*	*62.0%*	*61.4%*	*56.3%*	*56.2%*	*60.0%*	*56.0%*	*66.3%*	*62.4%*	*58.9%*	*59.7%*
Accounting Fees	100	100	100	100	100	100	100	100	100	100	100	100	1,200
Advertising													0
Auto Expenses	50	50	50	50	50	50	50	50	50	50	50	50	600
Bank Fees	25	25	25	25	25	25	25	25	25	25	25	25	300
Computer Expenses	100	100	100	100	100	100	100	100	100	100	100	100	1,200
Equipment													0
Insurance													0
Internet Services	150	150	150	150	150	150	150	150	1,500	150	150	150	3,150
Legal Fees													0
Marketing Expenses	100	250	500	500	500	1,000	1,000	500	750	500	500	500	6,600
Meals & Entertainment	75	75	75	75	75	75	75	75	75	75	75	75	900
Office Supplies													0
Phone	100	100	100	100	100	100	100	100	100	100	100	100	1,200
Freight													0
Rent	400	400	400	400	400	400	400	400	400	400	400	400	4,800
Sales Commissions													0
Sales Expenses													0
Travel							750				1,500		2,250
Utilities	50	50	50	50	50	50	50	50	50	50	50	50	600
Non-Staff Expenses	1,150	1,300	1,550	1,550	1,550	2,050	2,800	1,550	3,150	1,550	3,050	1,550	22,800
Non-Staff Percent	*32.9%*	*32.5%*	*34.4%*	*31.0%*	*28.2%*	*34.2%*	*43.1%*	*22.1%*	*42.0%*	*19.4%*	*35.9%*	*17.2%*	*30.4%*
Total Overhead	3,480	3,630	3,880	4,650	4,925	5,425	6,450	5,750	7,350	6,850	8,350	6,850	67,590
Total Overhead Percent	*99.4%*	*90.8%*	*86.2%*	*93.0%*	*89.5%*	*90.4%*	*99.2%*	*82.1%*	*98.0%*	*85.6%*	*98.2%*	*76.1%*	*90.1%*
Profit before Tax	20	370	620	350	575	575	50	1,250	150	1,150	150	2,150	7,410
Profit before Tax Percent	*0.6%*	*9.3%*	*13.8%*	*7.0%*	*10.5%*	*9.6%*	*0.8%*	*17.9%*	*2.0%*	*14.4%*	*1.8%*	*23.9%*	*9.9%*

Figure 3.6: Sample budget worksheet of a consulting services business. *Reprinted with permission of The One Page Business Plan Company®.*

annual revenues (money she's bringing in) are $75,000. After all her expenses (totaling $67,590) have been paid, she is left with $7,410 ($75,000 - $67,590). This is her annual profit before tax. Note that this "profit" takes into account that she has paid herself a salary of $36,900. Salary is simply another expense, like rent or utilities. The higher the salary you pay yourself, the smaller the profit.

Figure 3.7 is a sample of a general budget worksheet that you can use to forecast the 12-month cash flow for your start-up business.

PURCHASING TIPS

Many of us have learned "to do more with less" in the course of our everyday lives. If this is the case for you, you have an advantage because you'll be in the same mindset about business expenses. If not, it's critical to understand now that every dollar spent must be scruti-

		Month 1	Month 2	Month 3	Month 4	Month 5	Month 6	Month 7	Month 8	Month 9	Month 10	Month 11	Month 12	Total
Revenue														
	Discounts													
	Miscl													
Net Sales														
Overhead														
	Wages													
	Payroll exp. (taxes, etc.)													
	Benefits													
Total Staffing														
Non-Staffing Expenses														
	Accounting													
	Advertising													
	Computer													
	Professional Consulting													
	Equipment													
	Legal													
	Insurance													
	Marketing													
	Telephone													
	Internet													
	Office Supplies													
	Banking													
	Travel													
	Sales Expenses													
	Rent													
	Other													
	Other													
	Other													
	Other													
Total Non-Staff														
Total Overhead														
Profit Before Tax														

Figure 3.7: Budget worksheet: business cash flow 12-month forecast.

nized. Banks are more cautious than ever in making loans, investors want to see their money go further than before, and, out of necessity, vendors have shied away from offering extended payment terms. Two rules I suggest you employ as you create your own modeling are:

1. Budget at least 20 percent extra on top of everything you estimate spending if you pay standard rates.
2. Expect to pay upon receipt.

After you have completed your modeling, arranged financing, and started operations, there are three guidelines I recommend:

1. Before buying any business product or service, ask yourself, "Is this essential, or would this just be nice to have?" If you answer "nice to have," don't buy it.
2. If you decide that something is essential, buy it only once you

have found a way to do so for at least 20 percent less than standard rates.

3. If you buy, find a way to pay no sooner than 30 days out—and ideally delay payments for 60+ days.

EXPECT THE UNEXPECTED

You obviously can't know what unexpected costs you'll have—but it is important to know there will be some! For me, it was product liability insurance and product testing costs that most major retail buyers require prior to accepting your product. As you are writing out your costs in your budget worksheet, include a category for "surprises" or "unknown," often labeled "miscellaneous." If you're very cautious or risk-averse, assign a specific dollar amount or percentage to create a safety "cushion" for your overall budget. The size of the cushion will be determined by your tolerance for risk—from zero percent to as much as you need to feel comfortable while still being able to build your business.

Other under-the-radar costs to consider are things like new trademark filings for products that you add to your product line (you may only have one business idea now, but trust me—more ideas will surface as your business evolves), new development plans to upgrade your Web site, new product prototypes, engineering and computer-aided drawings (CAD), packaging costs, language translation costs for the packaging, factory costs (the cost of production), freight forwarding, customs brokerage, warehousing, shipping to customers, health insurance, marketing, bookkeeping and accounting, and so on. Other important costs to consider are the ongoing legal and professional consulting expenses needed when owning a business; most business owners I speak to drastically underestimate these costs. As you can see, the list continues to grow. But by thinking through your costs from the beginning, you will have a better grasp of how much money you will need to launch your business. And by budgeting now, you can spread future development costs out over time.

KEEP AN OPEN MIND

No matter what you've planned, though, it's important to be open to the necessity of changing course. From experiencing and observing the challenges faced by small businesses during the 2007–2009 downturn, it is easy to see that:

1. Commitment and passion are essential to success.

2. A willingness to let go of certain plans and to change direction sometimes or accept delays are both essential if you're to survive and to thrive.

For example, it may make sense to keep a day job longer than initially anticipated. Or, accepting a slower growth plan may make more sense than taking out a second (or third) mortgage to fund more rapid growth. After you have done the hard number crunching, you may conclude that your current business idea is not going to work, and you may choose to abandon it in favor of a new plan.

Now that you have done the necessary work to determine what you currently have, what you are building, and how much money you need, you can start looking at the most probable options for financing your business—all covered in the next chapter!

Finding the Funding

So now that you've examined where you stand in terms of money—and what it takes to finance your business—which funding sources make sense? Before you begin searching for anything, you need to know specifically what you are looking for. While most businesses need capital at some level, there are substantial differences in funding levels for different kinds of businesses. Small, home-based start-ups, for instance, aren't typically in a position to pursue venture capital, whereas microloans are small potatoes for big business start-ups that require millions in financing.

In this chapter, you will find a matrix to help you organize your thinking about funding. Once you've pinpointed your own business on this matrix, you can begin exploring the options and resources available to decide which of them make sense for you.

To determine the appropriate resources for financing, first figure out where your business falls on this continuum (Table 4.1), working from left to right. For instance, do you consider yourself a business type A, B, C, or D? Once you've identified the correct column, the next section suggests some potential funding resources for your business. There are always exceptions, but these suggestions are intended to give you an overview.

Investment Description	Pay As You Grow	Modest Investment	Meaningful Investment	Significant Investment
Revenue	Immediate	Immediate with less early on	Spending more than earning "burn" for 12 to 24 months	"Burn" until sale of business
Risk	Low	Low to modest	Modest to meaningful	Substantial risk
Examples	Local business, consultancy, Web site	Public business (e.g., retail outlet, franchise)	Larger franchise, product business, invention, retail chain	Hi-tech, software, biotech, media publication, large Web site
Nature of Business	Lifestyle, side business earns $10,000 to $50,000 per year	Lifestyle business but principal source of income $30,000 to $200,000 per year	Significant income $200,000 to $5 million per year, long-term sale potential	Speculative, built to sell, $5 million plus
Need Type	A	B	C	D

Table 4.1: Business Type and Financial Needs Continuum Chart, © Mom Invented 2010

RESOURCES FOR TYPE A: SMALL/HOME-BASED BUSINESS

These types of businesses have a low-risk, "pay as you grow" model. Examples include a marketing consultancy, an eBay store, or a business selling roasted almonds to your local farmers' market. You may still have another source of income and are creating this side business to bring in additional income, or because you've always enjoyed "dog-walking," for example. You will most likely be your first investor, using personal savings, credit cards, and home equity loans (mortgage) to start up and grow the business, supplemented by the profits from your initial sales. Many people at this stage also approach family and friends for loans. Other options include bartering and credit.

BARTERING

Modern-day bartering is about creating partnerships with vendors. For example, a business coach might offer coaching services to a print shop owner, trading "coaching" for "printing" (brochures and business cards). If you choose this route, make sure that the terms are clearly spelled out and that you have a simple agreement in place to avoid misunderstandings. Few people realize it, but bartering actually is subject to income taxes. See www.irs.gov/taxtopics/tc420.html.

CREDIT

Vendor credit is something else that you can negotiate when you are bootstrapping. For instance, you may arrange to buy a needed service from a vendor if they are willing to permit you to pay over time. Vendor credit is perhaps the greatest source of capital available to business start-ups. The key is to find quality vendors who see the validity of what you are creating and have the capacity to offer you service without jeopardizing their cash paying clients. The best way to create a positive partnership using vendor credit is to be very clear in your communications. If your vendor is expecting payment terms that differ from the terms you are offering, your relationship can be jeopardized.

TIPS FOR GROUP A

Borrowing from friends and family can become awkward if the terms are not spelled out clearly. One resource to counter this outcome is a business called Virgin Money (www.virginmoneyus.com). Virgin Money manages business loans between relatives and friends. They handle the legal documents, transfer of payments, and provide year-end reporting. Their system is flexible, enabling you and your partner to determine the repayment terms. Putting these agreements in writing provides peace of mind all around.

SMARTYPIG IS ONE FUN WAY TO SAVE MONEY

SmartyPig (www.smartypig.com) is a fantastic Web business that will help you save money in a new way (Figure 4.1). This site's innovation is that it helps people save for specific goals. You provide the date by which you would like to achieve this goal, and SmartyPig will work backward to come up with the appropriate monthly payment necessary to achieve it. Once you agree with

Figure 4.1: SmartyPig.
com home page.

the payments that
you can afford,
SmartyPig will auto-
matically withdraw
the amount you des-
ignate from your checking account and deposit it into your
SmartyPig savings account.

If you have determined that you are not in a position to launch
your business yet, this is a brilliant tool for saving for your start-
up costs. For example, if you know that you'll need a new computer, BlackBerry, and business cards in the next few months,
then add up the costs and open up a free SmartyPig account.

SmartyPig also lets you reach out and share your goal publicly
with friends or family via your social networks or your blog (see
Figure 4.2). (See Chapters 9, 10, and 11 on how to use social networks to your business advantage.) You can cancel your account at
any time without incurring any fees or charges. This savings
account can also be listed
within your Mint.com money
management account. Your
funds are FDIC-insured when
you invest them through
SmartyPig.

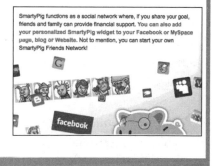

Figure 4.2: Social networking on
SmartyPig.

RESOURCES FOR TYPE B:
SMALL- TO MEDIUM-SIZE BUSINESS
Type B are small- to medium-size businesses looking for a modest
investment. Starting a type B business is a low-to-modest risk.

Examples might include making chocolates that are sold to retail chains; developing and manufacturing products that are sold locally; or building a marketing business, repair shop, or a full-time professional bookkeeping or warehousing consultancy.

Obtaining a small scale loan is a good approach for financing a type B business. The following are some options.

PEER-TO-PEER LOANS

Peer-to-peer loans are an increasingly popular way to borrow money, and they are typically facilitated through Web-based services created for this purpose. You state publicly on such a site how much money you're seeking and what you plan to use it for, and your "peers" (investors) on the site will fund you if they like what you are creating. You will need to have a good credit rating to participate, as investors will not know you personally and will look at your credit as a way of establishing your credibility. One positive side to peer-to-peer lending is that you can often get better loan rates than you would from a brick-and-mortar bank. Well respected resources include www.lending club.com and www.prosper.com.

MICROLOANS

Microloans are another good funding source for type B businesses. These loans are typically offered by nonprofit agencies, although there are exceptions. There is a large demand for microloans, which may make it competitive; however, if you fit their criteria, it's definitely worth applying.

One microlender of note is **Accion USA** (www.accionusa.org), which offers loans from $500 to $25,000 at competitive rates to launch your small business. While banks typically require three years of financials to qualify, Accion USA offers loans for true start-ups that have been in business for less than six months.

Another nonprofit loan program, **Opportunity Fund** (www.oppor tunityfund.org), provides small business loans to low-income entrepreneurs who cannot qualify for a traditional bank loan. They lend on your merit, not just your credit. Opportunity Fund's loan amounts range from $1,000 to $10,000. Larger loans up to $200,000 are available by exception for clients with existing businesses, good credit, and collateral.

Another microlender, **Women's Venture Fund** (www.wvf-ny.org), offers financial assistance for women. This fund is backed by a nonprofit organization that helps women of diverse backgrounds establish thriving businesses in urban communities. WVF also offers training, small business loans, and a network of business advisors to help women reach their business goals.

OUR Microlending (ourmicrolending.com) is neither a nonprofit nor a bank, but a microlending agency that offers loans for small businesses. Loans range from $1,500 to $25,000 for working capital, purchase of assets, raw materials, expansion, or redesign of your business.

Innovative Bank (www.innovativebank.com) offers a special loan program for small businesses called a SOHO loan. SOHO stands for small office/home office and is geared to small- to medium-size businesses in all geographic areas of the United States. A SOHO loan offers the potential qualified small business owner financing that ranges from $5,000 up to $50,000.

Finally, look to your local community for potential microloan funding. **TMC Working Solutions** (www.tmcworkingsolutions.org), for example, is a regional nonprofit microlender offering loans from $5,000 to $25,000 at reasonable rates. Although they offer loans only to San Francisco Bay Area companies, there are organizations like this across the country that are specifically motivated to support local businesses within their communities. A Web site to help you find an organization like TMC in your area is www.microenterpriseworks.org.

Another interesting source for small loans may be a religious organization, such as your local Jewish/Hebrew Free Loan association. They offer interest-free loans to people in their communities for various purposes. (Note that they do not limit themselves to Jewish borrowers.) Do a Google search to learn more about the different local free loan organizations.

GRANT MONEY

Grants are "free" money—and everyone knows that "free" money is hard to find. Finding grants requires lengthy Internet searches, and they are often specific to industries or business niches. However, there are a couple of general grant programs worth mentioning here. One such treasure is a program offered by Eileen Fisher that opens for applications just once per year and annually makes five $10,000 grants to women entrepreneurs. To learn more, visit www.eileenfisher.com. Yahoo! offers another grant program called Seeds for Success. The winner receives a $20,000 cash grant to be used to accelerate the business; up to $5,000 in free technical services from Yahoo! Small Business to build a company Web site; mentoring from business leaders; free Yahoo! Web Hosting services for two years; and promotional support from Yahoo! to help drive attention to the business.

PERSONAL LOANS

Family and friends are still one of your best and most important sources for the initial funding you need for your type B business. If you have a good track record with them, if they have the money, and if they believe in your idea, they are much easier to convince than acquaintances or people who don't know you. Plus, their loan is usually driven by their wish to help you, not to earn an astronomical interest rate.

You can also consider selling shares of your business to friends and family in exchange for funding. They may consider lending you the money with the possibility of converting it to company stock—also called a "convertible bridge loan." It should be noted that offering shares in your business introduces new legal and other costs and complexities as mentioned later in this chapter.

TIPS FOR TYPE B

Don't forget: you are an entrepreneur, so you can write your own rules except for the rules that the U.S. Securities and Exchange Commission (www.sec.gov) and Internal Revenue Service (www.irs.gov) write for you. While I caution new business people about giving away too much of their companies at this stage, there are many ways to get what you need. Trade for services, bring on a partner, ask for donations, ask others to waive fees, or even ask for free support—none of these ideas are out of the question. Sometimes we must swallow our pride to get where we need to go!

RESOURCES FOR TYPE C: MID-SIZE BUSINESSES

A type C business will require a meaningful investment, and the expectation with this size business is that you will spend more than you will earn in the first 12 to 24 months. Type C businesses include companies like high-end franchises, retail chain stores, and restaurants with high initial setup costs. Therefore, a large infusion of capital is necessary from the beginning.

All the resources discussed for type A and type B businesses can be explored at this level (for example, friends may want to invest), but unless you have substantial savings (or very wealthy family and friends), most likely you will need to look to banks and vendors to secure enough capital.

SBA LOANS

There are a lot of misconceptions about Small Business Administration (SBA) loans. First, a clarification: the SBA is an agency of the U.S. federal government and does not lend money. It does support small business owners, however, in obtaining loans from traditional lenders like banks by giving lenders an incentive to offer small business loans. That incentive is to guarantee these loans so that the bank won't lose its money in the event your business fails. While they're commonly referred to as "SBA loans," they are more accurately termed "SBA-backed loans." To get an SBA-backed loan, an entrepreneur must fit the SBA profile and go through a rigorous application process.

An SBA-backed loan is a good option for companies that fit the profile. However, it's still essentially a bank loan for a company that can meet stringent requirements relating to a history of operational success, demonstrable ability to repay the loan, and varying collateral requirements. This kind of loan can be ideal for companies challenged to grow because they need to purchase new equipment or a facility (collateral) to continue the growth of their production. In my experience, the criteria for an SBA-backed loan are not too different from the criteria for standard business loans: adequate collateral, a solid business plan with proven revenue, and an ability to repay the loan.

BANK LOANS

A bank loan is just what it sounds like—you take out a traditional loan at a given interest rate with the promise to pay it back. Traditional bank loans can be difficult to secure for businesses in the early stages of growth because they are considered high risk.

There are literally thousands of banks and credit unions, many of which have special programs to support women, minorities, small businesses, and other groups. It can be worth the time to ask the loan agents at local branches about any programs they might have that would be good for you to pursue. In addition, if you visit the Office of Small Business Development Centers, which is part of the U.S. government's Small Business Administration, they may have information on special programs and lenders in your region. For a list of microloan intermediaries at SBA, visit www.sba.gov.

In addition to the SOHO loans mentioned in the small business section, **Innovative Bank** (www.innovativebank.com) also offers larger loan amounts for mid-size companies.

FACTORING

Factoring is an interesting option for businesses with receivables (money owed by customers at a future date). This is how it works: some financial service companies will "factor" your accounts receivable, giving you access right away to money you're owed at a future date. Say your company ships a container-load of product to a retail store chain. That retailer will pay you any time from 30 to 120 days later. If the delay between the time you ship to the retailer and the time you're paid is hindering operations, factoring may be worthwhile. In this example, the "factor" (financial service company) would pay you 80 percent of the invoice right away. Your retailer would now be responsible for paying the "factor" instead of paying you. In return, the factor earns a percentage of those receivables, anything from 1 to 15 percent. The factor then has the burden of collecting on the debt. Once the retailer pays the factor, you get back the 20 percent reserve—minus the factor's interest and fees. Your banker can often introduce you to companies that factor receivables. Resources include www.factor money.com, www.justintimecash.com, www.inzap.com, and www.btb capital.com.

PROFESSIONAL ANGEL INVESTORS

Angel investors are generally high net worth "qualified" professional investors who put money into companies expecting to earn exceptionally high returns—much greater than they can find with more conservative investment options. There are securities rules that stipulate what it means to be "qualified." These rules pertain to the investor's personal wealth, income, and presumptive ability to make prudent investment decisions as well as the investor's ability to absorb the loss of the investment without undue negative personal consequences. Before approaching angel investors as an option, ask yourself if it's realistic to anticipate the high return they are expecting. Think through your growth potential and be thoughtful in estimating the ultimate return your investors are likely to earn. Also, know that finding angel investors is a time-consuming process; this approach makes the most sense if and only if you've tapped into everything else first.

In addition, you should understand that by accepting this type of investment, you'll have someone to answer to. Your angel investors, essentially shareholders in your company, will expect to be kept informed and may want to share their opinions and recommend strategies. If you became an entrepreneur strictly to avoid answering to others, obtaining your funding from outside investors—angel or otherwise—may not be the right option for you.

How Do I Find Angel Investors?

The key to finding angels is to talk to people. Ask others what they think about your business and about who might want to offer advice on growing your company. A wise person once said, "The best way to get money is to ask for advice. The best way to get advice is to ask for money." So do whatever you can to expand your circle of advisors. Many times these advisors will become your investors!

Other potential sources that can help you identify prospective angel investors include local business groups or the local chapter of the trade association under which your business operates. Introduce yourself and establish relationships. Also, ask your advisors—your attorney, accountant, banker, marketing consultant, even professors—whom they would recommend to you. Your local chamber of commerce, county, or even state government may have lists of angel groups and entrepreneur financing programs they can tell you about. All these people are likely to have an interest in your success; they also have their own networks and generally want to help.

Also, as the process of raising seed or start-up capital has matured, the sophistication of angel investors has also increased. One result has been a growing population of organized angel "groups." They tend to fit four different models: regionally based (e.g., Sacramento Angels), sector-based (e.g., Life Science Angels), cause-related (e.g., Investors Circle, Golden Seeds), or general (e.g., Angel Deals, Active Capital, Keiretsu Forum).

Even if angel groups do not invest in your business, there's still an opportunity to connect with individual members who *are* interested. I have found several angels this way. Because you've had to go through a rigorous screening process to be invited to present to the group, it can provide some comfort to individual angels who have the knowledge that you've been prescreened by a group they respect.

The downside to presenting to angel groups is that there is often a fee associated with being "invited" to present. For bootstrapping entrepreneurs, these fees can be prohibitive. If your company is a "perfect" fit for this particular group of investors, then it may be worth the risk; only you can make this choice.

Additional Web sites to help you begin your research on angel investors include www.gobignetwork.com and www.angelcapitalassociation.org.

OTHER ENTREPRENEURS AS ANGELS?

If you consider the fact that you are building a business that has promise for substantial returns, you might assume one group of people is likely to buy into your business: other successful entrepreneurs. However, I have personally found that this is not necessarily the case. When approaching other entrepreneurs, I've found that unless they have fully cashed out and now consider themselves full-time investors, active successful entrepreneurs are not very likely to invest. I believe this is because they usually would prefer to use that capital to grow or expand their own businesses. And, if they join your company, they usually want to do so as board members or advisors in return for equity, rather than cash.

TIPS FOR TYPE C BUSINESSES

Take time to review carefully all the information above about bank loans, factoring, and angel investor groups to figure out what makes the best sense for you.

Also remember that "I'm getting an investor" falls under the category of "famous last words." There are three reasons for that comparison here: First, with the abundance of investment opportunities ranging from high-tech start-ups to real estate development projects to U.S. and foreign stock markets, people with money can be very selective. Getting them to perceive the positive potential of your venture in competition with so many others—especially in light of the risk—is no small achievement. Second, the level of success investors will expect given the heightened risk of a start-up is not as easy as one might assume. Third, when you sell or give an investor shares of stock in your company, you enter a whole new realm of business and legal complexity. High-priced attorneys make their living on structuring and overseeing these kinds of transactions. Even when you have figured out precisely what you will sell and for what price, you will find that the investor will invariably have his or her own concept in mind.

I have no doubt that this process can be carried through to a successful conclusion by anyone; I have been through it personally, raising more than $500,000 in angel investment over the past few years. However, I want you to take full account of the amount of time, energy, and money that goes into this process so that you first consider all other options, including adapting your business model.

RESOURCES FOR TYPE D: BIG BUSINESSES

Type Ds are big businesses that require big capital. Typically, these types of businesses are defined by their need for "venture capital." Venture capitalists or "VCs" differ from angel investors in the sense that VCs exist strictly to invest money. VCs are sophisticated organizations (usually organized as limited partnerships) run by professional financial businesspeople—often entrepreneurs themselves—or MBA types who have pooled investment dollars into a "fund" that can total tens of millions to billions of dollars. This money typically comes from outside groups and individuals who want to invest with the help of professional managers in rapidly growing companies offering the potential of especially high rates of return (20 to 50 percent per year) within a five- to seven-year time frame. The companies that VCs invest in generally represent a higher degree of risk than larger, established, slower-growing companies.

The VCs will invest money in several companies each year that fit their investment criteria such as industry, stage of growth, and strategic plans, with the expectation that maybe 1 of 10 will hit big. It's typically pretty big money—not less than $1 million per investment, and usually over $5 million. In turn, VCs will often assist in the development of new products and services, and seek to add value to a company through active participation on the corporation's board of directors.

RESOURCES TO HELP YOU PREPARE
FOR VENTURE CAPITAL PRESENTATIONS

For start-up and very early-stage companies, venture capital is generally not appropriate. There are additional issues at play for women-owned companies that make venture capital seem even more improbable. Women are making progress in getting a larger share of VC funding, but it is still a male-dominated world. More organizations are rising up to overcome this, like Springboard Enterprises (www.springboardenterprises.org), which has matched up women business owners with $3.45 billion of venture capital money to date. Another program that supports women entrepreneurs is Astia (www.astia.org). Astia is a unique, international, not-for-profit organization that provides innovative programs that ensure companies gain access to capital, achieve and sustain high growth, and develop the executive leadership of the founding team.

PRESENTATION TIPS

Guy Kawasaki is a managing director of Garage Technology Ventures, an early-stage venture capital firm and a columnist for *Entrepreneur* magazine. Previously, he was an Apple Fellow at Apple Computer, Inc. Kawasaki is the author of *The Art of the Start*, in which he teaches how to pitch successfully to investors. His points are summarized here:

The Art of Pitching

For an entrepreneur, pitching is almost as important as breathing. Not only is pitching a great tool for raising money, it is essential for reaching agreements. Needless to say, agreements are common to any entrepreneur's daily life.

Here are some tips to help you make a perfect pitch:

1. **Explain Yourself in the First Minute.** Every single time you make your pitch, keep in mind that your audience is waiting for you to answer one question: "What does your organization do?"

2. **Answer the Little Man.** Picture a little man sitting on your shoulder. Imagine the little man whispering, "So what?" Always answer the little man's question.

3. **Know Your Audience.** Find out who you would be pitching to and learn what's important to your audience.

4. **Observe the 10/20/30 Rule.** Use the following the next time you are giving a presentation: 10 slides, 20 minutes, 30-point font text. The 10 slides that are necessary for a pitch to investors are:
   - Title slide
   - Problem
   - Solution
   - Business model
   - Underlying magic
   - Marketing and sales
   - Competition
   - Management team
   - Financial projections and key metrics
   - Current status, accomplishments, timeline, and use of funds

5. **Set the Stage.** Remember that everything and anything that goes wrong would be your fault. Therefore, you must be prepared. Bring back-up copies of everything.

6. **Let One Person Do the Talking.** In a pitch, it would be advisable for the CEO to do 80 percent of the talking.

7. **Pitch Constantly.** The best way to achieve familiarity is to keep doing your pitch over and over again.

(Source: www.bizsum.com/trial/html/TheArtoftheStart.htm)

For more in-depth guidelines, see "Perfecting Your Pitch" (www.garage.com/files/PerfectingYourPitch.pdf) by Bill Reichert, managing director of Garage Technology Ventures.

Pinpointing VCs

Like angel investors, VCs tend to have market-sector focus areas that can be as general as technology, energy, or consumer goods, or as specific as "business software applications" or "green energy." This is important to note so that you focus on firms that specialize in your area. Just like the process for finding angels, often the best way to start is locally—through business contacts and other networks. For instance, I asked my local banker and one of my microlenders for recommendations. Both put me in touch with several potential investors and allowed me to use their names as referrals. In a world where VCs are besieged with unsolicited business plans, a recommendation carries substantial weight.

You can also use the Internet to search for VCs in your specific industry. A number of Web sites offer centralized directories with VC groups seeking "deal flow"—i.e., companies in which to invest. Start with the National Venture Capital Association (www.nvca.com) for a list of venture capital firms investing in your business sector.

SBIC PROGRAM

Another source of investors is the Small Business Investment Company (SBIC) program. SBICs are encouraged through government incentives to invest in small businesses. It's a bit similar to the way government supports banks to make SBA loans.

The goal of the SBIC program, which is part of the U.S. Small Business Administration (SBA), is to improve and stimulate the national economy and small businesses by stimulating and supplementing the flow of private equity capital and long-term loan funds. The goal is the sound financing, growth, expansion, and modernization of small business operations while ensuring the maximum participation of private financing sources.

The 50-year-old program funds only small businesses—companies with no more than $18 million in net worth. Any business that fits this description can apply for funding, and there is a diverse group of VCs included that fund businesses in virtually every sector and at every investment stage, from start-ups to mature companies.

Recently, the Obama administration signed the American Recovery and Reinvestment Act, which put even more SBIC money into circulation, and there are plans to streamline the process for qualifying for an SBIC loan. For more information, go to www.sba.gov/aboutsba/sbaprograms/inv/esf/inv_sbic_financing.html.

You can also find a comprehensive list of SBIC investors by visiting www.sba.gov/aboutsba/sbaprograms/inv/inv_directory_sbic.html. The list of operating SBICs is organized by state. Another source of SBIC information can be found within the member listing of the National Association of Small Business Investment Companies (NASBIC) at www.nasbic.org. A third source is the National Association of Investment Companies (NAIC) Web site at www.naicvc.com. Finally, you might want to check out The Funding Post (www.fundingpost.com), which connects thousands of angel and venture capital investors with entrepreneurs.

TIPS FOR TYPE D BUSINESSES

I've spent hundreds of hours preparing for and making VC presentations, but I have found much more success in raising money from angel groups and individual angels, microloans, and friends and family. Finding VC investors is a time-consuming, drawn-out process that requires patience and a very thick skin—two things that I have had to develop over time.

This is not to say you shouldn't pursue VC investments as an option, but you should be prepared for a competitive and often grueling process that may not yield the results you anticipate. However, as with every aspect related to your entrepreneurial pursuit, it is up to you to use your business acumen and instincts to decide on the right path for you.

CONCLUSION

Now that you've begun getting a clear picture of the money it will take to fund your business, the next part, with chapters on marketing and sales, will cover strategies on how to bring it in! While sales can be a daunting task for some entrepreneurs, for others it's just what they've been waiting for. We have strategies and tactics to recommend that will help entrepreneurs of every type excel at one of the most important aspects of the business—selling your service or product, and maximizing your marketing to support those sales.

PART 2

❖

Making the Most of Today's Marketing and Sales Tools

Creating Value
and Building Your Brand

One of the most critical parts of defining your business lies in pinpointing what value it provides to your customers. In this chapter, we will explore how to determine your company's value—the distinct "thing" you are offering customers that no one else is—and discuss how to build your brand to support that value message. This is your first step in marketing your business, which will help support your sales and everything you do!

The most simple and effective way to break down the marketing process is via the following **three core components**. These are the primary elements that will enable you to begin selling your product or service successfully:

1. Know your customers.
2. Focus on providing value.
3. Create a marketing plan.

The following sections will explain each of these in detail so you can be on your way to supporting your sales!

1. KNOW YOUR CUSTOMER

First things first: a key truth to understand before you even begin to sell your product or service is that it's actually not about you, your service, or your product at all. It is also not about how well, how elegantly, or how loudly you can tout your products or services. It is, instead, about your customers.

But what exactly does that mean? If you don't know your prospective customers, don't go into business, because who they are and what matters to them is the only thing that should matter to you (as it pertains to marketing). It is all about your customer. If you are not supplying something that they need, want, and value—or you don't know who they are—there is no need to be in business.

When you think of "who they are," you should be able to describe them in some detail. What is their age, gender, socioeconomic status? These are called "demographics." Where do they live, what do they drive, what is their marital or family status?

Next, you need to go a little deeper to understand their needs, motives, and concerns. What do they like to do for fun? What has made them successful? What do they fear? What publications do they read? To what groups do they belong? Who are their industry opinion leaders? Who are their partners, allies, and competitors? These are often termed "psychographics."

At this point you're probably wondering, "How do I get this information?" Excellent question. The answer to that may be the most useful secret shared in this book. This is highly confidential advice, so please read carefully. Here is the answer: **Ask them and listen.**

Yes, it may sound obvious. But time after time, entrepreneurs simply assume that they know their customers. After all, we all have the same basic needs and concerns, right? Wrong! I have been guilty of believing this too many times myself.

Here's an example. One time we spent three weeks creating an online seminar series thinking we knew what courses and topics our community wanted and needed. When we launched the series, eagerly awaiting the imminent rush of registrations, what happened was quite surprising. There *were* a lot of registrations. However, those registrations were for only three of the dozen or so courses we offered. While these were filled to capacity, others did not get even a single registrant. This came after weeks of work in creating the entire program, and I would have saved a lot of time and money had I just taken time to find out first, from my community, what mattered to them.

DISCOVERING WHAT MAKES YOUR CUSTOMERS TICK

There are a number of ways to "ask" your potential customers for information. To some degree, the methods you choose will be driven by the nature of your business, your target customer, and your own comfort level.

When you contact existing customers or those you think fit the profile, do so solely with the intention of gaining more information about their needs—and do not turn it into a surprise sales call. You will find that people will be surprisingly forthcoming, as long as your task remains on course. Make it crystal clear that this is not a sales pitch and that you have no intention of making it one. Then ask them a series of questions you have prepared in advance. Here's how to create an effective list of questions:

- First, brainstorm every question you can think of, and write it on a board or notepad.
- Next, reread each question and look for ways to extend or deepen it. For example, if your product is a gizmo for the consumer market, you might ask, "What stores would you expect to carry a product such as this gizmo?" Then you might go further and ask, "In which departments would you expect to find it?" and "How would you feel about this store if they did not carry this item?"
- Consider the negative or opposite of each question as well. Continuing the example above, you might ask, "Where would you *not* expect to find this product?"
- Be sure to ask financial questions. "How much would you pay for this service or product?" Then ask the opposite question, "What price would be too high?"
- Include questions that focus on the customers' needs, not just the product's or service's attributes. For example, "Describe any issues you

face daily, weekly, monthly that relate to [insert language describing the need your product or service addresses]?" "How big an issue is this for you?" "Have you ever discussed this issue with friends, colleagues, and peers?" "How have you addressed this need in the past?"

Once you have a long list of possible questions, go through and select the ones most relevant to you. Then tighten the language of each question so it is as clear and brief as possible.

During the interview (covered next), carefully document the answers. Also be sure to make any notes you can about the individuals (your potential customers) that could prove useful in your later analysis, such as their gender, ethnicity, estimated age and economic status, marital and parenthood status, and anything else that comes to mind. People will often deviate from your expectations—but in so doing will share the most useful tidbit you get out of the entire interview. The key is to be quiet and listen, even after the interview is over. Often this is when people will drop their guard and make some of their most interesting and useful comments.

WHERE TO FIND YOUR INTERVIEWEES

There are any number of creative ways to find potential interview subjects/customers. The best method is the one that gets you the information you need in the most efficient way possible. Here are a few proven methods.

Intercepts

If you are selling directly to a fairly general consumer base, place yourself in a location where people congregate, such as shopping areas, parks, etc., with clipboard in hand, and ask if they would be willing to share their views on a few questions. You can also use this approach by posting questions in online forums where your target customers may gather. For example, if you have a wedding product or service, go to a wedding site like www.theknot.com and access a chat room or forum. Visit my site, www.yourmilliondollardream.com, for new and updated resources. Be mindful of site rules and etiquette regarding sales-related postings. Remember, to be effective, you are not selling but instead seeking and listening to people's opinions.

Focus Groups

Focus groups can be incredibly valuable. Not only do you get people's direct feedback, but you can observe them as they interact with each other about your business, product, or service.

It is important to create a focus group atmosphere where people will be comfortable sharing their most candid opinions. You gain little value if they censor their views to make you feel good. That's why it may be beneficial to have a third party conduct the focus group. To do this, you need to find a venue, preferably other than your home, where people can feel they are on safe, neutral ground. (Often local libraries and civic or community centers will rent rooms at a reasonable rate.) Then invite attendees to share their feedback on the business, product, or service.

To make a focus group more manageable for your guests, schedule it during a time that you think would be most convenient for them, such as lunchtime. If you aren't sure what would be most convenient, ask them. Also let them know there will be a time limit, and feel free to provide payment or other perks as an incentive. For example, when we held a focus group for our new online business, we promised that we would be finished in two hours and we provided lunch.

Targeted Interviews

If you are selling to other businesses rather than directly to consumers (for example, you've developed new software for the restaurant industry), you will likely need to schedule one-on-one meetings or phone calls with individual owners, managers, or buyers in your target market. One effective way of getting a lot of information at one time is to find out when and where the industry association conventions are for these companies. You can then look into sponsoring a lunch meeting with several of them at one time. Or, just attend the event and meet them one-on-one. An added benefit is that you can catch executives or business owners in a venue that is distant from the constant pull of their day-to-day business operations.

Once you've collected a good sample of data, carefully analyze it. Start by labeling response types. For example, to the question, "Have you discussed this with friends?" you might categorize responses such that 1 = yes, 2 = no, 3 = on occasion, and 4 = don't recall. Once you have read and categorized your data, look for common patterns. Ideally, you will get insights as to what is most and least important to your target customers. This will enable you to identify the optimal features, benefits, and pricing—the intersection between your highest profit and their perceived value. It will also enable you to craft your marketing messaging in a way that most appeals to the customers, and structure your service or product to deliver true value to them.

2. FOCUS ON PROVIDING VALUE

In developing your sales and marketing approach, the first thing to consider is your core philosophy and how you deliver value to your customers. Being mindful of your approach and how you project your commitment to the customers' well-being, versus your own success, is essential. As I said earlier, the only thing that matters is what the customers need. Your focus must be on giving them what they need rather than "getting the sale"—even when you don't get the sale.

In their important book *The Go-Giver*, Bob Burg and John David Mann creatively and powerfully communicate this essential message through a five-part story that illustrates their five core concepts. The first and third concepts, addressed here, are:

The Law of Value: *Your true worth is determined by how much more you give in value than you take in payment.*

The Law of Influence: *Your influence is determined by how abundantly you place other people's interests first.*

After learning about your customers, consider the "laws" above and take the time to think about the value you bring to them. Ask yourself questions like:

- What do I "like" about them?
- What can I give them?
- How can I make them successful in their own pursuits?

This approach can help lead you to new ways to hone your product or service and deliver more value. How you do this will involve the specific features of your offering and how you describe them, your price, and how you will deliver your product or service. Traditional marketing professionals call this your "marketing mix." Think of it in terms of the value you will deliver.

One thing it's important to be clear on is the difference between "price" and "value." Value is not objective. What does that mean? Put it this way: Most people get a haircut on a regular basis. Every barber and stylist has access to the same tools and for the most part uses the same ones: a comb, scissors, shampoo, dryer, etc. So, why will one person pay $500 for a haircut and feel like it is completely worth it, while another, like my husband, feels that spending more than $20 borders on obscenity? Value is completely subjective to the perspective of the customer. One person may value the experience, skill, and bragging rights offered by a celebrity hairstylist; another may think he can do it himself just fine. Survey after survey has shown that most consumers—from all aspects of life, not just the wealthy set—are willing to spend more money on a similar product or service if they "perceive" there to be added value. So your task is to understand your customers' perception of value and deliver it.

MARGINS

A critical aspect of this idea will have to be fleshed out in your business plan (Chapter 13). It is your obligation to have a crystal clear understanding of your own costs and profit margins (the amount of money left over after paying all your own costs and expenses). In addition to your hard costs, such as materials, production, and shipping, you need to include the cost of your own time and effort. I raise this here so that you have a clear understanding of the ramifications of any commitment (both time and money) that you make.

Once you are clear on the value you plan to deliver, it's time to create a sales and marketing plan that folds into your philosophy.

3. CREATING A MARKETING PLAN

Your marketing plan will be the map you use to create an effective approach to communicating your mission and brand to your target customers and stakeholders. The plan should include your unique story, how your message will be carried, and how you will ultimately engage in sales transactions. There are a few key elements that will go into your marketing/sales plan.

YOUR MESSAGE

In your business plan (covered in Chapter 13), you will create a mission statement. This is the heart and soul of your business. In some cases, the mission statement will be your message. However, there will be other messages you develop for specific purposes and varied audiences. While the messages may vary, they should not contradict your mission statement.

For example, my company, Mom Inventors, Inc., has two parts. For the online and educational portion of my business, the mission is to "inspire, inform, and boldly promote courageous women in business." For the consumer products side of my business, the mission is to "celebrate the creativity of moms by launching innovative Mom Invented® products around the world."

My message in various situations has varied. For instance, I have sought to convey to the media the intrinsic importance of our Mom Invented brand as it relates to women by saying, "The Mom Invented brand recognizes and celebrates the intellect and creativity of Moms."

To a retailer considering our line of products, I have said, "The Mom Invented brand communicates both innovation and trust to your most important customer, Moms."

And to investors, I have said, "The Mom Invented brand creates a meaningful connection with a brand-loyal consumer base—Moms." None of these messages contradicts my mission. Instead, I modify my mission to best communicate to the respective audience. The key in developing a plan is to adapt your message carefully to your audience and what they care about most.

BUILDING YOUR BRAND

Your brand is an extension of your mission as well. The most successful brands—think Apple, Coke, Target—elicit reactions and feelings before a word is even spoken or communicated. Strong brands, simply put, are easier to sell. And strong brands engender long-term loyalty, translating into repeat sales.

Creating your "brand" is all about instilling the impression that you want your target customers to have of you and your product or service— and connecting with your customers through ideals they care about. Ideally, you would have a chance to share your messages—the ones we covered in the prior section—directly with every person. However, you can't reach every person, and it generally takes more than a single communication for the meaning of your brand to settle in, even with the people you do reach. So, here we will discuss some strategies for creating and strengthening your brand, which, in turn, supports your success at selling.

While your message will initially come from you in some form, your success will ultimately be determined more by what *other* people say about you, your product, or service than what you say yourself. This is the elusive and highly valuable "word of mouth." Apple didn't sell a gazillion iPods because CEO Steve Jobs said it was hot. They sold *some* because of what he said, but they sold a *gazillion* because of what users said to each other.

But you need to start that word-of-mouth somewhere, and there are numerous ways to send your "message" to your target audience. Here I want to distinguish between two broad categories (and then put most of my focus on the second): (1) advertising, and (2) earned marketing, often referred to as "guerilla marketing," based on Jay Levinson's outstanding book of the same name.

ADVERTISING

This might be an overstatement, but not by much: there are almost an infinite number of places you can buy advertising. Most people think of newspapers, television, radio, Internet, and magazines as advertising venues because these are the major media outlets we see every day. However, if you stop to think of the number of ways marketers reach us every day, it's dizzying: direct mail, coupons, e-mail, telemarketers, bus signs, Web site ads, billboards, inserts in your bills, catalogs, window displays, flyers, counter signs, signs in elevators, ads on grocery carts and on the sides of cars, and on and on. That ubiquity is also one of the principal problems with advertising from the advertisers' perspective. The sheer number of messages creates clutter and makes it difficult for any one message to get through.

However, there are also strengths to paid advertising. First, with paid advertising, you have 100 percent control over your message. You write the content, design the ad, and choose the music, message, and visuals.

Second, because there are so many possible places to buy advertising, it is often possible to get your message in front of a very specific or niche target audience. If you sell a product for scrapbooking, for example, there are magazines, Web sites, and catalogs that serve scrapbooking enthusiasts. And you could likely even narrow your ads to scrapbooking enthusiasts within a specific geographic region.

Getting your own carefully crafted message in front of your target customer is helpful in the process of creating the desired perception of you, your product, or your service. However, because advertising is well understood to be bought by the company promoting its own wares, it seldom will create, by itself, the kind of buzz and confidence that other methods can generate. If the impression of your brand is already solid and well established, advertising can be useful to communicate changes or special offers such as discounts, or to reinforce your brand and maintain top-of-mind awareness.

EARNED MARKETING

Because the economics of Internet marketing tools and social networks are so compelling, much of earned marketing is now done through these means. Each of these topics is covered in depth in Chapters 7 through 11.

However, there are a number of powerful methods that can be used to help build your brand and get others talking about you, your product, or your service as either a complement to, or instead of, your paid advertising.

The essential nature of earned marketing is reaching individuals directly who will voluntarily share your message with others. Think of this as a process of building your reputation and gaining supporters, one by one, among the relevant audience. It all starts with you. You, or representatives of your company, first need to communicate and project your brand to your target customers and identified opinion leaders. The positive word of mouth and brand-building inevitably follows. A few of these methods are listed here.

Become an Expert

For a few reasons, becoming an expert helps you connect with people on a level beyond your own success. It is enormously gratifying to share information that people truly appreciate and from which they benefit—and at the same time reinforce your company and brand perception. Becoming an "expert" in an area in which you are knowledgeable is much more achievable than most people would imagine. In fact, it can be achieved in four basic steps:

1. Start by thinking about what you know. Make sure there is a logical connection to the mission you ultimately want to convey. For example, if you're a hairstylist, convey your expertise in hair color.

2. Identify venues where your knowledge might be useful. Given the number of Web sites, magazines, newsletters, and social and business groups, the demand for content is insatiable. This is another good reason to know your customers and the publications, newsletters, or online communities to which they subscribe.

3. Write up a couple of brief columns and approach the editor with a proposal that you provide a regular column.

4. Offer yourself to relevant local groups as a speaker. The groups you speak to will depend on your own market. Virtually every industry has associations that serve as central places for sharing industry

information. Contact the association(s) that your customers belong to, and offer to write an article for its newsletter and to speak at its monthly get-together or at its annual conference. Local groups that are typically open to guest columnists and speakers include chamber of commerce networking groups, Toastmasters, Rotary and Lion's clubs, PTA and mommy groups, and of course groups dedicated to specific hobbies and interests. Don't expect to be paid at this point. However, when you do a good job and actually "move" an audience, it is not unusual to be approached afterward with an invitation to deliver a paid speech.

Earn Recognition

Winning contests or recognition can be a simple way to build buzz around your business. Many business publications, associations, industry or demographic groups (e.g., women, seniors, etc.), chambers of commerce, and state, city, and county entities create honors, awards, and events to draw attention to their own efforts and to support entrepreneurs. Oftentimes these groups get far fewer applications for their "business of the year" and other awards than you might expect. Be sure to try to leverage this type of "free" recognition. In fact, whether you become a finalist or not, your mere entry can be used to create some buzz with your local media. The time and effort spent researching these kinds of opportunities can be well worth it. You'll find plenty of examples in the online resources section in the back of this book.

Align with a Cause

Cause marketing is closely associating your business or product with a social cause, in an effort to do good and connect with your target audience. Business has a responsibility to give back to the community beyond the jobs and taxes it creates. Also, if done well, cause marketing can truly enhance your brand and help with your objectives. An example of this is one I've used myself: every time someone purchases one of our Mom Invented products, they are both validating the creativity of women and directing a percentage of the sale to an independent mom inventor.

Ten or fifteen years ago, cause marketing was a new, creative way to build a positive impression and media interest in a brand. Today virtually every company, large and small, has adopted one or more "causes." This has made it increasingly difficult to stand out by using this technique by itself. Simply noting that "a percentage of proceeds will go toward [name your cause]" will not have the same cachet it once had. But it can still have a big impact on your marketing and branding mix, especially if you get creative. For example, instead of giving a percentage of proceeds to a given cause, involve all your employees as volunteers instead—and let your customers know about your initiatives.

When looking at using cause marketing, there are two things to consider. First, choose a cause or causes that you can personally feel passionate about. Second, choose causes that your customers will likely feel drawn toward as well.

PUBLIC RELATIONS

The deliberate process of generating press is known as "public relations" or "PR." While it's a massive subject with many elements and layers, you will still benefit from an overview as well as the valuable resources below.

Start-ups often have big ambitions and slim marketing budgets. In comparison to paid advertising, press coverage can be much more cost efficient. Also, media coverage—when positive—carries tremendous credibility. Unlike paid advertising, which may state claims about your product or service, an article about your business in the news media comes across as unbiased and can be far more persuasive.

So if it's that easy, why would anyone pay for advertising at all? The answer is that advertising, if done well and placed intelligently, does work to make sales for you directly or indirectly. Like any business tactic you take on, it does take time and finesse to make PR work. Here are some tips.

Find Your "Hook"

There are challenges associated with getting the media's attention. The media, especially large broadcast and print publications, need to select stories that are interesting and/or of value to their audiences. While your product or service is extremely interesting to you, it isn't automatically interesting to the media—and its angle can't be overly commercial in nature. That said, there are many possible angles or "hooks" that can make it interesting.

First, consider the type of media you want to reach. Let's say you are a CEO who wants to recapture market share from a competitor by selling a new computer storage device that has breakthrough technical features. Undoubtedly technology magazines, Web sites, TV, and radio programs will be keenly interested in interviewing you. Oprah's producers, on the other hand, would not likely be interested. However, if you were to create a technology job-training program for underprivileged or low-income women, Oprah might be interested. This is an extreme example, but making these kinds of decisions is where your creativity should come in.

To pinpoint your hook, think about how your product or service can tie in to current events. For example, recently there was a news program that featured an interview with the coach of the new men's national baseball team in Iraq. In the interview it was noted that the new team owned just one bat and a hodgepodge of old used gloves. Several American companies leapt at this opportunity. One company donated bats and equipment, including baseball shoes and gloves for every player. Another donated lightweight uniforms, while a third donated a freight service to deliver it all to Iraq. On the same news program the following week, the newscaster glowingly spoke to a multimillion viewer national audience about these companies, repeating their names, touting their products and their generosity, and displaying their logos and their Web sites. This media value would be impossible to purchase at any price—and they probably got it for just a few thousand dollars in donations. This is just one example. There are opportunities like this every month, especially if you pay attention to local events and holidays. For an online directory of holidays, visit www.altiusdirectory.com/Society/united-states-holidays-2009.html.

Another angle to consider is your personal story. If it is a stretch to generate interest in your product or service alone, perhaps your own story will intrigue the media. Are you a "mommy"? Try publications that want to feature success stories about mothers. Have you overcome personal obstacles? Is your personal story completely unique or newsworthy in another way? Try pitching these angles to the appropriate media.

Also, remember that you can pitch stories related to your cause marketing efforts or any recognition you have earned—both elements we discussed in prior sections.

When you do come up with your angle, typically there are two ways to present it to the media: a press release and a personal "pitch."

Make It Shine

A press release is a brief document that is written to introduce editors and reporters to your story. The goal is to pique their interest and provide your contact information. A press release is not intended to tell the entire story although publications sometimes publish releases in lieu of reported stories. Make it easy for them to do so, by writing them well and succinctly. Many media outlets rely on a relentless supply of news in order to keep their offerings to their own customers fresh and interesting.

Press releases can also have a secondary purpose, which often ends up being the main benefit of a release. Even if the news media does not pick up your story, you can still post your release to your Web site and send it to your own stakeholders, such as investors, customers, and vendors, to help convey a message of strength, success, and momentum.

The most important aspect of the release is the headline. It must catch an editor's or reporter's interest. The most common mistake is making your headline too long. A seasoned reporter will decide if the story warrants follow up after reading about two to three sentences—that's it. Everything beyond those first sentences is for the other audiences I mentioned above, who will actually read more because of their personal stake in the company, or for publications that choose to publish your release in its complete form.

Once you write a great press release (prweb.com offers free, excellent guidelines in "The Quick Guide to Writing Your First Online Press Release"), it's time to distribute it. Choose two or three free press release distribution sites and see which one works best for you. When I began selling my first product—the TP Saver, a toilet paper saver that prevents kids and pets from unraveling the family toilet paper—I sent out a free press release on www.prweb.com, and my story was picked up by the *Today Show*. That led to my first TV interview with Katie Couric! There are an abundance of these free press release services, and you will find plenty of them listed in the additional resources section in the back of this book.

Also, create a slightly different version for your local press, with a local spin on the story. Local media are always looking for interesting stories to feature about people in their respective communities. Niche or industry publications, Web sites, and blogs may also be a perfect fit for your story. Finally, make sure that you have a press room on your own site, so that people and reporters can read your latest news announcements.

Make It Personal

Above and beyond sending out your press releases, you should try to make personal contact with an editor or reporter. Your success is more likely if you identify specific reporters at particular magazines, newspapers, and television shows that cover stories like yours. Send them your brief, meaty press release that teases them with your unique "hook," and then follow up by phone to "pitch" your story.

When you make your pitch, remember how busy these people are and what their goal is: to cover stories that will interest their audience. When you make phone contact with reporters, you have about 20 seconds to grab them. Assume they have not read your release but use it as your reason to call, and hit them with substance immediately—e.g., "I sent you a press release today. I wanted to be certain you saw that [compelling fact with real-world example]!"

Another great way to get free press is via Web sites that aggressively pursue sources for stories. HARO (www.helpareporter.com), ProfNet (profnet.prnewswire.com), and Reporter's Source (www.reporterssource.com) give you access to queries directly from reporters about the stories they are working on right now. If you see one that fits your business and expertise perfectly, call or e-mail the reporter with the relevant info, being sure to answer all questions fully and directly and provide all your contact details. Also make sure you're playing by the site's rules and not spamming journalists and adding them to distribution lists without their permission. Remember, this is a delicate dance, so don't bombard a reporter with e-mails. Instead, respond to the query and then follow up once in about three to five days if they do not respond. Don't burn your bridges; your story may not interest them now, but down the road you may have an angle that captures their attention. Be gracious even if you feel that they haven't been.

Bring in the Pros

Because PR is so cost effective, there is a huge industry of public relations professionals, also called "publicists," who are paid to secure and manage media for companies. Although I have used the steps outlined in this chapter to secure press for myself, I have also worked with publicists. Because of the sheer number of media outlets and the time it can take to pursue this type of coverage, hiring a professional can be a wise move if getting free press is part of your marketing plan. There are a number of ways to find a good publicist. The best is through referrals from other people in your industry or local area. In addition, you can find PR firms by visiting the Web site directory provided by the Public Relations Society of America (www.prsa.org).

CONCLUSION

So you've determined what value you provide—and you're on your way to creating your distinct brand. In the next chapter, you'll learn how you can use this marketing to get your "feet on the street," so to speak—and begin making actual sales.

Getting Your
"Feet on the Street":
Making the Sale

Sales is a cornerstone of your business. There are few things that make a bigger impact on whether you succeed than your ability to generate paying customers.

Yet for many entrepreneurs, the sales process can be intimidating. This chapter will show you that it doesn't have to be. If you're passionate about your product or service and understand the real value you are providing to customers—and if you then create the proper channels for reaching your target customers—it's a much simpler process than it seems at the outset.

Of course, sales challenges and methods are as varied as the types of businesses and their customers. An interior home designer will sell her services to a different type of client than will the owner of a computer consulting company, or someone selling jars of homemade jam online. That means the way you approach sales will be uniquely your own.

But there are some universal concepts, nonetheless, and I will share the ideas and approaches that can be applied to almost any sales

LESLIE HAYWOOD'S FIRST SALE

Leslie Haywood, founder and CEO of Charmed Life Products (www.grillcharms.com), shares her "first sale" story. She calls it, "Doing Business Topless."

Very shortly after my "light bulb" moment, I was diagnosed with breast cancer at the age of 34. My passion for my product was so strong that cancer really didn't slow me down much. One day I was having my final "procedure," if you will, for my breast reconstruction. I'm the queen of TMI (too much information), but even *I* won't come right out and say what the gal was doing. I had known these health-care professionals for over a year, pretty intimately, as you can imagine, so in an effort to help me think about anything other than what she was doing that day, she asked about how my little invention was coming along. It worked. I instantly forgot the discomfort and gave her the complete rundown of Grill Charms—and then asked if she wanted to see a set, which I happened to have in my purse! By the time she was done waving her buzzing magic wand, she said, "I need five of those!" I pretty much jumped off the table right then and there, opened my cell phone calculator (yep, still topless), and totaled up everything. She wrote the check on the spot. Only after our business was done did I put my clothes back on! Now part of my proceeds goes to the Breast Cancer Research Foundation.

process. Know, however, that you should adapt all these concepts to your own individual style. One of the most important aspects of your million dollar dream is that you enjoy the process and that it fits *you*, not the other way around.

That's why the information provided here is meant to increase your knowledge base and give you examples of how others have overcome sales challenges. Rather than viewing them as inflexible instructions, know that your creativity, inspiration, and guile are *the* critical elements to your success. Entrepreneurs regularly find new ways to sell their wares that would not likely get air time in an MBA sales curriculum. This is what sales—and entrepreneurship—is all about, which is why this chapter includes some interesting, unusual, and inspiring "first sale" stories from our online community.

PSYCHOLOGY OF SALES

Most people's discomfort with selling is at least partly based on a misperception as to what exactly constitutes selling. It takes just three words to sum up what many people envision when they think of selling: "used car salesman." This image, fair or not, carries with it the idea of a fast-talking person who, once he gets you on his car lot, will stop at nothing to see you drive off with a car for which you overpaid, and that will likely break down within the next two or three blocks. (FYI, though—I've had nothing but great experiences buying "pre-owned" cars!)

While there are salespeople who have no compunction about selling like the proverbial used car salesman—and such people tend to sell all kinds of products and services—this strategy does not reflect the activity of "sales" in a satisfactory way.

Perhaps the biggest misperception is that to be successful at sales, one must have some kind of innate or genetic skill. Often I have heard, "Oh, he's just a natural salesman," which carries with it the unspoken belief that others are *not* natural salespeople. But know that this is really just a myth. Your genetic makeup will *not* prevent you from being successful. It's much more a matter of hard work than it is DNA. Sales is a learned skill, and *you* can learn what you need to know to be successful even if you are a naturally shy, introverted, or quiet person. You can get a lot of advice, guidance, and education to be effective. But mostly, you can teach yourself. Being successful at sales is a choice; if you decide to sell successfully, then you will.

"BUYING" VERSUS "SELLING"

One helpful way of looking at sales is to consider the concept of "buying" versus "selling." You will undoubtedly get your first order because you "sell." But what does that really mean? For example, recall the last time you went clothes shopping and bought an outfit. If someone assisted you, say, in finding pants to match the shirt you'd chosen or got you the correct size, you probably didn't think of this in terms of being "sold." Rather, you were "buying," which is the way most successful salespeople want their customers to feel.

Even if an attentive salesperson is feeding "options" over the changing room door, seldom would you consider it "selling." The next time you saw your friends, you would talk about the new sweater that you just "bought." Don't be fooled, though—you were sold, and you are happy about it.

Generating "buying" customers will result from your overall sales efforts. Despite the fact that we have been sold to since an early age, and most of these experiences have been positive, many are uncomfortable with the notion of selling and accepting money for their products or services. This is mostly based on a deep-seated, negative view as to what sales and selling is all about. Therefore, before jumping into sales planning, process, and techniques, this chapter demystifies and redefines how sales should be approached and interpreted.

WHAT IS "SALES"?

If "sales" is not some kind of manipulation supported by a high-gloss brochure and loud advertisements—and then closed by a natural-born fast-talking salesperson—then what is it?

Every business will have drastically different targets—some will be selling to consumers, some to retailers or wholesalers—and that means a different approach to selling. Also, some businesses will need to generate a large quantity of sales to make a profit, whereas others have higher-ticket products or services that make highly targeted sales strategies more critical.

No matter what your product or service, there are some universal concepts that you can adopt and apply to your business to find success. In this section, I'll outline some direct sales strategies (i.e., where you or an employee is charged with making sales) as well as indirect sales strategies, where you employ other methods, such as partnerships or independent sales reps to generate sales. Most of these concepts can be applied, in some way, to any type of business. Use this information as a guide, and tailor it to your own specific products or services sales requirements.

CUSTOMERS GENERATE CUSTOMERS

In the beginning of any new business, there's a process we'll call "creating your market." This is about building sales upon your initial sales. The idea is that when you first begin to sell, some customers will be more willing to try your new product or service than others. These customers are referred to as "early adopters." These sales will usually require some extra attention, and feedback from your early adopters should be carefully considered. Then, by using these customers as references, you can begin to sell to a broader mix of customers using more of a formalized approach.

DIRECT SALES START WITH YOU

As an entrepreneur, it is very likely that in some way, you will need to sell directly to a buyer. That buyer may be a consumer, a retail buyer, or a wholesaler. Direct sales means you, or an assigned salesperson, will be actively identifying and selling directly to customers. Typically this method of sales is used when the value of a single sale is large enough to justify the cost of a person's time to make a sale. In other words, if it takes a week of full-time effort for a salesperson to make a sale, and you pay him $1,000 per week, the sale he or she lands must be worth a great deal more than the $1,000 you have paid. This is one reason that entrepreneurs are usually their own first salespeople.

FINDING SALES LEADS

Generating direct sales must begin with a list of target customers. Historically "lead" lists and contact lists were hard to come by, as most of this information was compiled and sold in the form of large lead publications. These books are still produced and are readily available at most business libraries. If you will be making direct sales and need customer leads, take advantage of this resource and the librarians on staff to assist you. Business librarians are often extremely happy to help unearth the ideal resources for your needs. In addition, many industry associations provide Web directories of their members and will even sell lists of "buyers" that attend their trade shows.

BUILD YOUR NETWORK

Deliberately and methodically building your network, one person at a time, is essential to developing leads. To do this, attend organized networking events, mixers, and gatherings for businesses. There are two general "secrets" to successfully using these events:

1. Identify networking groups that attract the type of people you want to be connected with and then "show up." This is really half the battle; afterward, you will still need to become a regular. Introduce yourself to people and before you know it, you will have become a leader with tremendous influence with this new "network." And at the events themselves, recognize that nobody attends for the snacks; they are there to meet people. But most people feel a bit shy, so your boldness will be appreciated.

2. Understand what "networking" is about. People will complain that they attended a mixer but didn't sell anything. Networking events are *not* about selling to people, though. They are about creating a network that will help you succeed over the long term. These people can aid you in amplifying and transmitting your message. So the larger and stronger your network is, the better your chances are for success. Approach these events with this in mind.

There are a few additional techniques that will add to your effectiveness as you attend these events:

- Go early and stay late. If you are going to network, then do it right.
- Make sure your 30-second elevator pitch is honed and clear.
- Listen more than you talk. After you briefly introduce yourself and what you do, listen to other people. Really learn about them, their business, and what they are trying to accomplish.
- Think about helping others you meet, and pretty quickly you will be someone they remember. In your discussion, focus on how you might be able to help them. Is there a contact that you can give them? Do you have any ideas to help them land a deal they are working on?

LAURA CASTILLO'S FIRST SALE

Laura Castillo, founder of Sassy Soles (www.sassysolesonline), tells her "first sale" story.

I often get asked how I got Sassy Soles, my ridged design shoe inserts, on the shelves of H-E-B grocery stores. The answer is simple: I called the main switchboard of the company. With this one phone call, I got the name of the foot care buyer and her e-mail address. The operator transferred me to the buyer's voice mail. On the buyer's voice mail, she stated that e-mail was the best way to communicate with her and gave out her address. I was then able to confirm the information given to me by the operator.

I left her a voice mail stating I would also be sending an e-mail to introduce a new product. A couple of months later, we were in 33 of their stores.

So, that wasn't too bad, was it?

- Making four solid contacts is better than making many marginal ones. So take your time with people and make a connection, rather than giving and collecting as many business cards as possible.
- Give up the "I am bad with names" excuse. When you meet someone, repeat the name to yourself and reuse it two or three times within your initial meeting. You will be surprised to find out that you are not "bad with names," just not in the habit of remembering them.
- Follow up and stay in touch. Many times contacts with great networking potential are made but then not maintained.
- If you find that a particular group isn't strong enough to be worth your time, move on quickly to find others.
- Networking takes time and is a serious sales activity. If this is to be part of your plan to build your business, be sure to dedicate enough time to it.

SALES IS A NUMBERS GAME

No matter how it is approached, success at sales is about activity. The more opportunities people have to buy from you, the better chance you have to make money. If you have a retail store, you will get more sales if you stay open longer. If you are selling advertising, you will close more deals if you call more people. As part of your plan, you will want to start by measuring the effort that leads to your desired results. For example, how many calls did it take to get each appointment? How many appointments did it take to earn a sale?

THE ART OF THE COLD CALL

One of your best tools is likely to be the research you do on your own through the Internet and the cold calls you make as a result. Few industries exist that don't have an industry directory that can be found with a few Google searches. Your biggest challenge will probably be identifying the individual decision maker at the companies you want to contact. Typically, though, it just takes a little detective work, such as a couple calls to the company, to get the information you need. When it comes to direct sales, though, cold calling skills are essential, whether you will be doing any actual selling over the phone or making appointments to meet in person.

For some reason, many people fear having to make cold calls. Perhaps that fear is driven by the fact that most of us, at one time or another, have been less than "gentle" with a caller who has interrupted our dinner or happened to call in the middle of a family discussion to ask, "How'd you like to save money on your phone bill?"

Click.

But the more you cold call, the better you'll get. You'll not only become more confident as you do it more frequently, but you'll also become more comfortable with the actual content of what you are saying. In the meantime, here are several techniques and tips to consider:

- Get over your fear by turning cold calls into a game. No matter how badly someone treats you, realize that the minute the call is over, they will forget about you, so you can do the same.
- Understand that telephone cold calling is a numbers game. You may need a hundred "no's" to get to a single "yes." When viewed this way, each "no" simply becomes one more step toward your "yes."
- Set aside enough time to get into a rhythm, allowing at least two hours per calling block. Also, plan to get through a set number of calls. Mornings tend to be better than afternoons for reaching people, but before or after work hours can also be very good. Oftentimes, decision makers work during holidays while gatekeepers do not, so this can also be a good time to make calls. Note, however, that if you are selling directly to consumers, calling them at home can be dicey. They won't appreciate it, and they may be listed on "do not call" lists. Typically calls of this nature are best made to businesses.
- Keep good notes. Next to each name, note the date you called,

what was said, or if you left a message. When it is time to follow up, you will be surprised at how glad you are to have some basic notes to refer to—e.g., "I called last Thursday and mentioned I would be in town later this week . . ."

- Prior to your call, be clear about your objective. It should be limited and narrow. If your objective is to set up a sales appointment, for instance, craft your script to reflect this, and stick to it. If your goal is to get an appointment, don't try to close a sale. By focusing on the objective and avoiding getting drawn into random discussions, you will both improve your success and earn credibility with the target.

- Businesspeople and their gatekeepers may be courteous toward amateurs, but they like to do business with professionals. Your voice can convey either. When we are nervous, our voices rise. In addition, nerves increase the speed of our speaking. To counteract these tendencies, lower your voice. Think of yourself as a very important person about to call another important person, and speak extra slowly. Be polite but not to the point of being apologetic. And smile when you speak, as this will add warmth.

Your script should be uncomplicated and direct. Introduce yourself with confidence and credibility, provide a brief explanation as to why you are calling, and ask for whatever your objective is:

Hi John, this is Mary Jones, President of XYZ Company.

I have a product that we use with several other companies like yours [such as _____.]

I am working in your area next Tuesday and Thursday morning and would like to show you briefly how we saved these companies $_____. I have a slot at 9 a.m. on Tuesday. Would that work?

(Note: when you get a question, one good technique is to answer directly and briefly and follow with a question. For example, if they ask, "How do you save us money?" you could say something like, "We have a new proprietary system that reduces waste by over 50 percent. I see I also have an 11 a.m. slot; does 9 or 11 work best?")

The gatekeeper is the person whose job it is to shield your target from unwanted telephone calls. This person is not your friend, but don't make him or her your enemy. Your first call to a gatekeeper will be indicative of how hard your target will be to get on the telephone. Assuming you have already figured out who your target is, be polite but authoritative when the receptionist or assistant answers:

You: "This is Mary Jones; is John in?" (Using first names connotes familiarity. You may get passed through because the gatekeeper assumes you have a relationship with the target.)
Gatekeeper: "Who is this? What is it pertaining to?"
You: "Yes, Mary Jones with XYZ. Is he there, or should I call back?"

You will figure out fairly quickly how challenging it will be to get through. Only leave messages on a cold call as a last resort, though; most contacts will not call back. Instead, you can and should try to get useful information from your interaction with the gatekeeper. For example:

Gatekeeper: "I can take a message if you like."
You: "Oh, thank you. I am on my way out but can try back later. What time do you expect him?"
Gatekeeper: "About 4 p.m."
You: "OK, how late is someone there answering the phone? And what time can I reach you in the morning?"

These types of questions are the key to avoiding the gatekeeper on future calls. You see, often executives and owners work after and before the gatekeeper, and they will frequently answer the phone themselves then. And many phone systems have an individual extension directory that you can access after hours. In this case, you will simply search the directory for your contact's direct extension and dial it.

If this doesn't work, another strategy is to call and ask the switchboard operator for the sales department. Virtually every receptionist in

America knows that when someone calls for sales, they should be transferred immediately to a salesperson. Then, when they answer, say,

"Oh, I must have gotten the wrong extension—I was trying to reach John. What is his extension?" Don't be surprised if this person simply transfers you directly to the boss. And when he does, be ready to launch into your script in a tone that assumes he would be happy to hear from you: "Oh, hi, John. Mary Jones here with XYZ company. I have . . ."

Once you achieve your objective, say, "Thank you, I will see you at 9 a.m. on Tuesday. Goodbye." Once you achieve your goal, stop talking and hang up—or risk having the whole transaction unravel.

Most offices have caller ID. Find out what shows up when you make a call. If it says, "XYZ Sales Company," for instance, you are starting off with a disadvantage. If it has your personal name or "private," you are much more likely to pique their curiosity enough to answer.

Get started now! The anticipation of making calls is a hundred times worse than making them. While you may make mistakes and won't succeed every time, you will get better—and if you keep making calls, you will generate business.

HIT MULTIPLE TARGETS AT ONCE

Sales is a time- and resource-intensive process. Therefore, it makes sense to leverage as many shortcuts in this process as possible. Trade shows, networking events, and other special programs are some ways entrepreneurs can expand their networks and leads and, in so doing, accelerate their progress. Here's the rundown on each of them.

TAKING ON THE TRADE SHOWS

Trade shows provide a venue where all the people who buy specific products or services (say, consumer electronics) are invited to a single place during a condensed period of time (typically one to four days). Companies who sell industry-relevant products or services rent space to display their wares and meet these buyers. The benefit of this arrangement is hard to miss. With so many trade shows from which to choose, there are inevitably multiple opportunities that would be of benefit to your business.

Generally speaking, there are three types of trade shows to consider: industry trade shows, consumer trade shows, and local events.

Industry Trade Shows

Most industries—whether it's plastics manufacturing, banking, juvenile products, medical devices, or software—have representation through a trade association (or multiple associations). Most of these trade associations organize a trade show, also known as a convention, each year. Members are invited to attend the show to get information relevant to their industry. At the same time, they are encouraged to "walk the show" and meet the companies offering services or products relevant to their businesses. For you, exhibiting at trade shows can be a highly efficient way to generate new sales leads. These events are also invaluable in terms of meeting other people in your industry, finding service providers, and even finding staff for your business. (At my own first trade show, I actually met one of my best sales reps and was also introduced to my future overseas manufacturer.)

Your main objective at these functions, of course, is generating sales. Say, for example, you sell corporate promotional products—pens, gadgets, T-shirts, or caps with company logos on them—and have decided to target banks. Trade shows may provide the perfect opportunity to reach them. By calling around and doing a little research, you can figure out which shows make sense for you to attend and which make sense for you to be an exhibitor. If you are going to be an exhibitor, be sure to book your booth as early as you can, because you'll often get a better rate, and, more importantly, because you'll get a better location within the exhibit hall. Getting a booth at the end of the very last row that attendees can visit is a sure way to get less bang for your buck.

If you have the luxury of time, it's a good idea to attend a trade show at least once before you decide to exhibit there, since attendance alone is much less expensive than exhibiting. A show might look like it would be a good venue for your product or service but turn out to be pitched to the wrong audience for your purposes.

SALLY CAMPBELL'S FIRST SALE

Sally Campbell of Chatterpants.com shares her first sale story.

I didn't have any prior experience in children's clothing, so it seemed very risky to launch to the retail trade until we had spoken to lots of parents first. Two months in, we exhibited at a popular consumer baby show attended by new parents and those with one on the way. We had to be very quick on our feet as we didn't know what to expect, particularly when, to our surprise, one lady said, "I could sell these." I could tell by the look in her eye that this lady wasn't your average new parent! But she needed to be sure that our product was ethically made and wouldn't have a wholesale discussion with us until we could prove it. Not that we had a clue how to set wholesale prices yet anyway. Unfortunately, I didn't ask for her business card, but her face was imprinted in my memory, and I resolved to come armed with the validation next time.

Four months later, we decided we were brave enough to exhibit at our first industry trade show. In the last few days before the show, the threat of an unusually severe snow-storm was all over the news, dampening our hopes for visitor levels. To our great surprise, having traveled what must have been two hours to get there with a good chance of not being able to get back, I spotted her approaching our stand. Then it became remarkably easy! I addressed her previous concerns and got our first ever trade order. She still doesn't know that she was our first, but now that she has become a regular customer, we will probably tell her one day.

Consumer Shows

Consumer shows, unlike industry trade shows, are attended by the general public—usually targeted groups like brides-to-be or moms. Here's a comparison: a popular industry trade show for the juvenile market is the All Baby and Child Expo (www.theabcshow.com) in Las Vegas. Buyers from juvenile departments of most major and independent retailers attend this show looking for products to be sold in their stores.

On the other hand, there are consumer shows serving the juvenile market such as those produced by Bebe Paluzza Productions (www.bebepaluzza.com). Mothers and mothers-to-be in the cities where these shows are held will attend the shows expecting to buy a wide range of retail products for their own use. Whereas companies/retail buyers that sell products to their customers would attend and "shop" the All Baby and Child Expo, actual end-customers (individuals) would shop at the Bebe Paluzza shows. Events like this can be found in most major cities throughout the world.

If you sell directly to consumers (say, handmade baby blankets or baby photography), a consumer show can be a great opportunity for you to begin getting exposure and making contacts and sales.

Local Fairs

Many small businesses sell to a general local population and simply need opportunities to meet local people. These might include businesses that provide homemade food items, home improvement services, or other locally focused consumer-oriented products or services. Local fairs can provide an effective opportunity to make lots of contacts and begin building your market. Often these events will be organized by civic groups such as a chamber of commerce. They might even complement another local community event, conference, or organized gathering such as a farmers' market, charity event, flea market, or a women's conference.

SPECIAL PROGRAMS

Entrepreneurs must seek out every advantage and shortcut they can find. In this vein, there are a number of special programs that are worth considering. If you sell a product, find out when major retailers offer special new vendor days. Also, take advantage of programs designed for people within specific socioeconomic or demographic categories. There are often opportunities to sell to large companies and government entities for certain types of people. To learn about minority-owned, women-owned, disabled-owned, and other certifications, visit www.wbenc.org and www.mwbe.com.

EXPANDING INTO INDIRECT SALES

As your business grows and you take on more tasks and responsibilities, one-on-one sales by you or your own staff salespeople may not be the most cost-effective approach. One way to generate cost-effective sales is to take advantage of opportunities to generate sales indirectly—meaning that you get other people to do your selling for you. There are no absolute rules, so you can create new models that work. However, there are a number of established indirect sales models described below.

AFFINITY PARTNERSHIP

If you have ever received a mailer from your college alma mater, social group, or industry association offering you a special discount on auto insurance, you have seen affinity marketing. A company, in this example the auto insurance company, will partner with another company or organization that has existing customer or member relationships. The insurance company will then pay a referral fee to the organization for any new customers generated through this mailing. Virtually every organization is looking for new sources of revenue. If you can identify organizations whose members would benefit from your product, it may be a marketing approach that you should pursue. One note: most large organizations and associations have been besieged by companies making affinity offers, so they may be slow to accept even an obvious win-win situation. One way to accelerate this process is to sell to some of their members first—then enlist these customers' support in persuading the organization or association of the benefits to both the organization and its customers/members.

AFFILIATE PARTNERSHIP

An affiliate partnership is nearly identical in concept to an affinity partnership, except it's typically used to describe online relationships. For instance, you place a link on someone else's Web site, and then you pay them a commission for every click or purchase made through that link. There are a number of companies that have built infrastructure to streamline this process on both sides of the affiliate relationship. I have used one called Commission Junction (www.cj.com) myself.

INDEPENDENT MANUFACTURERS'
SALES REPRESENTATIVES

Most manufactured products ranging from gardening tools to baby products have an entire field of independent manufacturers' representatives, sometimes referred to as just "sales reps." These may be individuals, or they may be professional companies with extensive corporate structures. These people or companies "represent" product lines made by other companies and, as experts in their respective fields with strong relationships within the sales channels in their industry, get compensated for what they sell. They sell the products to customers such as retail stores, but the manufacturer (in this case, you) still invoices the customer and pays a commission to the manufacturer's representative. For example, I have a sales rep that specializes in selling to Toys"R"Us. He understands this retailer very well and has a special relationship with various category buyers. On a regular basis, he presents the product lines he represents, including ours, to the appropriate buyers. When they buy, we ship and invoice the customer ourselves, and he is paid a commission on the sale. His job is purely sales.

Once again, the industry associations representing your product category (from technology to textiles to toys) can often be a useful source of knowledge about the industry and often provide a directory or links to manufacturers' reps that service the industry. A few examples of these associations are the International Housewares Association (www.housewares.org), the Juvenile Products Manufacturing Association (www.jpma.org), and the Toy Industry Association (www.toyassociation.org).

SUZANN COWING'S FIRST SALE

Suzann Cowing, founder of SaniManiPedi (www.sanimanipedi .com), tells her "first sale" story.

After pounding the pavement for a few days and coming up short, my family got a new Chesapeake Bay Retriever puppy. Because the seven-week-old puppy was too little to leave at home, I started bringing her with me on all errands. I happened to have her with me when I popped into a store I had been meaning to contact about carrying my line of products. I don't think they even looked at what I was trying to sell them. They fell in love with the dog and placed a huge order. Who knew?

DISTRIBUTORS

A distributor is a company that, like an independent manufacturer's representative, sells products produced by another company to retailers. The key difference between a distributor and a sales rep is that the distributor takes on more financial risk and requires a larger piece of the pie. A distributor will actually buy products directly from the manufacturer (you), stock the inventory at its warehouse, sell and ship to the retailer-customer, and invoice the customer. In fact, the distributor may have its own sales reps selling to retailers on its behalf. Because of the increased risk and cost of services incurred by distributors, they generally require a greater wholesale discount so they can sell to their retail customers and still earn a profit. The best way to identify proper distributors for you is by asking target retailers which distributors they work with. The role of distributors varies depending on the sales channel.

VALUE ADDED RESELLERS (VARs)

Similar to the manufacturers' representatives discussed above, a VAR is an expert in a particular field, usually technology or professional, who provides value-added services to his or her customers. The VAR requires a menu of products and services they can provide beyond their own services. Generally you will give them a wholesale price, like you might give a retailer for a consumer product, and they, in turn, will sell your product/service to their customers at a marked-up price in conjunction with their other services.

Whereas direct sales can be quite time consuming because you and your salespeople have to be involved in each and every sale, indirect sales can help your small company grow much more rapidly. Finding these partner companies can be challenging, however. The best source for finding them can be your current or target customers. For example, if you are trying to sell a housewares product through your regional supermarket chain, ask them which organizations, manufacturers' representatives, distributors, or resellers they'd recommend. As with affinity partnerships, it can sometimes be challenging to persuade these distrib-

DO YOU LOVE SALES?

Consider this: If you are in the process of identifying your own new business, these intermediary businesses described above are viable business models if you love to sell and want to be your own boss. In other words, you could become a VAR or manufacturer's rep.

utors or reps to begin championing your product or service to their customers immediately, but there are ways to accelerate their interest. One way is to present them with a current prospective customer and let them participate in the sale (and get paid for it); the second is to sell directly to one of their customers without their assistance. When they experience the latter—seeing their customer go around them to buy your product or service—they will become much more interested in working with you. We landed our largest retail account this way!

By starting small and identifying one or two indirect sales approaches to try, you will quickly learn if this is a way you can sell more rapidly. If you are currently going it alone, just imagine having a team of indirect salespeople, who are paid on results, working for you!

IT'S ALL ABOUT CLOSING

"Closing a sale" is getting the customer to agree to buy. When done properly, closing a sale should not be a major event. If you have addressed each of your customers' needs, and they are convinced of the value you have offered, finalizing the transaction—closing—is a natural next step. As illustrated in some of our "first sale" stories, this can actually be quite fun for both parties involved. The main thing worth mentioning here is that you must be sure that you do, indeed, finalize the agreement.

When you reach that point in the sales process where agreement must be secured, but you feel uncomfortable saying, "Please sign here," it is perfectly acceptable to use less direct language that means the same thing. For example, "How would you like to pay for that?" or "Would you like that shipped this week or next week?" will do just fine.

Just don't leave without a clear agreement that the sale is final!

POST-SALES STRATEGIES

Of course, once you make the sale, it's not quite over yet. Here are some strategies to ensure things continue to go smoothly with your new customer—and to generate ongoing loyalty and future sales:

Getting paid. Payment standards will vary depending on your business. However, in today's environment when credit is tight, cash is key— so I prefer getting paid quickly. In fact, I nearly always offer customers an incentive to pay in advance. In my consumer products business, I have found that as a matter of practice, most customers (typically, retailers) expect and tend to pay in 60 or 90 days. But if I offer a meaningful discount, they will pay up front or within 10 days. Getting the cash in hand and avoiding the costs and headaches of invoicing and collections is always worth it to me, and the cash can be used to fuel other parts of my business right away!

Following through. Once you have earned customers, you need to keep them. That means exceeding their expectations. In the process of keeping your customers happy, look for new ways to fulfill their needs and sell more to them. Some companies always add a free little gift to every purchase—and customers always feel good about receiving their orders. This creates loyalty.

Also, if there is any complication at all, overcommunicate. People will tend to forgive a hiccup if you apologize and communicate about it. On the other hand, they are unforgiving if the matter is handled less openly. In addition, keep in mind that your easiest future sale is made to an already satisfied customer.

Showing gratitude. When you make a sale, understand that your customer is putting his or her faith in you and your business. By making an effort to express your gratitude, you will continue to set yourself apart from prospective competitors. One way to do this is by using a handwritten note. Think about this: how many handwritten thank you cards have you received this month? If you received one, you'd remember who sent it. With the advent of e-mails, texting, and more, handwritten notes are rare—and you can use that to your advantage.

Another thing that has become all but extinct in business is authentic communication between customers and vendors. This doesn't mean you should introduce heated political or religious debates. However, frank comments that express your feelings can have an impact far beyond the financial benefits you receive from one another. A simple statement like, "You know, I really appreciate working with you because you always do what you say," will have a surprising impact.

ANOTHER FABULOUS BUSINESS TOOL FOR YOUR SALES AND MARKETING TOOLBOX

Animoto.com is a powerful video creation platform. Business owners can create stunning videos (without a video camera) that bring their products and services to life. Simply add photos, text, and select music (from the site's 500+ songs), and the program automatically generates a flawless, professional-looking video. The videos can be used to "Enhance your Web site, help your e-newsletter go viral, create killer PowerPoint presentations, spice up your blog, create promotional videos for trade shows . . . and more." It is a great way to attract customers, clients, and sponsors.

CONCLUSION

The nature and methods of selling will be as varied as the businesspeople who create them. No book can capture the essence of all of them, but this chapter has provided insights on some of the main concepts and tools available in the process of generating sales. It is up to you to choose and adapt those that you find relevant and dismiss those that you do not. And no matter how you use this information, you should approach sales with pride, as this is the essence of entrepreneurship!

In the next chapter, you'll find more tactics on how to support your sales efforts, including specific ideas on how to bring customers to you via the Internet.

Your Web Site
and Online Marketing

As a business owner, I had read and heard about Internet marketing for a long time before truly diving in. I simply couldn't grasp the magnitude of it until I began researching it and using it personally. I soon learned that the Internet is a marketing world unto itself. If you are not a part of it, then you are missing out on an enormous opportunity. In fact, creating a powerful presence on the Internet may be the single most important thing you do to help your business succeed. The challenge is figuring out how to get started.

One way to think of "online marketing" is to divide it into two parts. The first involves using the Internet and associated tools to get your message out—similar to traditional marketing. This chapter and the next will begin to address those methods. The second part of Internet marketing involves the phenomenon of social networking; because it's such a big topic unto itself, it's covered in Chapters 9, 10, and 11. But no matter what stage you're at—whether you are launching your business or looking for new techniques to reach new customers/clients—it is time to explore what Internet marketing can do for your business.

There is only one thing in the world worse than being
talked about, and that is not being talked about.
—Oscar Wilde

Specifically, this chapter will answer the following questions. What is online or Internet marketing? How does Internet marketing work, and how do I create a Web site presence, create e-commerce capability, and bring customers to me? How do I use online marketing to reach out to customers? What are some of the best online resources and tools available to help me build and grow my business? The answers to these questions will lead you well on your way to finding Internet marketing success!

INTERNET MARKETING: A (VERY) BRIEF HISTORY

First, it's important to keep in mind that the concepts and methods of online marketing are constantly changing. What was cutting edge just a few years ago is practically archaic today. Remember when not too long ago people began using e-mail, then e-mail list managers (such as LISTSERV), then group e-mails? Web sites and "portals" such as Yahoo.com popped up in virtually every category with free news content, chat groups, and online display advertising. Next came directories and classified listings such as Craigslist.org, individual e-commerce sites, auctions and marketplaces like eBay.com and Amazon.com, and e-mail marketing services such as Constant Contact and Internet radio. It seems like only yesterday that blogs were the "new" big thing, and then social networks like Facebook and LinkedIn exploded. After that it was YouTube, mobile phone applications, Twitter—the list goes on!

Possibly the biggest change that has occurred over the past decade is the ability for people to interact with one another online. All of the services that permit and promote that intercommunication are collectively referred to as Web 2.0. With Web 2.0, users can change Web site content (by, say, commenting on a blog or posting info to Facebook) in contrast to noninteractive Web sites, where users are limited to viewing information passively. Web 2.0 created a whole new set of opportunities for businesses. Since the rapid pace of technology can feel daunting and overwhelming, the intention of this chapter is to slow everything down and establish a foundation. As you read through all of this information, do not feel the need to do everything at once. Start with one or two options to see how they work. Learn about what is available, research where your target market is actively spending time, and start where you feel most comfortable.

INTERNET MARKETING DEFINED

You've probably heard that Internet marketing is the great equalizer. If so, you heard correctly. You can be just as—or more—powerful wearing flip-flops in your home office as large corporations are with their abundant resources. The low cost and the greater capabilities for distributing information and media provide each of us with tremendous resources that require only Internet access, personal focus, creativity, time, and determination to make an impact.

Internet marketing can be as simple as sending an e-mail message to a group of friends or colleagues about your business—or as complex as developing a high-concept Web site with video posts on YouTube, a blog, an online forum, and your own weekly newsletter—all promoted via Twitter and your Facebook fan page. It's up to you how much you want to do, based on the results you're seeking.

When compared to the cost of reaching people via traditional media (brochures, direct mail campaigns, billboards, television, and print ads, for instance), Internet marketing is inexpensive, and its reach is global. Imagine driving by a billboard. You may read it and think about it, but you can't take any immediate action, and you often will forget about it until you drive by the next time. With Internet marketing, on the other hand, you read it and think about it—and then you can buy the product or service instantly, and you can also share the information about that product or service with friends, expanding the advertiser's reach in one fell swoop.

Ten years ago, building a significant Web presence was a major marketing decision, while few businesses would have questioned whether they needed a printed brochure. As things change, businesses tend to migrate toward the tools that are the most cost effective. Today, the Internet has become a utility relied on as heavily, or more so, than the telephone.

Understand that without my crystal ball, I am only able to share some of the tools available today. Undoubtedly new tools will continue to surface, as rapidly as they have already. The point, though, is that you must start somewhere. Choose the method that feels the most comfortable to you, and test it out and see how it works. Also, don't feel shy about asking others to help you get started—even borrow your friend's teenager if you don't have one!

FIRST STOP: YOUR OWN WEB SITE

If you don't already have a Web site or blog (blogs will be discussed later in this chapter), it is time. Web sites have become essential, must-have marketing tools, as important as a phone line or a business card. It gives customers a place to learn about your business, the products and services that you offer, and how you can help them. It tells your customers that you are legitimate, that you care about them, and that pricing is reasonable and fair. In the past, this role would have been fulfilled by your company brochure. Consider your Web site an online brochure that you can update moment by moment with a great deal more potential for exposure. Plus, it gives you a place to tell your "story," and that helps you connect with customers, the media, and the world at large.

So what should your Web site include? Put yourself in your customers' shoes, and imagine that they are seeing your Web site for the first time. What do you want them to take away after spending time there? What will bring them back again?

YOUR DIGITAL ADDRESS

First things first—before you can create your Web site (or blog), you will need a URL. "URL" stands for uniform resource locator. Translated into English, that means a Web site address. It is also called a "domain name." Most businesses choose their company name to function as their URL. For example, my company is Mom Inventors, Inc., and therefore my URL or domain name is www.mom inventors.com. To purchase a domain name, you will need to search online to see if it's available. Many sites offer this service, including www.whois.com, www.dyndns.com/services/pricing/#domains, www .1and1.com, www.godaddy.com, www.hostgator.com, and www.name cheap.com. If the URL for your company name is already taken by someone else, you need to consider either buying the URL from them or finding a way to modify your company name. For example, if www.joesgym.com isn't available, you could try www.joes-gym.com, www.joesgym.net, or www.joesfitness.com, or you might consider changing your company name. You'll be investing a tremendous amount of time and money in building your business, and you don't want to find yourself in the position in six months or in two years of having to change the name of your business because it violates some-one else's intellectual property.

If your "address" is available, you will be able to buy it for a set period of time, say one to three years. You will also have choices as to the "extension" after your Web site name, the best known and most desirable of which is ".com." If this one is available, you should buy it. The next most often used are ".net" and ".org" (although the latter typically indicates that the Web site is associated with a nonprofit organization). Given the prominence of video on the Web, ".tv" is an increasingly popular extension, although it currently costs more.

You would be well off to buy any names that you anticipate potential customers may use to look for you. For example, I also own www.mominvented.com, www.mominventors.net, as well as www.tp saver.com (named for my first product). You should also buy your personal name. If your name is Sally Rose Smith, you should buy sally-smith.com, sallyrosesmith.com, and sallyrsmith.com. Some people even go to the length of buying common misspellings of their business name. Note, though, that the costs of buying so many domain names can really add up, so use your best judgment.

THE SKINNY ON WEB TEMPLATE COMPANIES

Here are a few sites that offer templates that you can use to get up and running quickly:

- 1 & 1 (www.1and1.com) offers a program called MyBusiness Site. There is a video tutorial that will demonstrate how to set up your site.
- Homestead (www.homestead.com) offers 2,000 free templates to choose from, as well as a simple video tutorial that will walk you through the steps. (Owned by Intuit.)
- GoDaddy (www.godaddy.com) may be the most comprehensive. It offers Web templates and industry-specific Flash introductions (Flash technology uses animation and/or video to add spice to your Web pages) that can be easily incorporated into your Web site. You also get free e-mail and Web hosting when you buy a Web template. Again, a video tutorial is available for guidance.
- Yahoo! also has an online tool called Yahoo! SiteBuilder at smallbusiness.yahoo.com/webhosting/websitetemplates.php that offers 380 templates to choose from.

Check each of these sites out—as well as others—to see which one is the clearest and easiest to understand.

For your Web site to be connected to the Internet, it has to be "hosted" by a Web service—i.e., the software has to be loaded onto a server, which is like a big hard drive, and connected to the Internet. Each of the companies mentioned above and many others offer hosting services. We use Media Temple (www.mediatemple.com). They offer excellent service, they're affordable, and they have great customer service.

WEB SITE 101

You can always hire a Web designer to build a Web site for you. However, if you go this route, expect to pay a few hundred to many thousands of dollars. This support is worth it if you can afford the help. But if you can't, there are many low-cost solutions that will allow you to build a Web site easily with no prior technical background. (Yes, really!) A great place to start is with a Web template company, which can help you get something up and running quickly. As your business grows, you may want to have a more sophisticated, individualized Web site, at which time hiring a Web designer or consultant with knowledge in search engine optimization (explained below) can be the way to go. Be sure to work with someone who will show you how to make updates and changes yourself if you wish.

DO YOU NEED TO KNOW CODING AND HTML?

As you begin your online explorations, you'll inevitably start hearing terms like XML, HTML, Drupal, Ruby on Rails, Java, and PHP coding. These are all terms describing software language and development environments. These are "under the hood" technologies that are useful to know something about if you want to get into the building blocks of your Web site. You can get definitions for these terms on Wikipedia (www.wikipedia.org). Fortunately, you can have a Web site without any expertise in these areas. For instance, my Web site was created on WordPress (www.wordpress.com), which gives users the option to make updates easily in plain English.

**MAKE IT EASY FOR PEOPLE
TO BUY FROM YOU WITH E-COMMERCE**

PAYPAL

If you're selling a product or service, you will need an easy way for customers to pay you. There are two main ways to deal with getting paid. The first is to set up an account with a company that handles online payment exchanges between people such as PayPal or Google Checkout. This can be set up almost immediately, requires very little administrative work, and, thanks to eBay, is a very well-accepted method of processing payment.

The downside to this approach is that customers will be taken away from your site to make the actual transaction. Also, the payment can take time to "clear," and then it takes additional time to be transferred to your bank account. While bank transfers are usually free, the cost per transaction can be rather high for credit cards. For a low volume of sales, these gateways can help a small business get up and running quickly, provide secure and trusted transactions, and bypass merchant account and security fees associated with doing your own credit card processing.

MERCHANT ACCOUNTS

The second way of getting paid is by setting up your own merchant account. If you create your own merchant account, you gain a much greater degree of flexibility. You can accept most credit cards both through your e-commerce Web site as well as directly from people who need to pay for your products in person or over the phone. The money is generally cleared and in your bank account within a couple of days, and a customer can pay you directly on your site with your secure ordering form.

The downside is that there is a bit more administrative work to do to get set up. To get started, you will need to set up three things: a merchant account at a bank that allows you to accept credit cards; an online payment gateway or processing service, like www.authorize.net and www.verisign.com, that allows you to take payments online; and a secure, SSL (secure sockets layer) certified Web site to handle your e-commerce needs.

You can find merchant account companies through your industry association or bank, by searching online, or even through discount clubs such as Costco. In addition to signing up with a merchant account service, you will need to open a bank account with the capability to link to a global payment-processing service. Some banks may offer the entire package. A merchant account costs approximately $50 per month plus a per-transaction fee. Some banks also charge initial setup fees.

BUILDING YOUR ONLINE STORE

Being able to accept credit cards won't help you if you have no place to sell. There are many different shopping cart solutions out there, some much more complex than others. Solutions to look into, from the simple to the complex, include PayPal Shopping Cart, E-junkie, Shopify, WebStore by Amazon, 1ShoppingCart (www.1shopping cart.com), 3D Cart (www.3dcart.com), and Magento. Some options integrate with your existing site, like PayPal Shopping Cart (www.paypal.com) and E-junkie (www.e-junkie.com), while others help you create a separate, stand-alone shopping site, like www.Shopify.com, WebStore by Amazon (webstore.amazon.com), and Magento (www.magentocommerce.com). Prices vary drastically depending on the complexity of your e-commerce site, how many products you're selling, and how much custom setup help you need from a designer or developer.

CREATE COMMERCE AND TRAFFIC VIA ONLINE MARKETPLACES

If you sell products, you need to sell in multiple places beyond your own Web site to gain traction and visibility. Today, there are more options than ever, including sites like Amazon and eBay that allow individual sellers to post their products. Remember, you need to be where your customers are—so find them and use the sites that reach them.

Given its size, technology, and fee structure, Amazon is likely one of the best general marketplaces to sell your products online. You can either post your products on Amazon and pay only when your item sells, or you can create your own Amazon WebStore. An Amazon WebStore will become your own branded, custom store that can reside on your own Web site yet use Amazon's high-powered technology, which handles e-commerce and payment transactions for you. Amazon WebStore costs just under $100 per month, but they offer a free 30-day trial. Even if you don't have your own products to sell, you can select and sell Amazon products in your WebStore and earn commissions on sales.

Amazon has a special program for high volume sellers called Pro Merchant to help you manage inventory and sales. Features include fulfillment centers to store and ship your inventory (if you don't want 2,000 units sitting in your garage) and a complete e-commerce check-out solution that provides your customers with the same secure check-out feature as on Amazon.

The advantage of marketplaces like Amazon is that not only do they bring prospective customers to you, they also provide a professional Web presence with e-commerce capabilities so that you can be up and running quickly and present yourself well. Check out the other marketplaces to see their advantages in the resources section at the end of the book. You can also use these sites to drive people back to your own Web site. Try it by posting a few of your best or favorite items on different marketplaces, with your Web link in your contact information. It exposes people to your creations, products, or services and entices them to visit your Web site to see more.

The disadvantage of listing in these marketplaces is their sheer size. One jewelry maker I recently spoke with said she's never sold a piece of jewelry on a popular marketplace site (www.etsy.com) because she was just one of 14,000 pages of jewelry designs. However, I know some entrepreneurs have great success. I happen to know another jewelry maker who gets 8 percent of her sales from www.yelp.com. Although it is a review site and not a marketplace, she found, through testing various sites, that this worked best for her. In fact, Yelp worked so well that she reinforced her sales by taking the next step and advertising there. By purchasing an ad space, she also earned extras from Yelp like a rotating slideshow of photographs of her jewelry—which again helped reinforce sales.

Even though it's good to be listed in multiple places, it will require plenty of stamina and personal determination to drive people to your Web site, store, or marketplace listings.

DRIVING PEOPLE TO YOUR SITE
SEARCH ENGINE OPTIMIZATION

When you print a brochure, you can do things to ensure customers see it. You can hand them out at events, display them in offices, and even send them through the mail. The formatting and layout of the brochure itself should be designed to draw someone in and entice them to read what's written. With a Web site, you have a similar challenge in getting people to view it and, once there, to spend enough time to see and read what you'd like them to see and read. Even if you hand out your URL, people still must proactively make the decision to visit your site. But, most potential Web site visitors are likely to find you by searching for the subject of your site—i.e., the product or service you are offering.

One technique to get them there is search engine optimization (SEO). In a nutshell, SEO helps ensure that when people are online "searching" via, say, Google, MSN, or Yahoo, and they enter search terms relevant to your site, your Web site/URL shows up as high in the search results as possible.

SEO is the process of modifying your Web site in a manner that improves its chances of showing high up in the search rankings when searchers enter the appropriate search terms in search engines like Google, Yahoo!, AOL, Ask, MSN, and bing. For many online companies, using SEO techniques to achieve a high search engine ranking is essential for survival. If your Web site ranks very high and therefore comes up in the first page of search results in any online search, chances are good that the searcher will click through to visit your site. If it doesn't come up on the first page, chances are greatly diminished that the searcher will pay attention to your site. When a user types in a search term, the unpaid results that come up are called "natural search." Because it may not be possible to modify your site in a manner that will bring your site up in the first page of the natural search results, then you'll want to consider taking out a paid advertisement that will show up in conjunction with the natural search results. That strategy is discussed below in the section on online advertising.

Search engines find your Web site by "spidering" the Internet—i.e., continually searching for all Web sites that are part of the great web of content known as the Internet and then indexing them. Note that the World Wide Web (the famous "www" that appears at the beginning of most Web URLs) is a subset of all of the content on the Internet. The search engines continue to spider the Web 24/7, looking not only for newly launched Web sites but for any changes in existing Web sites. There are a great number of factors involved in optimizing your Web site so that it's more likely to come up in the top natural search results. I won't get too detailed here, as an effective SEO program usually requires a fair amount of expertise, but it's worth having an understanding of what's involved so you can decide how best to approach SEO.

SEO involves creating keyword-rich pages that are indexed by search engines. Search engines use rather complex algorithms and rules for determining each Web site's place in the search rankings. In addition to looking at the keywords on a Web site, the search engines will look at factors such as the metadata (descriptive information placed into the Web site coding that doesn't appear to visitors but can be read by search engines), whether there are links to your site from other quality sites, how long your Web site's been around (search engines are skeptical of new domains), and how often the content on your site is updated (that's why blogs do so well—because they tend to have lots of new content and get spidered by search engines often). You also want to have an appropriately keyword-rich site title and description that will look coherent, polished, and enticing in search results.

To get a sense of how you show up on search engines right now, check out MoreVisibility (www.morevisibility.com) for a free search engine visibility report. You can also download the Google toolbar at www.toolbar.google.com, which will allow you to see your "rank" on a scale of 1 to 10 and monitor it each day. (Note, however, that this metric is not as important as the number of visitors, bounce rates, and time spent on your site, all of which are discussed later.)

WHAT'S UP WITH WEB SITE METRICS?

How do you know if anyone is visiting your site? How many pages are they visiting? How much time are they spending on it? Which pages are they clicking on? What other Web sites referred them to you? How many "bounce" away from your site? How many people return again? And how many are new, unique visitors?

The numbers that answer these questions are called Web site metrics. These metrics can provide you with invaluable feedback that will inform you about what's working—and what isn't—on your Web site so that you can make informed decisions and modifications to improve the experience of your visitors, boost traffic, and ultimately increase sales. If you know what your visitors/customers are most interested in, where they came from, and what keywords they used to find your Web site, then you can offer more in that particular area to help others like them find you—and to keep all visitors engaged, telling their friends, and coming back.

One of the most popular Web site metrics tools is Google Analytics (www.googleanalytics.com). It is a free service that shows you how your customers find you and how they navigate through your site. There are many different ways to view your data, and you can select the chart type that makes the most sense to you. In addition, if you use Google AdWords to advertise (discussed later in this chapter), Google Analytics can look at who you are reaching, where your best customers are coming from, and who is purchasing products/services from you the most. For instance, if you discover that the majority of your customers are coming from San Francisco, you could then purchase Google AdWords to target the San Francisco area. Another great Web site that offers a free toolbar that tracks metrics of your Web site both in the United States and around the world is www.alexa.com.

While you're gathering all this data, it's important to find out what you can about your Web competition. Businesses that have been up and running for a while usually know their competitors but often lack information about the Web traffic they are generating. Fortunately, there are free Web sites that enable you to compare your Web site metrics to other Web sites. These include www.statsaholic.com and www.compete.com.

BRING PEOPLE TO YOUR WEB SITE THROUGH ONLINE ADVERTISING

Online advertising receives mixed reviews. Some people swear by the results, while others will tell you not to spend a dime. I suspect that the real answer is, "It depends." Ads will work for some businesses better than others. I'll outline your options here, and then it is up to you to explore and choose what is right for your business. There are many different ways to advertise online, and like any advertising purchase, it makes sense to buy ad space based on where you think your customers are. Some options include Google AdWords, Facebook ads, display/banner ads, and classified ads.

With any type of online advertising, terms that are important to understand are CPC (cost per click) and CPM (cost per thousand impressions, with "M" representing the Roman numeral 1,000). CPM advertising is preferred by advertisers who care more about visibility than clicks. Advertisers (that's you) set the maximum amount they are willing to pay for each 1,000 impressions their ad receives. The price paid is the same whether users click the ad or not. If your primary goal is to make your brand name visible to potential customers, for instance, then you might want to consider CPM bidding. In CPC campaigns, you pay only when someone clicks on your ad. If you are mainly interested in having users click through to your Web site—for instance, if you operate an online store—then you may prefer CPC pricing that will allow you to pay only when a potential customer actually visits your Web site.

Google AdWords

Remember how we distinguished between natural search results and the paid advertising that can appear alongside those natural results? Well, this section is about that particular form of paid advertising. This is probably the most effective type of advertising you can find on the Web, because your ad is appearing in exactly the context you want: when a searcher types in a particular search term that is relevant to your business.

Google's paid advertising program is the best-known and probably the most successful. It's called AdWords. It's a simple process to sign up and create Google AdWords. Consider first whether this approach makes sense for your business. Google AdWords promises to reach people looking for your product or service; allows you to keep full control of your advertising budget; offers the capability for you to design and edit your ads easily; and enables you to see your ads on Google within minutes after creating them. You can sign up at www.adwords.google.com.

Pricing works via your "daily budget"—the amount that you're willing to spend on a specific AdWords campaign each day. AdWords displays your ads as often as possible while staying within your daily budget. When the budget limit is reached, your ads will typically stop showing for that day. How quickly your ads are shown during a given day is determined by your ad delivery setting.

The downside is that you pay either way, whether you use CPM or CPC. It may make more sense for you to use other free methods first (mentioned later in this section), at least in the beginning.

Facebook Ads

While Facebook is covered in great detail in Chapter 9, it also makes sense to discuss Facebook ads specifically here. With 350 million members and growing, Facebook can be a highly effective tool if that's where your customers are.

The ads can be created quickly, you can define your target audience very specifically (e.g., gender, marital status, region, etc.), and Facebook will automatically post your ads to a specific niche market of

5. Keep your ad simple

Create your ad so that it is as simple and easy to read as possible. Avoid long sentences or complex punctuation. Use simple, grammatically correct, complete sentences and language. Use proper punctuation, punctuate the end of sentences, put spaces after periods and commas, and don't use hyphens in place of periods.

Don't try to fit every detail about your product or service into the ad. Make it clear what your product or service is so a user can tell what your website will be about, but save the details for your landing page.

Incorrect:	Correct:
Ecro Flowers	**Ecro Flowers**
The best flower store around – delivery all day – phone 598 555 1246 – email: flowers at hotmail.com!	Ecro Flowers is the best flower store around! Check out our special sales this week.

6. Use a strong call-to-action

Your ad should convey a call-to-action along with the benefits of your product or service. A call-to-action encourages users to click on your ad and should explain to the user exactly what you expect them to do when they reach your landing page. Some call-to-action phrases include: buy, sell, order, browse, sign up, and get a quote.

Incorrect:	Correct:
Textbook Store	**Textbook Store**
We have cheaper textbooks than anyone else. Guaranteed.	We have cheaper textbooks than anyone else. Browse our selection for next semester now!

Figure 7.1: Facebook offers suggestions for creating effective ads. *Source: Suggested Best Practices for Advertising on Facebook"* (*www.facebook.com/ ads/best_practices.php*).

your choosing. To create ads on Facebook, click the advertising tab at the bottom of your Facebook page.

Another helpful tool that Facebook offers is a guide called "Suggested Best Practices for Advertising on Facebook." This is worth reading if you advertise on Facebook or anywhere else, such as via classified ads. This guide provides concrete steps on developing effective ads with examples of "incorrect" ads and "correct" ads (see Figure 7.1).

Display/Banner Ads

Display advertisements, otherwise known as banner ads, are placed on individual Web sites appropriate for your market. To make it work, find sites that target your ideal customer and complement your product/service, then contact the Web site to find out how much it would cost to "display" your ad on their site. The cost will range dramatically depending on the popularity of the site and size of your ad. Web sites typically provide ad slots with specified dimensions. Be sure to find out their ad "specs" (shape and size) before you spend time and money developing your ad. Most online display ads will follow industry standards. There

Figure 7.2: Online display ad types: medium rectangle (300 pixels by 250 pixels). *Source: MomInvented.com*

Figure 7.3: Online display ad types: full banner (468 pixels by 60 pixels). *Source: MomInvented.com*

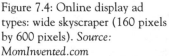

Figure 7.4: Online display ad types: wide skyscraper (160 pixels by 600 pixels). *Source: MomInvented.com*

are three basic categories of online display ads: rectangles and pop-ups, banners and bulletins, and skyscrapers (see Figures 7.2, 7.3, and 7.4).

Within each category are between three and nine various sizes measured in pixels. If the ad is to include any animation, the recommended length is 15 seconds. The maximum recommended download size is 40k.

You can find many more examples, variations, and sizes with specific guidelines and industry standards—at the Interactive Advertising Bureau (www.iab.net). Click on the "guidelines" tab along the top navigation bar or simply search "ad unit guidelines."

Finding a graphic designer to create your ad is relatively easy on the Internet; just search for graphic designers. My preference, though, is word of mouth; if you like someone else's ad, ask the company who designed it. Another great resource that is often overlooked is local business groups, like the chamber of commerce.

Also know that some Web sites are glad to exchange banner ads for free if it's mutually beneficial for both companies. For example, if I own a cookware Web site and I am contacted by a company that sells apparel for people who love to cook, it might be beneficial to cross-promote each other.

You may also want to consider creating a banner ad for your own Web site to introduce or highlight new products or services that you are launching. People are attracted to different things, and an ad can attract people to click and read about or buy what's new on your site. This is something that should be updated regularly, perhaps once every few weeks, to keep things new and fresh on your Web site.

Online Classified Ads

Many of you will be familiar with Craigslist (www.craigslist.org). Craigslist is a centralized network of online communities featuring free online classified advertisements, with sections devoted to jobs, housing, personals, for sale, services, and more. Craigslist was started by Craig Newmark in 1995 as a free e-mail distribution list of friends, featuring local events in the San Francisco Bay Area. As of April 2009, Craigslist has established itself in approximately 570 cities in 50 countries and generates more than $100 million in annual revenue.

This is a free and easy way to post an ad for your business and may be one of the best examples of how the Internet can be used to level the playing field among tiny businesses and large companies alike. As a matter of fact, Craigslist is where I found our patent attorney, whom we have worked with now for seven years.

Other free classified advertising sites have sprung up as well, including www.kijiji.com and www.usfreeads.com. An Internet search will probably turn up even more.

ONLINE MARKETING ALLIANCES: SHARING CONTENT

Another way to use online partnerships to drive visitors to your site is to seek out other sites that complement yours and offer to share content. Let's say you specialize in writing about safe, fun, and inexpensive day trips for your family. You may want to contact other popular parenting sites that offer tips for families and ask if you can share content with proper attribution and cross-links. Make it simple for people to tell others about your site and add "share this" or "tell a friend" links on each page.

Here's where to start to find potential customers or referral partners, both online and in person. In the beginning, unless your Web site is extremely unique, it will likely be difficult to get large online portals to cross-link or build referral arrangements with you. Therefore, just like the networking I spoke about in Chapter 6 on sales, you can employ similar grassroots tactics online. Many of your alliances can be built online, but start with contacts and networks you already have in "real" life:

- Family and friends
- Neighbors
- High school classmates
- College alumni groups
- Chamber of commerce
- Local business organizations
- Women's organizations
- Professional networking groups
- Book clubs
- Professionals you come into contact with (doctor, lawyer, accountant)
- PTAs & other mom/parent groups
- Sports or other activities that you are involved with (yoga, Pilates, Jazzercise, boot camp, the gym, reading club, bridge club, cooking, other hobbies)
- Activities your kids are involved with (soccer, martial arts, dance, music, art, foreign languages)
- Religious affiliations (church, temple, mosque)

Ideas for Reaching Out to These Groups

Let them know what you do. To get people to recognize your business, you need to be able to tell people what you do in a succinct, easy-to-understand, and repeatable way. Whether you call it your mission, your elevator pitch, your unique selling proposal, or just "what you do," ensure it makes sense and is intriguing. You want people to remember it and be able to repeat it, because even if they aren't in the market for something you provide, someone they know might be. Really, as the first step, this also includes just being friendly and willing to start conversations. If you're at a meeting, sports event, or other gathering where you are comfortable talking to the organizer, ask to make a quick announcement. You can tell people about a big event or sale, giving them a personal invitation, or you can tell them about the launch of a new product that would be relevant to them.

Always carry business cards. Even though you may encounter many of these groups via social occasions, this old-fashioned marketing tool is still one of the best ways to give contacts your info and remind them who you are. Having a catchy design and high-quality card is definitely a plus. You can also bring along small brochures if appropriate. Don't forget to get business cards from contacts too. Put them in your address book, but don't subscribe them to your newsletter unless they specifically ask you to do so. Send a friendly note and make sure your e-mail signature includes your contact information, Web site, blog, and possibly even some social sites you're active on.

Offer to speak. A great way to get some attention and establish yourself as an expert is to speak in front of a group. Or you can even ask to tack on a special talk or seminar at the end of an event for interested members, to generate interest in your field of expertise or business. If you have a low-cost product or can give away some sort of samples, bring them along to give to members of the group. They may just get hooked and order more. Plus, it'll be easier for them to tell others about your product if they have actual physical experience with it.

Donate a product/service to an auction/fund-raising event. Many organizations, schools, and religious groups hold auctions to raise money, and if your product/service is a fit for the event, make a donation. It's tax deductible, you'll get your product in front of a lot of people, and you may also get credit in the auction brochure. If you have a high-ticket item, seeing your product will also likely inspire custom orders.

Sponsor/host an event. Many organizations look for event sponsors or hosts. Getting people to your business location is a great way to create interest in what you do, and if you provide snacks or some sort of giveaway item, see if the event organizer will mention you as a sponsor on their Web site and then link from your Web site to that page. If you take a few minutes to mention on your blog that you went to an event, say a few words about it, and mention the people you met—with links to their sites (get their business cards!)—you'll likely get plenty of links back as well.

Buy ads in local newsletters/publications. Local organizations need your financial support, and they can help you reach your community if you buy ads in their publications. These low-cost ads reach a targeted audience and not only let people know about your business but also let them know you support a particular organization. You may also consider offering a special discount for members of an organization you belong to.

If your group doesn't have an online presence, start one. If there is an organization or group you are connected with that does not have its own online presence, or if it has a Web site but isn't on social sites, take some initiative and start a Facebook fan page, for example, that is "sponsored by" your business. Your cost is minimal, but you get very positive recognition, and it will help you to continue connecting with members outside of meetings. You'll be seen as a leader, and people will have one more place to go to find your site/personal info.

OTHER TRAFFIC-DRIVING METHODS TO CONSIDER

Of course there are other ways, as well, to help drive traffic to your Web site. Here a few of them with explanations.

LISTS AND DIRECTORIES

Online directory listings and review sites such as The Open Directory Project (www.dmoz.com) can also create exposure and bring you customers. The Open Directory Project is a Web directory of Internet resources that's like a huge reference library. You can submit your business to be included, but the publisher ultimately chooses who is included. Each Web site is handpicked to maintain quality. However, it is free, so it may be worthwhile to check out for your business.

Other directories to consider are www.citysearch.com, www.angieslist.com, and www.google.com/local/add. Google's service is free, and you can list your business in your local city. Google's search engine is used by 82 percent of people, so it's a good idea to list your business in their directory. Google even offers you a free report to let you know where your customers are coming from! Also, Google Local is attached to the Google maps feature, which a lot of people use on their computers *and* on their mobile phones, so you definitely want your information listed there.

You may even consider submitting your URL to paid directories like www.yahoo.com and www.joeant.com. I already mentioned www.craigslist.com, but because your ads expire every seven days there, this can be time consuming. However, it still may be worth using, especially if you have different individual services or products you can list.

REVIEW WEB SITES

People may already be talking about your business on review sites. You need to know what they're saying and participate in the conversation proactively. This will help you take control of your online identity and "claim" your business's profile on review sites. If you're in the Yellow Pages, you're likely already on www.yelp.com, www.citysearch.com, www.insiderpages.com, www.tripadvisor.com, and other local sites like www.angieslist.com. Make sure all the information is correct and up to date, and claim your listing by adding images, listing your Web site and promotions (sometimes for a small fee), and by responding to users' reviews, both positive and negative. On some sites, you can respond publicly, and on others you can respond publicly or privately. This can help you resolve issues, counteract any negative reviews with good customer service, and earn you more loyal customers.

Some of the review sites let you see your business's stats, such as how many people are viewing your page. You can also pay extra to advertise on these sites with sponsored search results or, in the case of Angie's List, coupons.

These review sites are perfect for small businesses because people really rave about their one-of-a-kind finds, which helps other people find those businesses. And companies that are reviewed typically get more business than those that aren't, so encourage customers to write about you, though don't offer incentives for reviews—that's typically against review sites' policies. Publicize your good reviews on your site and blog.

The more you get reviewed, the more your business will show up on review sites' local home pages, and the more views it can get. These sites get tons of viewers. Claiming your business and improving your listing are relatively quick and easy tasks that can really create a big impact for your business.

Negative Reviews: How to Deal with Them

Although negative reviews can be hard to take, they can provide invaluable information about the experience your customers are having with your business and provide a hidden opportunity to respond. For example, if a reviewer says they love your restaurant but service is slow, it will give you the opportunity to apologize; tell them that you are aware of the issue and are hiring new people to improve service; and offer a coupon for them to return and enjoy dessert on the house. This will give the reviewer the opportunity to update the review and share with everyone how well things were handled.

If you're receiving great reviews, on the other hand, you can add a link from your Web site to your business profile on review sites so that people who visit your site can read candid reviews from "real" people about your business. Also, as people see the exchange of reviews, they will be more inclined to check out your business.

CONCLUSION

Hopefully you can adopt some of the tactics shared in this chapter to support your marketing and sales strategies. In the next chapter, we'll delve further into some Internet tools that can help your business, including the power of blogging and finding partners to create affiliate revenue sources.

Reaching Customers through E-mail Marketing and Blogs

So far, we have focused on many different ways to help people find and come to your Web site and business. In this chapter, our focus will shift toward the ways you can proactively reach out and convey messages to your customers using the tools of the Internet, specifically e-mail campaigns and blogging. In addition, this chapter covers how to utilize affiliate marketing strategies to generate additional revenue for your blog (which can also be used for your Web site, or for both!).

THE POWER OF THE INBOX

E-mail is still one of the most important, effective, and inexpensive Internet tools for reaching out and communicating with people. When messages are well constructed, e-mail campaigns can lead to dramatic results. Depending on your business type, your e-mails should include insightful information, discounts, viral coupons (ones that can be forwarded and used over and over by friends of friends), invitations to special events, and/or a monthly newsletter. The intention of these special offers and tidbits of information is to encourage your readers to click through to your Web site and ultimately purchase your products and services.

In *Word of Mouth Marketing*, in the section "Put It in an E-mail," author Andy Sernovitz touts the power of e-mail and offers great tips:

Make sure it's forwardable. Far too many overdesigned e-mails fall apart when forwarded, with broken graphics and links. Send it to yourself on different accounts and computers, and make sure it looks great when passed along.

Write it for the second recipient. Make sure that your e-mail makes sense to pass along to readers who get it from a friend. They may not know who you are. Add sections such as "About the Company," "About This Newsletter," and anything else that tells your exciting story to someone who is seeing you for the first time.

Capture new talkers. Every e-mail should have sign-up instructions right in the message. Don't expect secondhand recipients to go to your site and search for how to get on the list. Grab them while they are hot and ready to act.

Tell recipients to tell a friend. Put a big, bold call to action right at the top. Remember, talkers talk when you ask them to. Include a link to a Tell-a-Friend form right in the message.

Be funny. Put something amusing at the end of every message just to get it forwarded.

Tell readers NOT to forward the message. Works every time. My most-forwarded messages all start with the phrase "PRIVATE: DO NOT FORWARD."

VIRAL STRATEGIES

The beauty of the Internet is that it is viral. In other words, if you craft messages well and people like what they see, they will want to forward it to others.

One person I know included a "viral" coupon for her product in her e-mail and sent it out to her network. The coupon had real value—

it offered a significant discount off her normal pricing. She told people the coupon could be used by anyone who received it and encouraged them to forward it to their friends. It took off like wildfire. She said it's the most effective and dramatic sales tactic she's used to date.

Think about what value *you* have to offer. If you don't know, ask! Send a message to your community or to a select sample of your community members and ask them what discount or added value you can offer that would interest them in your service or product. For example, you might offer them $10 off, a free consultation, or a buy-one-get-one-free deal. Look at your community as a sounding board; most people love to be asked for advice, and the best part is that you'll get valuable feedback for free!

ASK FOR PERMISSION

Before you start blasting people with e-mails, however, make sure that you ask for permission first. While it's all right to send e-mails to people that you've met at a mixer or party if they gave you a business card and suggested that you contact them, you may anger or turn off others who haven't given you permission. In your initial e-mail, give recipients an opportunity to sign up (through a big sign-up button or link), but don't automatically add them to your database unless they "opt-in" themselves.

Here are the results from a woman entrepreneur who took her first stab at Internet marketing and had excellent results. Maureen H., creator of the Magic Sleepsuit (www.magicsleepsuit.com), generated her first sales by using a simple e-mail blast to family and friends:

> I always believed that word-of-mouth advertising was going to be one of my most effective, low-cost marketing tools. When I was approaching the launch of my online business, I wanted to let all my friends and family know that my product was available for sale on my Web site.
>
> I created a Web blast e-mail that I sent out to about 390 friends and family. This e-mail told everyone about the launch of my business, and I asked that they share the e-mail with

everyone they knew to help me spread the word. From this e-mail, I received my first sale, from a friend of my brother-in-law. To this day, months after my e-mail, I continue to get sales from this initial announcement from both friends and family and those who were contacted by them.

Using the example above, Maureen H. might consider following up with another e-mail blast that includes a coupon for "50 percent off the first Magic Sleepsuit ordered" or "Buy one, get one free—this offer available only with this e-mail." And she could also add a call to action, like a tell-a-friend button, to share the great discount offer with a friend.

While you can initially send out small e-mail blasts using your Outlook e-mail program, most Internet service providers (ISPs) will not permit e-mail blasts to large lists of people. One of the best ways to send out e-mails to larger groups is by using service bureau companies that are specifically designed for this purpose such as Constant Contact (www.constantcontact.com), iContact (www.icontact.com), Bronto (www.bronto.com), VerticalResponse (www.verticalresponse.com), and Emma (www.myemma.com). These companies offer tools to manage your lists, provide well-designed message templates, offer open-rate reports, and work with ISPs to reduce spam and improve your delivery and open rates.

I do not recommend the purchase and use of e-mail lists for building and growing your own list. The last thing you want to do is spam people about you and your company without their permission as this creates a feeling of being treated without consideration. Here are some ideas for building your list organically first:

- Include a sign-up form (or at least a link to one) on every page of your site—near the top.
- Offer a free download or coupon for signing up for the list.
- Display a few sample e-mail newsletters on your site so people know what to expect.

USING THE INTERNET TO GET PRESS RELEASE COVERAGE

Press releases are one of the best things that you can do to promote your business—especially online. Due to the sheer volume of online portals, blogs, and news Web sites, the opportunities to get press coverage online are enormous. See the resources directory at the end of this book for a list of online press release distribution companies, as well as tips on crafting your release.

Once you send out your release, there are several methods of monitoring your "hits" so you know what people are saying about you and your business. The easiest way to do this is to set up a Google Alert (www.google.com/alerts), which will e-mail you when your search term (e.g., your name, your business name) shows up somewhere new online.

WHAT ARE RSS FEEDS?

RSS stands for real simple syndication. It is a tool that lets you bring content created on one site onto another site to be read there. When you subscribe to a Web site's feed by RSS, you'll receive a summary of new content from that Web site in your e-mail, with links to full versions of that content. You will need to use an RSS reader like Google Reader (www.google.com/reader), FeedDemon (www.newsgator.com/Individuals/FeedDemon/Default.aspx), or Sage (https://addons.mozilla.org/en-US/firefox/addon/77), or you can add the feeds to a customizable home page like iGoogle (www.google.com/ig), My Yahoo!, or My MSN. For example, my own Web browser opens to my www.igoogle.com account, where all my alerts and RSS feeds are organized and displayed. This is basically an alternative to getting e-mail alerts that fill your inbox; instead, you can view them unobtrusively and in your own time. They're a great way to bring together a number of different sources in one place and get an overview of the news that's important to you.

You can also use Social Mention (www.socialmention.com) to monitor social site mentions of your name/company name more closely and subscribe to the feed via RSS. Other Web sites that monitor links, traffic, and comments made on blogs (more on that in the next section) are Technorati (www.technorati.com), BlogPulse (www.blogpulse.com), Yahoo! News (www.yahoonews.com), Askblogs (www.askblogs.com), and Feeds.com (www.feeds.com).

Feel free to respond to mentions of your name/business name if it seems appropriate. If someone is complaining, see if there's some way you can help. If someone is offering you praise, let them know you appreciate it. People love to know they're being heard.

ALL ABOUT BLOGGING

Because blogging has become such a widely used tool on the Internet, I am dedicating a separate section to explain what it is, why you should consider having a blog, how to use blogging for your business, and how to get started. When used for Internet marketing, blogging is about projecting yourself and your company onto the Internet with the intention of bringing people back to your site.

WHAT IS A BLOG?

No doubt you've heard the term "blog" countless times, but you still may not know exactly what it is, or how it differs from a regular old Web site. The word is shorthand for "Weblog," and it's like a combination of online diary and news column with some major additional functionality, as described below. A blog is essentially a communications stream between you and your customers—and anyone else who cares to look. It is a type of Web site or a section on a Web site that relies on frequent updates posted by one or many writers on a particular subject. The subject matter and the style can vary widely. Some people write about news in their field, others write about what their company is doing day to day, and still others don't actually write much but post lots of videos or photos to show what they're up to.

A blog gives a voice to you or your company, and most blogs enable people to comment on what you've written and interact with your business. Readers of your blog can also subscribe to it via an RSS feed or e-mail if you set up that functionality. In other words, they can receive your updates at the moment you create them. You can use your blog elsewhere on the Web via RSS using FriendFeed (www.friend feed.com) or FeedBurner (www.feedburner.com) and by adding it to the social networks on which you have a presence (such as Facebook or Twitter). If you are not on any social networks yet, or if you feel that you are not using them effectively for your business, the next three chapters will be of additional help.

WHY IS A BLOG IMPORTANT?

By letting customers connect with your business in a personal way, or by writing about the subject you know best, you're giving them a reason to keep coming back, hearing what you're up to, and learning about your new products or projects. A blog can help establish you as an expert in your field, and it can also help show off what you're doing in your business.

Your blog can also take the place of an actual Web site for your company—or it can act as a valuable addition to it, depending on your needs. Because of the frequent updates, blogs are great for SEO—and if you add keywords about your business, they can help drive new traffic to your site or your blog.

If you're not up to the challenge of making regular blog updates, you probably shouldn't start a blog. A dead blog can have a negative impact on the impression you make with your business. If you can't commit to updating at least once every week to two weeks, I wouldn't recommend blogging. You'll get the best results if you update multiple times per week.

HOW TO LAUNCH YOUR BLOG

You have a few options when getting started with blogging. First, you need to pick a blogging platform, like WordPress (www.wordpress.com),

TypePad (www.typepad.com), Movable Type (www.movabletype.com), or Blogger (www.blogger.com), and decide if you'd like to host your blog on your own site or on the blogging platform's site. For example, if you host the blog yourself, your URL could be mycompany.com/blog, while if you host it on WordPress, it'll be mycompanyblog.wordpress.com. Either way is fine; it just depends on your technical savvy and requirements.

ESSENTIAL STRUCTURAL ELEMENTS OF A BLOG

Here's a checklist for the bare minimum elements you should have for a successful blog (not including the content itself, which I will discuss below):

- Header with the title of your blog
- URL that includes the blog name/your company name
- Search box
- About page with your bio/business info
- Contact page/form/info, so people can contact you easily
- Link to RSS feed
- Links to your other sites (Web site and social sites)

CUSTOMIZING YOUR BLOG

On all the blog platforms I mentioned, there are both free and paid themes/templates to help you individualize your blog's look.

You can also add plug-ins (i.e., bits of software that add additional specialized functionality) to give your blog more appeal. These can include better tagging programs; "chiclets" (i.e., small icons or pictures that go beside a posting on a blog, an article, or a Web page) for your social sites; photo galleries; and more. If there's something your blog doesn't do that you want it to do, someone has probably created a free or low-cost plug-in that can help you out. If you want something even more customized, consider hiring a Web designer who specializes in the blog platform you want to use.

LEVERAGING BLOGS FOR BUSINESS
How to Get Readers
Here are a few ideas to hook in an audience:

- Let users subscribe via RSS or e-mail so they can read your blog in a format they prefer.
- Promote your blog on your Web site and other social sites. You can even republish your blog on LinkedIn, Facebook, Amazon (if you're an author), and other sites.
- Link to friends' and colleagues' blogs, and encourage them to link to yours to help build traffic.
- Be transparent with your clients to build trust.
- Issue press releases on your blog, or respond quickly to any negative press in a constructive, intelligent way.
- Write guest posts on others' blogs, and make sure they link back to your blog.
- Sell items directly from your blog with a store widget from PayPal, Amazon, or other shopping cart services.

What to Say
Once you have people tuning in, here's how to keep them coming back:

- Write about new product releases.
- Write about your area of expertise.
- Post videos and photos about your business.
- Post videos, photos, and positive feedback customers send in.
- Respond to customer questions.
- Write about your customers or people who have something interesting to say to your audience; you can even interview them, which could lead to them linking back to your blog post.
- Comment on news in your industry.
- Write about events at your office.
- Highlight press mentions of your business or interviews that have featured you.

BEST OF THE BUSINESS BLOGS

There are plenty of great business blogs, but these are some of my favorites:

Moo (www.moo.com/blog) is an online printing company that uses its blog to feature new products, innovative and artistic uses for its products that users send in, plus insights into its fun and open company culture. Multiple people inside the company contribute to the blog.

Chris Brogan (www.chrisbrogan.com), head of a new media marketing agency, writes insightful commentary about what's new in his field, shares his thought process, and often opens up questions to his readers—who, in turn, leave great comments on his posts.

IDEO's Design Thinking (designthinking.ideo.com) is an innovative blog about design, concept work, and prototyping from an IDEO labs designer.

Rose Beranbaum's baking blog (www.realbakingwithrose.com) includes recipes, musings on food and cooking, and more from the cookbook author.

Patricia Zapata's A Little Hut blog (www.alittlehut.blogspot .com) is a place where the artist and paper crafter shares her artistic creations, wonderful photos, and how-to tips.

- Write about what you have learned from a certain event/news item.
- Encourage comments to generate interaction.
- Comment on others' blogs to get more traffic back, and start building relationships with other bloggers in your field.
- Promote or hold contests via the blog; let users win your product for guessing an answer, leaving an insightful comment, etc.

- Write about helpful resources related to your business, and don't forget to link to them.
- Post polls to ask customers to weigh in on topics/do market research.

LINKING READERS TO YOUR BLOG

Getting people to link to your blog is one of the best ways to build its ranking and authority. A good way to start is by talking to friends within your industry who may be willing to do a mutual link exchange with you. Once you become more active in the blogging community and know which blogs are similar to yours and may benefit from a link from you, you can approach those bloggers, too, to see about exchanging links. You would typically put someone else's link in your "blogroll," a list of links on the side of your blog.

Another way to generate links is to participate in interviews (if you're interviewed by a blog/Web site, make sure they link to you and vice versa). Also be sure to put a link to your blog on your primary Web site if they are separate. Another good way to get links is to write great posts, promote them, and get links back from people who are quoting you. If you stay on top of trends and breaking news, write well, and develop a strong audience, people will start linking back to you.

Two of the biggest link generators are Digg (www.digg.com, discussed in detail later) and StumbleUpon (www.stumbleupon.com). These sites let users submit and vote on content. You should get a plug-in that will add links for readers to submit your stories on Digg and StumbleUpon as well as post them to Facebook or Twitter, which can also bring in a lot of views.

WRITING FOR OTHER SITES

If you write for other Web sites or blogs, make sure you always get a writer's bio that includes a link to your Web site and blog. It's a good idea to write for other sites to get links if:

- Your target market is similar to that site's.
- The site is well-respected, and your presence there can establish you as an expert.
- The time commitment isn't too great or can be seen as part of your marketing budget.
- You gain important referral relationships with the others you write for.

Writing for other sites can mean either a short-term, one-time, or occasional post commitment, which is almost always a good idea—especially if it's a well-respected site—or it can be a longer-term, regular commitment. Consider what you'll get out of the relationship, how much time it will take, and if you really have the drive to do it. You can also look into syndicating your blog content or articles you write and letting multiple sites use it, or even sell it for a fee.

SYNDICATING YOUR BLOG

A link that says "Syndicate this site," "RSS," or "XML" means that the headlines, a link, and an entry description for each new blog entry are made available for others to use on their Web sites or to access through a newsfeed reader program.

Your blog's RSS feed is your key to syndication. You can use this feed to run your blog on your LinkedIn page (by going to one of their blog applications that will pull your RSS feed). You can also run your blog on Facebook, with an application like Blogcast. On MySpace and other sites that accept HTML code, visit SpringWidgets (www.spring widgets.com) and go to "Express Widgets" to create a widget that links to your blog feed; you can even create a custom header. If you're an Amazon author, you can import your blog to show up on all your Amazon product listings, and if you have a YouTube channel, you can syndicate your blog there too.

Another great tool for syndicating your blog is FeedBurner (www.feedburner.com). Just put in your RSS feed, make sure you link/redirect to the Feedburner RSS feed from your blog, and start using its "Publicize" tools. You can create instant e-mail newsletters every time you post to your blog, build a headline animator to display a rotating array of your recent posts in your e-mail signature, and create SpringWidgets with your feeds to paste on other sites.

You can also notify friends of new blog posts on sites like FriendFeed (friendfeed.com), an aggregator for all the feeds from your social sites, and on Twitter. There are even plug-ins that will publish your posts directly to Twitter (well, the headlines, at least, since Twitter has a 140 character limit per "tweet," including the address). We'll discuss Twitter at length in Chapter 10.

SHOULD YOU PUT ADS ON YOUR BLOG?

In general, I'd recommend not putting ads on your blog or, at the most, running a minimal and unobtrusive Google AdWords spot. Ads on a blog that doesn't have a huge amount of traffic won't generate much extra income, and you may find competitors' products and services showing up in the Google Ads if they have bought the keywords that you write about.

There are ad programs other than Google AdSense that can generate a bit more money, like affiliate programs, but only put ads up that you feel can benefit your customers and won't detract from your business model. I've allowed a select group of handpicked companies to place display ads on my Web site and blog because they offer specific services that my members need.

STAYING INSPIRED TO BLOG

Blogging is a constant, ongoing task that requires energy and enthusiasm. Here are some ideas to keep it up and generate new topics:

- Keep up your blogging by talking with other bloggers. Consider attending a blogger event. Search www.meetup.com, which helps groups of people with shared interests plan meetings and form offline clubs in local communities around the world. Search Yahoo! Upcoming (upcoming.yahoo.com) to find a local event.
- Plan what you want to write about ahead of time.

- Create a list of go-to topics for slower news days.
- Take a break from your blog every once in a while and just post a picture or two without much text just to have *something* up.
- Post regularly, or else you'll lose readers and your traffic will take a major dive.

HIRING SOMEONE TO BLOG FOR YOU

Does the thought of daily writing seem daunting? An alternative option is to have someone do it for you. Unless you're giving one-on-one advice or your blog requires a very personal touch, blogging can be a task assigned to the marketing or PR department or outsourced to the right person. Assigning blog tasks and making the occasional cameo appearance should be enough. Just make sure you set clear guidelines for the style, tone, and type of posts you want; have someone whose grammar and copyediting you trust; and do a once-over before anything is published.

MAKE MONEY WITH YOUR BLOG

There are several different approaches to making money on your blog. Here are a few of the most reliable ones:

- Amazon's affiliate program (www.amazon.com/affiliate) is a good route for new blogs with little traffic. When readers click on the links you post to your blog, you get paid a commission.
- AdSense (www.adsense.com) enables Google to post relevant ads on your blog. You are paid if your readers click on ads, but it is a meaningful revenue source only if you have high traffic volume.
- Blogads (www.blogads.com) is easy to set up, but you don't get to choose who advertises on your site.
- PayPerPost (www.payperpost.com) enables you to write product reviews and get paid, but you have to disclose to your readers that you are getting paid for these reviews.

GENERATE REVENUE THROUGH AFFILIATE MARKETING

Affiliate marketing is a risk-free way of getting traffic to your Web site and another way to make money on your Web site or blog. If you want to offer products and services to your customers that don't fall under your area of expertise, and if you know other companies that offer those services and would feel comfortable recommending them, the solution is an affiliate marketing partnership. In other words, you can partner with other like-minded companies through an affiliate program and get paid for these referrals. Doing so allows you to offer their service to your customers through a link on your own Web site. When your customers sign up for those third-party services, you receive a payment. Arrangements vary, though, so you can also structure this plan in reverse. Affiliate partnerships can be a great way to provide excellent service to your customers and get another source of revenue coming into your business. (We touched briefly on affiliate marketing as part of your sales plan in Chapter 7.)

Figure 8.1 illustrates how affiliate marketing works. Step one: the customer comes to your Web site and clicks on the affiliate link to a

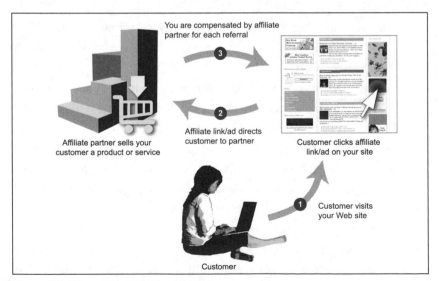

Figure 8.1: How affiliate marketing works.
Source: Wikipedia.

product or service that you have advertised or listed on your site. Step two: The affiliate link directs your customer to the affiliate partner and tracks electronically how many customers came from your Web site. Step three: The affiliate partner sells this referred customer a product or service, and you are compensated for each referral you send.

HOW DO I GET STARTED EARNING AFFILIATE COMMISSIONS?

One of the best ways to begin the process of adding affiliate links to your Web site and earning money is to apply for a free account on Commission Junction (www.cj.com) and become a "publisher." You are called a publisher because you are publishing advertisements from other companies on your Web site, and in return you will earn income from every referral that comes from your Web site to the advertising company. The companies that you select must already be registered as "advertisers" on Commission Junction. The best part is that you can select companies you think will be of interest to your audience and that offer the most compelling compensation structures. The ads or links (however you like them) have already been created and are ready for you to place on your Web site. Commission Junction manages the process: when you make money, Commission Junction earns a fee from the transaction and pays you royalty checks automatically. Each advertiser pays in a different way, but they state their terms clearly up front so you can decide if they work for you.

Will you definitely make money from affiliate partnerships? There is no way to know what will work best for you. As I've mentioned earlier, it's important to experiment. Commission sales tend to be small, but they can and do add up. If you have otherwise unused ad space, and it doesn't clutter up your Web site, it may be worth monetizing it. One of the goals of this book is to share possible ways that you can create multiple streams of revenue so that in the aggregate you are making the money that you want.

These types of marketing alliances can be created informally, too, by sharing content and cross-linking with others. If you create such arrangements, make sure to get the terms up front so that there are no misunderstandings. There is a downside to this model to consider, especially if you have a limited amount of space for ads. Most people acknowledge that it takes multiple advertising impressions before a consumer buys. If your visitor sees an affiliate ad for the first time on your Web site, he or she may buy after seeing it again on someone else's site. In this scenario, you have given away free advertising with no return.

SELLING YOUR OWN WEB SPACE

With the explosion in the number of new Web sites and the reduction in advertising budgets, making money by selling space on your Web site is not nearly as promising as it appeared to be in the late 1990s. However, it is still possible. One way to sell space is to join an ad network. These are companies that have banded together a large number of Web sites serving a specific demographic—say, "women." They sell a comprehensive package to advertisers and then "serve" the ads to the slots you have allocated to them on your Web site—and pay you based on the impressions or clicks your Web site delivers. As with affiliate marketing, your revenue versus the space you allocate to those ads can be rather small. However, the best way to monetize your ad space remains selling it directly. If you can identify companies that would benefit by reaching your audience, contact and sell them the space directly. By cutting out the "middlemen," it can be a good value for each of you. You can post ads directly on your Web site, or you can use a service such as OpenX (www.openx.org) to manage them for you. OpenX also will act as an ad network by offering you advertisers for your unsold inventory.

GOOGLE ADSENSE

Google AdSense (google.com/adsense) is entirely different from Google AdWords. With AdWords, you create advertisements that will appear on relevant Google search results pages and their partner sites. With Google AdSense, you get paid for allowing Google to place other

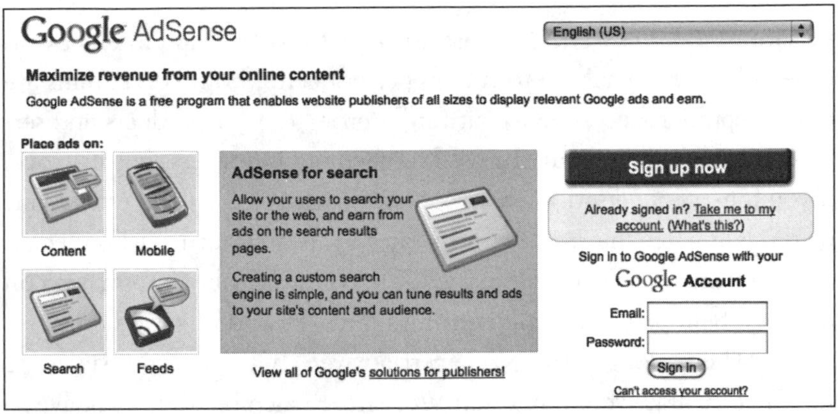

Figure 8.2: Google AdSense.
Source: google.com/adsense.

people's ads on your Web site. Google AdSense is a free program that enables Web site publishers (that's you: a person with a Web site) of all sizes to display relevant Google ads on their Web sites to earn money. When you sign up for AdSense, you describe the characteristics of your Web site, and Google will match appropriate ads to be placed there. Then, when people click on these ads, Google will pay you money. It's simple and may be one of the quickest ways to make some money. One word of caution: If you have too many ads, it can start to feel like spam—and you can jeopardize the environment that you have worked hard to create for your customers/clients. Plus, clicking on an ad takes visitors away from your site.

MORE INTERNET MARKETING STRATEGIES

If it seems like there's no end to the possibilities of the Internet, you may be right. Here are still other ways you can get your message out, drive traffic in, and build buzz for your business.

GET INVOLVED IN FORUMS

There are online forums (also known as bulletin boards and message boards) for virtually every topic and demographic; search your topic area to find forums that apply to your market. You can always join the conversations in forums, and it's a fast way to get involved and interact with others. Be sure to adhere to the proper etiquette, however. Forums are not an appropriate venue to outwardly promote your products and services; instead, they should be used to generate awareness. For instance, if you join a conversation on a topic in which you have expertise, start by providing free information. Let's say you are an attorney who specializes in incorporating new businesses. Try to post valuable information on forums where people are asking things like, "How do I set up my company?" Then, along with your expert answer, they'll see your signature line that includes your name and Web site. Remember that you have to be willing to give, give, and give before you receive anything. Once you have established yourself as an authority, people will come to you for advice. It is up to you then to show them the value of your services.

If you can't find the right fit, start a forum discussion and invite people to participate in the conversation with you. Start a discussion thread on a forum site, or even create your own forums on your Web site where you can field questions from users.

CREATE OR JOIN GROUPS

Joining or creating a group is a great way to connect with people. One place to do this is on Ning (www.ning.com), which has more than 4,000 social networks with new ones created daily. It's a place where people express their interests and passions. You can either join a group of people with similar interests or create your own network. If you want to create your own, Ning offers features that allow you to include videos, photos, chat, music, groups, events, and blogs as well as your own discussion forums.

Again, don't use these groups for blatant self-promotion but instead as a way to connect authentically with other group members.

GET YOUR CONTENT IN THE SPOTLIGHT

Digg (www.digg.com) is a place for people to discover and share content from anywhere on the Web. From the biggest online destinations to the most obscure blog, Digg surfaces the best content (determined by the votes of its users). It's a place where people can collectively determine the value of content.

Everything on Digg—from news to videos to images—is submitted by the community (that would be you). Once something is submitted, other people see it and "Digg" what they like best. If your submission receives enough "Diggs," it is promoted to the front page for millions of visitors to see.

Because Digg is all about sharing and discovery, there's a conversation that happens around the content. The site promotes this conversation and provides tools for the community to discuss the topics that it's passionate about. This gives every piece of content an equal shot at being the next big thing.

BLOGTALKRADIO

Do you have the gift of gab—and something to say? Let people get to know you through Internet radio. BlogTalkRadio (www.blogtalkradio .com) is a social radio network on the Internet that allows users to connect quickly and directly with their audience. Using an ordinary telephone and computer, radio hosts (you) can create free, live, call-in talk shows with unlimited participants that are automatically archived and made available as podcasts. No software download is required. Listeners can subscribe to shows via RSS with iTunes and other feed readers.

Not only is it free, but you can also place advertisements on your BlogTalkRadio host page as well as in your radio show (e.g., an ad break inserted every 15 minutes). BlogTalkRadio will share the revenue with you.

AUDIO AND VIDEO PODCASTS

Audio and video files are an attractive way to get people's attention, and they can be forwarded all over the Internet. This can be a powerful way to market yourself and reach out to more people. Hearing your voice or seeing you on video is a great way for your customers to get to know you personally. This trend is here to stay and will likely only get bigger as time goes on.

AudioAcrobat (www.audioacrobat.com) enables you to create your own audio and video podcasts (like radio programs, except people can download them to a portable media player such as an iPod or other mp3 player) instantly using your telephone, computer, and video camera without any additional software. The site offers free weekly tutorials. I have taken these classes myself and have found them to provide exactly what's needed to get started. They offer a free 30-day trial, and then it's a monthly fee. If you sign up for their affiliate program, you will be paid for referrals.

Another site to check out is Podbean (www.podbean.com), which focuses on hosting audio and video podcasts.

CONCLUSION

By now you can see that the opportunities and options for Internet marketing are vast, and I have only just scratched the surface. The most important thing in Internet marketing is tracking, testing, and optimizing everything that you do on your Web site and blog to maximize results. Make sure to set up a tracking system to figure out how your visitors found you, which marketing campaigns are bringing you profits, and which ones are losing you money. The best part of being in charge of your business is that you have the control and flexibility to make adjustments and changes quickly based on this feedback to enhance the effectiveness of your strategies. If something shows promise, focus on it. If it doesn't work, shift to other approaches quickly. And make it a point to read and learn about new opportunities that arise. I have little doubt that new tools and techniques will have surfaced by the time this book is published.

In the next three chapters, we are going to get even more focused on the Internet as we explore social networks and how to get started with Twitter, Facebook, LinkedIn, YouTube, and others to build your presence and connect with fans and customers in a powerful way. While social networks are certainly valuable components of online marketing, they are so massive, so unique, and so revolutionary in terms of how they can affect your business that they deserve their own chapters.

Social Network Basics + Facebook: Join the Party and Build Your Business!

The last two chapters on Internet marketing were full of examples of how traditional marketing techniques have been adapted to take advantage of the Internet. However, marketing your business through social networks is so new and such an extraordinary phenomenon that it's important to devote ample space to it, so you can see how using these networks will help you continue making money, your way.

If you haven't yet participated in social networking online, it is not too late, but don't delay, because your business can't afford to miss out on the exposure. And if you are already using social networks for your business, do not skip this chapter—you will walk away with at least a few new tips or ideas!

What surprised me the most, when I finally had the courage to sign up for Facebook and Twitter, was that many of my customers, community members, and competitors were already there. This whole universe in cyberspace was wildly active, and I, until then, was not a part of it. I had been aware of the phenomenon because I read about social networks regularly online and in magazines like *Fast Company*, *Inc.*, and

Fortune Small Business. However, reading about them is not the same as joining in and actively participating in them. My three favorites so far are Facebook (www.facebook.com/MomInvented), Twitter (find me at @MomInventors and follow me and I will follow you right back!), and my channel on YouTube.

In this chapter and the following two, you will learn what social networks are, how to find and use them to build your business presence, and how to get started right now on Facebook, Twitter, YouTube, LinkedIn, and MySpace. Finally, you'll also find out how to tie them all together and how to avoid costly and embarrassing mistakes through proper online etiquette. Let's go!

SOCIAL NETWORKS DEFINED

First, what exactly is a social network? Today's social networks (also known as social media) provide an online platform for people with common interests to connect with one another. There are social networks organized around virtually every subject imaginable, from geography (local businesses or events happening in your community) to special interests (music, swimming, travel, sexuality) to causes (politics, education, environmentalism) to personal connections (high school, college alumni) to meeting people with common interests (mommy groups, survivor groups, scientists, religion), and so on.

BE A SOCIAL HUMMINGBIRD

Using a social network is as much about connecting with people as it is about using a new set of tools to market your business. One day, as I was sitting in my backyard working on my outline for this chapter, I observed something in nature that serves as an interesting metaphor. We have a lot of bird life where we live, with many wild plants and flowers. At one point, I heard a crow insistently and persistently cawing loudly enough for every living thing to hear him, as if to say, "I have something you must hear! Look at me! Look at me!"

Not long after that I noticed a hummingbird as she gracefully and purposefully hovered over a blossoming plant at the edge of my patio.

As I watched her, she then quickly darted to another blossoming bush, then to a rose, pausing just long enough as if to introduce herself to each new flower and to cross-pollinate each plant in the process and move on quickly.

I drew a quick comparison to our own social world. To me, the flowers represent individual people. The crow got through to me. But it was the hummingbird's brief, personal connection with each individual flower in combination with the value she added to each flower's well-being (through pollination) that made an impact.

If you are marketing your business, and the goal is to grow and make money, there is certainly a place for the crow's approach. But when you use social networks, think of yourself as a hummingbird spreading pollen (your message) to as many flowers as possible in a thoughtful way (adding value). In fact, once a trusting connection has been made, it can even set the stage for the occasional (and effective) future "caw."

MIXING BUSINESS AND PLEASURE
THROUGH SOCIAL NETWORKS

While strictly social when they began, networks like Facebook and MySpace are being increasingly used for promoting businesses of every type, from small one-person businesses to mega corporations like Starbucks, Southwest Airlines, and countless others. In this manner, business has become personal. People expect you to be approachable and accessible. When I use the word "personal," however, I'm not suggesting that you share your personal life with your customers, clients, or community. It means, instead, connecting in an authentic and real way, answering questions that come your way, asking questions about your products or services, and being warm and gracious and doing your best to make each person who connects with you feel that you are interested in them and that you make them feel welcome.

Prolific author and online expert Seth Godin offered this valuable piece of advice in his blog: "Respond. This is the single biggest advantage you have over the big guys . . . Just be human."

Think of a billboard, brochure, TV or radio commercial, a Web site, or a flyer in your mailbox. These are all one-directional ways of communicating with a large audience. Advertisers remind me of those crows cawing loudly, "Look at me! Look at me!" All of it is directed *at* you. Social networks have changed communication forever by creating a mass, interactive dialogue. Although communication has always been an interaction between people, social networks have magnified communication to a new level, which makes it much more influential. People today expect you to respond immediately, and an important part of this dialogue is "transparency." When used by social media experts, this means letting people see who you really are. In his latest book, *Crush It,* Gary Vaynerchuk says,

> No matter how big or small you want to go, your authenticity will be at the root of your appeal and is what will keep people coming to your site and spreading the word about your personal brand, service, or whatever you are offering. If you want to dominate the social media game, all of your effort has to come from the heart.

PETER SHANKMAN AND HARO

Though not necessarily a social network, Help a Reporter Out (www.helpareporter.com) can really help your business by connecting you with members of the media. Here's how it works: you sign up to get queries from reporters about stories they're working on and promise to respond only to relevant queries with helpful answers. If you use it right, you can get press for your business— a great form of free marketing. Founded in 2008 by serial entrepreneur Peter Shankman, HARO has quickly grown to send out 1,200 queries to 100,000 sources each week, and it's growing every day. In addition, Shankman is a terrific example of how to use social networks successfully.

It's also about trust. One of the best ways to build trust is to treat each member of your social network with care, as you would any good friend. When they opt in and "follow" you on Twitter or ask to be a "friend" on Facebook, they are taking a first step in this new relationship. It is up to you to reciprocate, nurture, and value each person that joins you. If they trust you, they will share their experience with others.

SOCIAL NETWORKS: THE PERKS

There are undeniable benefits to social networks for all parties involved. Here are just a few:

They're mutually beneficial. The old model of communication was based on the idea that the loudest, funniest, most elaborate ad gets customers—to the benefit of the advertiser. Social networks are different. There is a mutual sharing of information and connection for each other's benefit.

They're free. One of the most powerful aspects of social networks is that for the most part they are free. One person, sitting at home at the kitchen table, can have tremendous power without spending a penny. This levels the playing field when you are competing against larger companies that carry similar products or services.

Their reach is unlimited. Social networks have tremendous reach—you no longer are tied to your desktop computer. With mobile phones and wireless technology, you can download social network applications directly onto your iPhone or BlackBerry and stay connected 24 hours a day with people around the world, if you wish. As a business mom, this is a relief, because I can take my kids to Tae Kwon Do and still get "business" done.

Their power is undeniable. Following are two examples of how social networks have been used to create extraordinary results: Zappos and the Obama campaign.

ZAPPOS

Many people have heard about Zappos (www.zappos.com), the online shoe store, launched in 1999 by Nick Swinmurn, which surpassed $1 billion in revenue and was purchased by Amazon for $928 million. This business has focused on making personal and emotional connections with its customers. Zappos has worked relentlessly at bringing the human touch to what can be an otherwise cold online experience. Soren Gordhamer (www.sorengordhamer.com) blogged about his interview with the current Zappos CEO, Tony Hsieh, and shared several lessons:

> **Your relationships are your brand.** "Whether it is engaging with someone on their blog, Twitter, or a vendor, Zappos believes that every interaction impacts how people view their company. 50 years ago a small group of marketing people would decide on your brand and then spend a lot of money on TV advertising—and that was your brand. Today anyone, whether it is an employee or a customer, if they have a good or bad experience with your company, they can blog about it or Twitter about it and it can be seen by millions of people. *It's what they say now that is your brand.*"
>
> **Embrace Transparency.** Transparency can take place in many ways. The staff at Zappos are encouraged to be themselves. "People can only get to know us if we let them, if we are transparent, if we bring 'who we are' into our work."

THE OBAMA CAMPAIGN

Irrespective of your political disposition, the Obama campaign is another extremely effective example of how social networks can be used to garner support by the millions. In a *New York Times* article entitled, "How Obama Tapped into Social Networks' Power," David Carr writes,

> Like a lot of Web innovators, the Obama campaign did not invent anything completely new. Instead, by bolting together social networking applications under the banner of a move-

ment, they created an unforeseen force to raise money, organize locally, fight smear campaigns, and get out the vote that
helped them topple the Clinton campaign and then John
McCain and the Republicans.

Unlike any other president-elect, Obama understood the Internet.
In the same article, Ranjit Mathoda, a lawyer and money manager, said,

When you think about it, a campaign is a start-up business. . . .
Thomas Jefferson used newspapers to win the presidency, F.D.R.
used radio to change the way he governed, J.F.K. was the first
president to understand television, and Howard Dean saw the
value of the Web for raising money. But Senator Barack Obama
understood that you could use the Web to lower the cost of building a political brand, create a sense of connection and engagement, and dispense with the command and control method of
governing to allow people to self-organize to do the work.

WHEN THE SOCIAL NETWORK IS THE BUSINESS

While you can and should use social networks to grow your business, in some cases the social network "is" the business. One of
the most innovative business ideas I've seen was created by Jason
Sadler, a regular person just like you and me (see www.iwear
yourshirt.com). Every day of the year, he wears someone else's
company T-shirt and promotes their business via social networks
for a fee. What's nice is that you can use his social networking
business to support yours. Just choose an available date on his calendar, mail him an XL size shirt, and this is what you get in return
on *your* day:

- Daily video on YouTube and Ustream (www.ustream.tv)
- Daily photos on Jason's blog and Flickr

- Daily posts on Jason's blog and Twitter
- Calendar (you/your company's logo and Web site)

Figure 9.1: Home page of Jason Sadler's Web site, I Wear Your Shirt. *Source: iwearyourshirt.com.*

In each of these venues, Jason appears in your T-shirt as he shares information about you, your company, and/or your product.

Jason has been featured on CNN and in the *Los Angeles Times,* the *Wall Street Journal,* and elsewhere, just for wearing someone else's T-shirt and talking about it all over the Internet using social networks for free! He pocketed more than $66,000 in 2009.

SOCIAL NETWORK BASICS

Most of this chapter and the next two will be dedicated to discussing the most popular social network sites in the United States: Facebook, Twitter, LinkedIn, MySpace, and YouTube. We'll go over what each network is, why you want to be on it, how to leverage it for business, and the first steps for getting started.

Of course, there are literally hundreds of other online social networks you can use to your benefit. In many cases, they will be more effective for your specific business than the major ones discussed here.

However, regardless which social networks you use, this information will be valuable because: (a) the fundamentals of using most social networks are similar; and (b) you will likely want to leverage a combination of online networks and tools to find the best mix for you.

HIRING A COMMUNITY MANAGER OR VIRTUAL ASSISTANT

You may consider hiring a community manager or virtual assistant to take on the task of social networking. If you do, be sure that you have clear expectations. A community manager should know your business inside and out, be able to respond to questions or complaints, be able to manage your presence across multiple social networks, and be able to provide valuable advice and information to your contacts. The person should also monitor any mentions across social sites and act as a part of your marketing team to get your message across to potential clients. If you are a sole proprietor or your business is based on giving one-on-one advice, you will most likely manage your sites yourself (though you can have someone help you get them set up and teach you about them).

THE RISKS OF USING SOCIAL NETWORKS

If you maintain a "personal professionalism" when on your social networks, there shouldn't be much of a downside. The key is deciding how you want to present yourself. My own criteria are to be authentic, warm, and approachable—yet I always think carefully about each and every comment that I share.

One risk is sharing too much. For example, two people I do business with have said things on Twitter and Facebook that have caused me to stop in my tracks. Without going into specifics, I will just say that stomach problems and divisive social viewpoints are best discussed in nonbusiness contexts. Unfortunately, every time I see their names pop up in my social networks or my e-mail inbox to do business, their remarks are still what come to mind. Has this prevented me from doing business with them? No, but it has impacted my feelings toward them in a way that they would probably regret if they knew. Therefore, it's important to think before you write! Only share when you have something newsworthy, relevant, or helpful for your community of friends and followers. Keep in mind that a post online is a post forever! Once you post something under your name or that can be traced to you, there's no pulling it back. It will be picked up by the search engines and cached (stored) on many different servers.

MY SOCIAL NETWORK DISCLAIMER

The danger in writing this chapter is that technology changes daily. From now until the time you read these pages, thousands of new features, tools, and entirely new social networks will have been created. Therefore, we'll stick with mostly basic concepts and go over how to leverage these tools at this given moment. People have their own allegiances and uses for social networking. There is no need to debate the subject here about which networks are the most relevant, as today's Facebook and Twitter could be something entirely different in the future.

MAKING MONEY ON SOCIAL NETWORKS

The idea of "making money on social networks" sounds like it could be a way to conduct e-commerce, but that is, of course, a misperception. When people talk about making money on social networks, they are referring to the ability to make connections with a lot of people and leverage their online profile and network to support their core business.

The fastest way to lose "friends" and "followers" on social networks is to blatantly market yourself and attempt to sell your products or services directly. As you start creating profiles on social networks, ask yourself how you can add value and share information *without* "selling" your product or service directly. Social networks are a powerful way to build your network—and yes, you can make money from creating these relationships.

If people like what you are saying, they will share it with their friends. You may be wondering, then, "How can I use social networks for my business?" The answer is that the more connections you make, the more people will check out what you do by following your links back to your blog or Web site. It is up to you to figure out how to offer value without resorting to self-promotion.

Here's an example of how one person became my "friend" and how she created value for me and turned me into a loyal customer: A few days after I signed up for my Facebook account, Margie Zable Fisher was recommended as a "friend." I didn't know her at the time, but Facebook will show you who your "mutual friends" are, and based on that, I decided to "friend" her back. Margie created a do-it-yourself PR service, Zable Fisher Public Relations (www.ZFPR.com). I learned about her service by reading her posts on Twitter and Facebook. She would share information by saying things like, "I'm prepping for my upcoming tele-seminar on how to set up your profile on Facebook." This way, she wasn't trying to sell me her service directly, but she was sharing what she was working on—which piqued my interest. She also sent links to articles that I found interesting and thought provoking. As it turns out, I did sign up and attended one of her tele-seminars. Promptly after it ended, she sent out a survey. I shared in the survey that although most of it was terrific, I was disappointed that I hadn't learned certain things. I expected that to be the end of it, but within two days, she had conducted a new interview with a different expert, and she made sure that my questions were addressed. Without requesting additional money, she sent me an audio link to the interview with a lovely message saying, "I hope this will address your questions." I was stunned by her proactive response to my experience and felt that she had given me tremendous value. Now I know that when I work with her again, I can expect excellent service beyond my expectations. She earned my trust and earned my money without me feeling that she was ever trying to "sell" me anything. The result was that I felt that my money was well spent, and I would work with Margie again without hesitation—and as a result I have no hesitation about further promoting her services here!

ALL ABOUT FACEBOOK

Facebook is the largest social network in the world, a site where 350 million people (so far) of all ages go to connect with friends and colleagues. When users sign up, they create a profile page, and whenever they update that page, their friends get notifications. Members can choose to make their pages public or private.

The site is really an all-in-one communications tool since you have all sorts of information about your contacts right at your fingertips. You can get information about where people are, what they like, who their friends are, and what sorts of businesses and groups they are involved in. Facebook can be lengthy or brief; it includes images; and, because of its visual nature, feels friendly and intuitive.

There is also an option to highlight businesses, products, and brands with Facebook pages that are similar to your personal profile page but focused on your business. Go to www.facebook.com and underneath the sign-up section, in smaller print, there is a link titled "Create a Page for a celebrity, band or business." Instead of users being "friends" with your business like they are with you, they can become "fans." The added benefit of a business page is that you can have an unlimited number of "fans," whereas today you are limited to 5,000 friends on your personal profile page. (Facebook plans to change this in the future.)

WHY YOU SHOULD USE FACEBOOK

Facebook is so large because of its strong appeal to people of all ages—and that means a big audience for you and nearly unlimited options for growing your business network. Facebook also has great tools for searching for people you may know, letting you search by school, location, name, e-mail, and more. And it continually identifies other users you may know, which will often lead you to find new friends.

Facebook is a great site to use for your personal network, and people will often only "friend" others they know, even if it is a casual or very old acquaintance. It can also work for your business. By building a Facebook page for your business, product, or brand, you are giving customers a great way to find you, become a fan, and promote your product through word of mouth via posts on their Facebook newsfeed (the broadcast of their activity on the site), which will reach their friends.

On your Facebook business profile page, customers can post feedback, ask questions, and discuss your business/product. You can also choose to step up your promotion by buying ads on Facebook or developing applications for the site, which other users can then add to their profiles.

In Figures 9.2 and 9.3, you can compare the differences between my personal page and my business page. The primary difference is that my business page is the place where I communicate directly with my "fans." They ask questions about business, and I do my best to answer them. They also share exciting milestones, roadblocks they've encountered, or challenges they are experiencing. We all jump in and share resources and information, and celebrate successes! Each page has a completely different personality.

STARBUCKS IS A GREAT SUCCESS STORY

One company using Facebook the right way is Starbucks. They have more than 3 million fans, send out invites to their events (like free coffee on Election Day), and encourage fans to leave comments about their favorite beverages. The Starbucks page promotes a positive brand identity, and it gets loyal customers involved and rewards them by cluing them in on promotions that they can then share with their friends. It also displays ideas from fans that the company is currently considering implementing in its business plan. That's a lot of engagement for essentially no cost beyond the effort you put into it.

You can also show a lot of personality on Facebook by joining groups, supporting causes, and posting photos, links, and more. It also makes it easy for you to leave public and private messages for your friends and others you may want to connect with. Facebook works especially well for sole proprietors because of its hyper-personal focus on you and your network.

HOW TO GET STARTED ON FACEBOOK

First go to www.facebook.com to sign up and create a profile (see Figure 9.4). You will have an option to create a personal page and/or a business page. I have both. My personal page is under my name, Tamara Monosoff, and my business page is under Mom Invented.

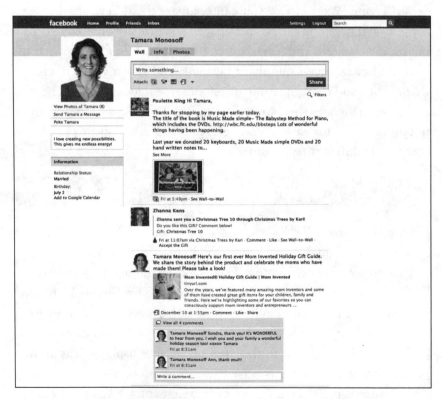

Figure 9.2: My personal page on Facebook.

Your Profile

Enter some information about yourself; leave blank what you don't want to include. Your profile can be edited at any time by clicking on the "Profile" link at the top of the page and going to the section you wish to edit and clicking the pencil icon.

Make sure to add a profile photo. You will be prompted to download a photo when you first sign up, and Facebook will walk you through the steps. If you decide to change the photo to a new one, you can simply hover your mouse over your current picture and a "Change Picture" icon will appear. You should also add a link to your Web site (go to the "Profile" tab along the top navigation bar and then click on the "Info" tab) and some contact information. You'll also need to decide what kind of privacy settings you'd like to have (under "Settings" in the top navigation bar). You can set different privacy levels for your friends by segregating them into groups.

Figure 9.3: My business page on Facebook.

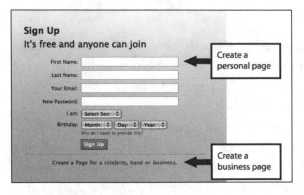

Figure 9.4: Facebook sign-up page. *Source: www.facebook.com.*

If you're using Facebook for business, you should be as open as possible and not block information from people unless you really feel uncomfortable about it. Facebook should be a positive extension of your personal and professional brand, and anything you put up there should reflect the image you'd like to portray. If other people post inappropriate content to your profile, like in a wall post, you can hide their updates from your newsfeed: hover your mouse near the post and an option will come up asking if you would like to see less of this person. If you actually want to delete a post from your profile page, hover over that post on your page and the word "Remove" will show up on the right side. Click "Remove" if you want to remove the post. If someone posts a photo of you that you don't want associated with you, you can remove the tag that links it to you.

Creating a Separate Page for Business

To create a Facebook page for your business, product, or brand, go to and select the type of business/product/brand that matches your business and then start setting up the page in a manner that's similar to how you set up your profile page. Once your page is set up with some basic information and an image (your logo or photo of you), you should start asking people to be fans. Start with your closest friends, and let other fans come to you organically over time.

To keep your page looking fresh, post about upcoming events and promotions, encourage fans to discuss your product/business, and respond to any questions your fans may ask.

Get Facebook Notifications in Your E-mail Inbox

It's a good idea to customize your e-mail notifications to match your preferences—you'll want to be notified of messages, friend requests, and likely about some other things, like wall posts. Just turn off the ones you don't want to receive, such as requests to add an application. You can always find those if you want them when you log into the site; this can be done under "Settings" (on the top navigation bar) by clicking on "Notifications."

TIME TO MAKE FRIENDS

Now comes the fun part: adding friends. Facebook offers a search box on the top right side of your profile page. To use it, type in your friend's name and search just like you would with Google. Search your e-mail contacts, search for people you know by name, and start searching your close friends' friend lists to find people you know you'd like to connect with. When you ask someone to be your friend, you can include a personal note with the request. (This is highly recommended if you're sending requests to people you haven't spoken to in a long time or people you think may not remember you.) And realize that others are also "searching," so make it easy for people to find and connect with you. If you have a married name, include your maiden name in your profile. Once you have a nice stable of friends, you'll notice that Facebook will recommend friends to you with the "People You May Know" tool, which shows up on the right-hand side of your "Home" page (where you see the newsfeed of information from all your contacts).

There are many ways to communicate with your friends on Facebook: You can send private messages; you can write on people's "walls" (essentially sending a public message); and you can instant message (IM) through "Chat." You can also comment on your friends' status updates, posted items (the external links they post), and photos. On Facebook, people tend to really enjoy public messages; it makes them feel popular, and it helps get them more attention.

To manage your friends, go to the "Friends" link in the top navigation bar. This will allow you to search for your friends, add them to groups (for personal reference or for sending out event invitations or creating group privacy settings), find their phone numbers, and search by location. Then, for instance, if you want to search for friends who are in a certain location (let's say you're traveling to Miami and want to see if there's anyone you should contact when you're there), go to "Browse" and then select "Browse By City" and then select the region you want to see.

You can also customize your newsfeed and hide people's updates and application updates you don't want to see by hovering over the items and selecting "Hide," which will pop up to the right of the item.

HOW TO LEVERAGE FACEBOOK FOR BUSINESS

Facebook is all about your connections, whether they're your friends, the people in the groups you belong to, or your business's fans. You don't need a huge group of friends to start seeing some returns from Facebook, but as you grow your network, you'll see more of an impact. Here are some specific tips:

- Create a page for your business/brand/product that's searchable, attracts fans, and can easily get feedback from customers.
- Network with people in your area or with people who have similar interests.
- Join groups for networking purposes or to support a certain cause.
- Support causes and show people what you care about.
- Create a group for a specific slice of your network.
- Send out event invitations to friends and group members for big sales, openings, and other events.
- Reconnect with friends and colleagues—you never know how they could help you now.
- Have links back to your Web site and blog.
- Find interns and employees by posting job listings on the Facebook Marketplace.
- Sell items or find items for your office on the Facebook Marketplace.

ADVERTISE ON THE SITE

We talked about this in Chapter 7, but I wanted to "show" you that this is yet another thing you can do to get visibility. On Facebook, there is a little link in the top right corner of your business profile page that says "Create an Ad." When you click on it, you will come to the Facebook advertising page, shown in Figure 9.5 (the "Create an Ad" link appears on this page too). A Facebook ad can be used to bring people to your Web site, promote a product or service, or let people know about an upcoming event. (This is a paid service.)

Facebook is a great place to establish a presence because of its popularity, and it is also relatively easy to maintain your presence. As long as you keep your business page and profile current and respond to messages, you're doing things right. You don't need to invest a lot of time in the site, but if you do want higher returns, the more energy you put into building your network and connecting with people, the more you'll get out of it.

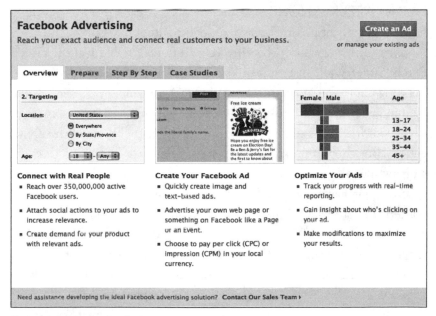

Figure 9.5: Facebook advertising page.
Source: www.facebook.com.

CREATING A GROUP

Facebook has a "groups" option available as well. You can post photos, have discussions, and invite group members to events. The groups feature is not as well developed as other Facebook features; for example, groups don't update to the newsfeed except when someone joins. Because they don't give you instant updates, it can be difficult to follow the conversation in a group because you have to remember to check it. However, you can use your group to promote events, create a network, and extend your reach on Facebook by offering some kind of support, community, and interaction beyond your profile and page.

To create a group, go to the groups application and click on "Create a New Group." You can also just go to www.facebook.com/ groups. Add the basic information for the group, including the name, network, description, and type. You don't have to add contact information if you don't want to. Then start inviting people. Be thoughtful and invite only friends of yours you really think would want to join.

USING APPLICATIONS

Facebook applications are a way to add extra items to your profile page. Applications range from the silly (e.g., Pirates vs. Ninjas, Lil Green Patch, Super Wall, and games like Scramble) to the serious (Blogcast, Lending Club, Calendar, To-Do, and Docs). In general, it's a good rule to limit your applications—they clutter up your page, and some can spam your friends by sending out invitations for them to add the application. But there are excellent business-related applications that are worthwhile. Blogcast, for example, can automatically connect your blog to your Facebook profile. This is a nice way to add some more content to your pages. Calendar is an application that gives you a full calendar with "to do" lists. You can also add connections to the other social sites you use, like Twitter, Flickr (a Web site that helps you organize and share your photos), and Google Shared Items (which allows you to share links and articles from Google Reader).

The bottom line with applications is to be careful what you add. If you're serious about using Facebook to grow your business, don't clutter your page with spammy nonsense, but if you find something you like or can use, go ahead and add it. You can adjust application privacy settings (i.e., who sees the application, whether it posts to your newsfeed, etc.) by selecting "Application Settings" from the "Settings" tab drop-down menu.

THE SKINNY ON STATUS UPDATES

One of Facebook's best and most popular features is status updates. By filling in the small text box at the top of your home page that says "What's on your mind?" you can update all your friends instantly about what you're working on and get feedback instantly as well. By updating your status, you stay at the top of people's minds. You can also include links in your status, which can help drive traffic back to your site. See Figure 9.6 for an example.

This is a great way to promote new additions to your Web site or blog and anything of interest to your friends.

If you're on Twitter and Facebook you can save time by using a Facebook application that will connect Twitter to your status updates (see Figure 9.7). This is fast and easy.

Figure 9.6: Facebook status update. *Source: www.facebook.com.*

Figure 9.7: Linking Facebook and Twitter. *Source: www.facebook.com.*

This works well if you're a light Twitter user and post mostly "what's on your mind" type messages, but if you get into a lot of long conversations and use a lot of @replies, it can look a little foreign for your non-Twitter Facebook friends.

FACEBOOK EVENTS

Facebook also enables you to send out event invitations and join open events. You can browse events you've been invited to and events your friends are hosting/attending, and you can search all events in the search box by keyword in the upper right-hand side of the page. Use this function to look for local networking or business events. If you get invited to an event, you can choose to respond yes, no, maybe, or just ignore the invitation. You can also leave a message on the event page to let people know why you're not coming, how excited you are to go, etc. Valuable connections can be made at live events.

If you are hosting an event and you want to let people know about it, click on the calendar; fill out the details; and hit the blue share button (see Figure 9.8). The message will go out to all of your friends and fans (see Figure 9.9).

THE FACEBOOK MARKETPLACE

The Facebook Marketplace is like Craigslist brought to Facebook. It lets you post and search for jobs (good for finding interns), housing, and other classified-type items you'd like to sell, such as your e-books.

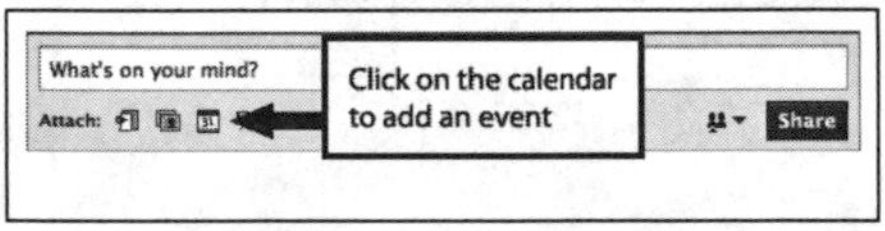

Figure 9.8: Adding a Facebook event, step one. *Source: www.facebook.com.*

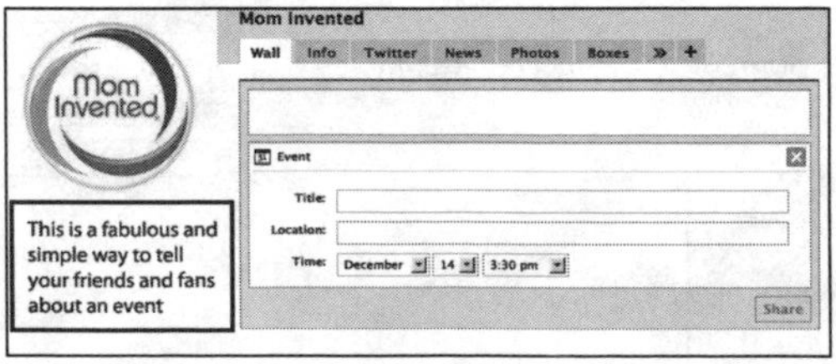

Figure 9.9: Adding a Facebook event, step two. *Source: www.facebook.com.*

Depending on your geographic area, your Marketplace network may or may not be very active, but it's worth a shot as a free place to post items and see what response you get.

Many people start with Facebook and then branch out to other social networks. Because of the size and nature of Facebook, the potential connections are extraordinary. While the business benefits are clear and often surprising, new networking opportunities result from reestablishing old connections with long-lost friends, distant relatives, acquaintances, and past colleagues. If you create a solid presence on Facebook, it can be used as a foundation from which to leverage into other social networks and platforms.

CONCLUSION

Now that you have an overview of social networks and the leverage they can give your business—plus a working knowledge of the world's most popular current network, Facebook—it's time to explore some of the other social networking tools available to you, including how they work and how they can specifically help your business. My personal favorite network, Twitter, is covered in full in the next chapter. Get ready for a real "tweet!"

Get Tweeting with Twitter

The last chapter covered social networking basics and explored the ins and outs of Facebook. This chapter will share tips, strategies, and benefits of what has become my own personal favorite social network—Twitter.

Initially, Twitter can look intimidating, and it may look a little "dumb" because of its condensed format. If you just don't understand Twitter right away, don't despair. This is a common reaction for people in the beginning. Twitter has a language all its own (e.g., DM, @reply, #hashtags, RT), and the conversation is always going. Because of the 140-character limit for each "tweet"—which is similar to a Facebook status update—various methods are used to squeeze as much information as possible into that small space. For instance, because of the condensed format, people tend to use shortened links that don't resemble the URLs we're used to (you'll learn how in this chapter). Things will start to make more sense once you start building your own community and following people you know. Although it can feel overwhelming at first, just remember that you don't need to read every tweet—nor should you try.

Twitter is technically a "microblogging" application, but if you are like I am, such terms have no meaning. Twitter is like a free-form chat room that you build with other members whose content you want to see. Essentially, it is a Web site where users post messages, called "tweets," that are no longer than 140 characters. These tweets can be straight text updates, links to other sites, or replies to other members. When you "follow" someone you know or someone who interests you, this means that you will receive their future tweets. Unlike more structured social networks like Facebook, MySpace, or LinkedIn, there's a looser concept of being "friends" on Twitter. "Following" people is more like subscribing to their blogs—you're just letting them know you want to receive their updates. It's up to them to "follow" you back. Once they follow you back, then you will each receive the other's updates, and a friendship can be forged. Once you are mutually following each other, you also have the option to send private, direct messages (the aforementioned DMs) to one another.

The power of Twitter lies in your powers of communication. As a completely stripped-down social site, Twitter relies on your short-form communication rather than lots of photos or a long profile. A side benefit is that with only 140 characters to work with, you don't have to think too long before you send your message—and you can still get a lot done.

WHY YOU WANT TO BE ON TWITTER

Twitter is a lively community full of business owners, marketing and news media people, and plenty of others who are just there to connect about the things they're personally interested in—whether it's traveling, pets, technology, or anything else. And it's a great place to find out about current ideas, trends, the latest news, and more.

Also, Twitter is not only portable in a physical sense, since it has good mobile phone integration, but it can also add another content stream for your Web site, blog, and other social network pages and act as a new way to make short, quick updates and keep people clued in to what you're doing.

The real power of Twitter, though, lies in the real-life connections it can help you make. People often have "tweetups"—impromptu events with open invitations to anyone who gets the message. These can range from a get-together for drinks to a more structured open group meeting to support a social cause or charity. By going to meet up with some people locally, you'll really be able to start building valuable business and personal relationships. I find Twitter to be an incredible tool that I use more than any other social media. Hopefully, you will see why in this next section.

GETTING STARTED WITH TWITTER

Setting up an account with Twitter is a snap. Here's how to do it. (If you already have a Twitter account, skip this section and go to "How to Use Twitter for Your Business").

Step 1: Sign Up

Click on "Sign up now" button (see Figure 10.1).

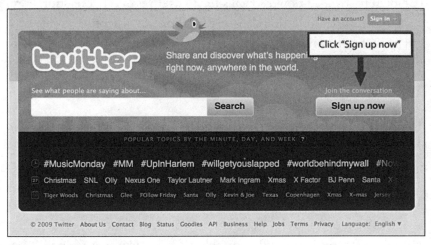

Figure 10.1: Twitter home page.
Source: Twitter.

Step 2: Choose Your Names and Password

In the "Full name" field, type in your real name. In the "Username" field, type in your business name. (See Figure 10.2.) This is the name everyone sees. If your business name is also your real name, then use

twitter

Join the Conversation   Already on Twitter? Sign in.
Already use Twitter on your phone? Finish signup now.

Full name ☐   → **Name Tip:** Use your REAL name

Username ☐   → **Username Tip:** Make your username your business name
Your URL: http://twitter.com/USERNAME

Password ☐

Email ☐   **Example:** My name is Tamara Monosoff, my username is MomInventors
☑ I want the inside scoop—please send me email upda

rosen Nel

Type the words above ☐   Powered by reCAPTCHA. Help

[Create my account]

Figure 10.2 Twitter sign-up page.
Source: Twitter.

your real name. This is important, because this will become your URL on Twitter (e.g., www.twitter.com/MomInventors).

Step 3: Create Your Profile
Next you will have an opportunity to create your profile (see mine in Figure 10.3). Be sure to include a link to your blog or Web site so people can easily learn more about you and your business. Also, be sure to fill in the "bio" information.

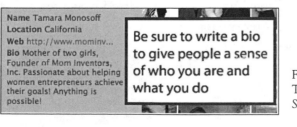

Name Tamara Monosoff
Location California
Web http://www.mominv...
Bio Mother of two girls, Founder of Mom Inventors, Inc. Passionate about helping women entrepreneurs achieve their goals! Anything is possible!

Be sure to write a bio to give people a sense of who you are and what you do

Figure 10.3: Tamara's Twitter profile.
Source: Twitter.

Step 4: Add a Photo

A headshot or company logo is best in the Settings > Picture tab. This represents to the world who you are. You can further customize your profile in the Settings > Design tab, where you can select a theme or create your own by uploading a background image and changing the colors on your page.

TURN ON E-MAIL NOTIFICATIONS

So that you don't have to check Twitter over and over again, just turn on your e-mail notifications (Settings > Notices) and you will receive a message in your e-mail inbox when you've received a new "follow" or direct message. This is important, as you will want to know about new followers and respond to direct messages.

When you receive notification of a new "follower," you will want to read their bio and decide whether or not to "follow" them back. When someone follows me and I follow them back, I send a direct message (DM) to them like the example in Figure 10.4.

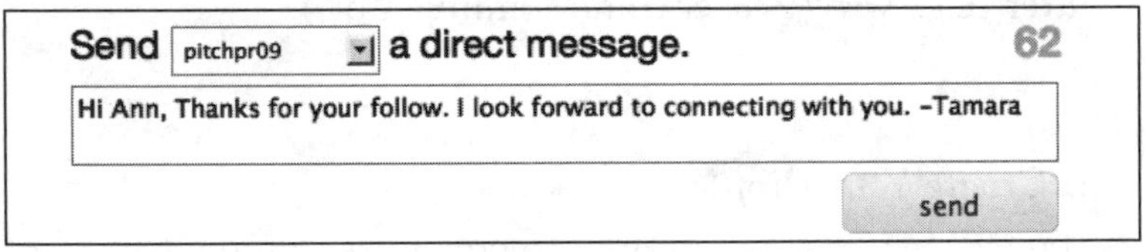

Send [pitchpr09 ▾] a direct message.   62

Hi Ann, Thanks for your follow. I look forward to connecting with you. –Tamara

                                                                    send

Figure 10.4: Example of a Twitter direct message (DM).
Source: Twitter.

You can make your Twitter stream private, but to some extent that defeats the point of joining the service and being able to interact with the full community. The only time I would recommend making your Twitter stream private is if you're creating an internal, private network of some sort, such as using Twitter as an interoffice communications tool. This setting can be changed at the bottom of the Settings > Account page.

Step 5: Find People to Follow and Let the Conversation Begin!
Now that you've done the easy part and you're eager and ready to get started, this is often where the confusion begins. I've seen first-time users on Twitter say things like, "Hello. Is anybody out there?" It's perfectly understandable to feel that way. In fact, when I logged on to Twitter for the first time, I said to myself, "I don't get it." At first you feel like you are dangling in cyberspace and have no idea who can hear what you are saying or how to connect with others. And when you do start finding friends to follow, you see pieces of their conversations and you have no idea who they're communicating with or what anyone is talking about! Don't worry. Give yourself two weeks and you will find that it will all start to make sense. You will begin having conversations with others, they will respond back to you, and you'll become the one having conservations that others will wonder about!

But before you begin the conversation, you have to find people. The first step is to click on the "Find People" button and start with people you know. Search by the person's name or, if you know it, their Twitter username. You can find me by searching for "Tamara Monosoff" or "MomInventors." (See Figure 10.5.) Once you click on

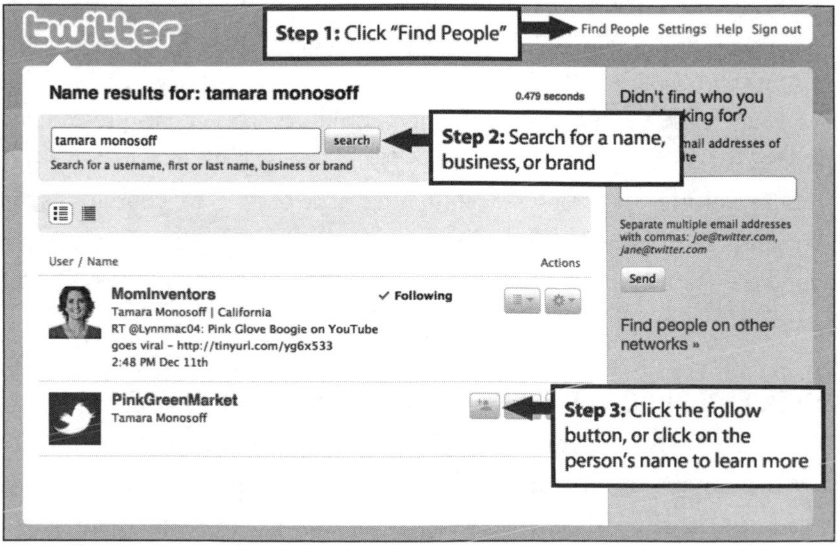

Figure 10.5: Twitter search page.
Source: Twitter.

Figure 10.6: To follow a Twitter user, click "Follow" on his or her profile page. *Source: Twitter.*

my username, it will take you to my profile page on Twitter and you will have an opportunity to "follow" me. (See Figure 10.6.)

Want to find more people, more efficiently? Twitter has a button to "Find People" that can search your Gmail, Yahoo!, Hotmail, AOL, and MSN address books to find matches.

You can also search for individuals using more advanced options, such as geographic location. The link to search is at the very bottom of your Twitter page, in the footer.

You can also look at lists of the most popular Twitterers to see if any of them seem interesting to you. Good places to find them are listed in the resources section at the end of this book.

Don't try to gain a huge list of followers on day one, or you'll look like a spammer. You should try to keep your "following" to "followers" ratio close to even.

Start with people you know or people you're very interested in, like top tweeters. Once you've established yourself a bit, you can then start searching for people in your area and people in your industry. Another good way to find people is by following the people your friends and other contacts talk to—their @replies are always a good source of new people to follow.

WHAT DO PEOPLE TALK ABOUT ON TWITTER?

Most people post a mix of business and personal information on Twitter, ranging from updates about where they are and what they're doing, to questions about how to do things, frustrations about what they're working on, comments about what their kids are up to, and anything else that's important to them. I have found out about deaths and marriage proposals on Twitter. I have also found out about new Web sites, companies, and breaking news.

In other words, you can talk about nearly anything on Twitter, and people do. Just be careful that what you say won't come back to haunt you. Don't tweet negative things about clients, share trade secrets, or embarrass yourself or your company. You can delete a tweet, but that won't take it away from all the people who have already seen it or any other places that may have published it.

WHAT TO TWEET

Here are some suggestions that will give you a better idea of what you should tweet about when you're first getting started:

Let people know what you're doing or what you're working on. Ask them for help, whether it's a restaurant recommendation for your area or someone to interview for an article or blog post.

Ask questions about how others do things you may be struggling with, especially when it comes to using Twitter. Also, if you tweet about problems with applications or companies, you may just get a response from them—Firefox, Comcast, Boingo, and other companies all provide customer service right over Twitter.

Use Twitter for customer service. If a customer posts about a problem with your company, respond! Whether it's troubleshooting, sending them a detailed FAQ, checking on a tracking number for a shipment, or telling them you can send out a technician—don't let problems go unresolved.

Be accessible to your customers. Twitter is an unobtrusive way for customers, clients, and/or community members to feel connected to you and communicate with you in a less formal way than via phone or e-mail. It makes you accessible and open, and it makes them feel like they know you better.

Respond to any problems customers have posted about your company—or any problems your company may be able to help with. A good way to get started is by setting up a search term alert in www.search.twitter.com. Put in a search term and then subscribe to the term's RSS feed via the right-hand "Feed for this query" link.

Events and conferences. You can search for events in the search box on your Twitter page by typing "events." Then use Twitter to connect with people at conferences and events—and find out about the after-parties. After the event, be sure to tweet about it and follow the new people that you just met. Or, let people know about your upcoming events and invite people to join you. Make sure to include your Twitter URL on your business card, e-mail signature, and your profiles on other social networks.

Use hashtags to make events searchable. If you're going to any conferences or events, let the community know so you can connect with others who are also going. See if there's a hashtag from the event's site or by searching Twitter, and start following it and contributing to the comments. Placing the "#" hashtag before an event helps people successfully bring together posts about the event in a single stream. Anyone can use the hashtag symbol to make something more searchable. For instance, if you wanted to meet other entrepreneurs at your local café at a certain time on a certain date, you would mark your event with a hashtag and give it a name like #yellowwood and include this in every tweet. You would encourage anyone who was joining the event to use that in every tweet as well. If someone wanted to easily search for the event details, they could click on #yellowwood in a tweet or put #yellowwood in the search box.

If you are following someone new and want to increase the odds of him or her following you back, send them an @reply saying hello, introducing yourself, or letting them know why you're following them.

Respond to other Twitterers' questions with @replies.

Post links to any particularly interesting or relevant articles or sites with a bit of description. Some URLs (especially those shortened ones) give no indication as to where they're leading, so some info is very helpful.

Establish yourself as a connector and a go-to person. If you write thoughtful @replies that give insight into topics people are asking about, you may end up getting some business.

Anything "newsy" you're experiencing.

BALANCING YOUR TWEETS

It's important to have a good balance of @replies, original posts, and posts with links. If you post too many links, it'll look like you don't care about conversation, just about promoting. If you have only text posts without @replies or links, it makes you look a little disconnected and like you may not know what you're doing on the site. Just try for a mix. The exact ratio isn't important. You just want to create interest, connections, and a strong network.

The Difference between a Direct Message (DM) and an @reply Message

See Figures 10.7 and 10.8 to see how to send your private direct messages and your public @reply messages.

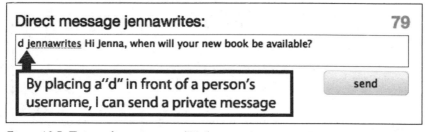

Figure 10.7: Twitter direct message (DM).
Source: Twitter.

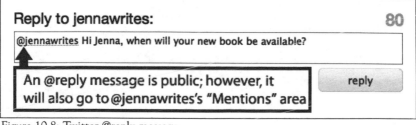

Figure 10.8: Twitter @reply message.
Source: Twitter.

HOW TO LEVERAGE TWITTER FOR BUSINESS

One invaluable way to use Twitter is as a "pointer site" to link to your site, blogs, videos, press articles, etc. You can place a link to point out some new content, or you can link to content that can help answer someone's question. Figure 10.9 offers examples of some of my tweets.

The last tweet in Figure 10.9 is an example of a "RT" message. The arrows symbolize that the message has been retweeted. This means that you've "retweeted" someone else's message. You liked what they shared so much that you forwarded their message to share with all of your followers. This is the highest compliment available, and you will be loved and appreciated for doing this. I do this only when I wholeheartedly believe in the content of the message. Your followers have chosen you because of the quality of your tweets, which is a trust that should be respected. Don't RT just to be "popular" because in the end you'll lose your faithful followers if they don't like what you are tweeting.

You can also use Twitter for social campaigns, like raising awareness for a bone marrow drive or for breast cancer research. When

@B_A_Bookworm I loved your blog post "What do kids really want!"
1:26 PM Dec 11th from web in reply to B_A_Bookworm

@textmessagebaby Thanks for your lovely message about mominvented.com! I love your products. I laughed out loud when I saw. Fabulous & Fun!
12:37 PM Dec 11th from web in reply to textmessagebaby

More wonderful peeps to follow. Thank you for your RTs. I'm sending my love @Kidzsack @mummypreneur @whynotsayhello @grillcharmer @KizzieFK
1:34 AM Dec 11th from web

Thanks for your RTs! You're wonderful peeps! @djthunder1 @MyGOMOM @Blue_Collar_U @4WheelParts @whynotsayhello @MirandaMcCage @OnTray2Go
1:32 AM Dec 11th from web

⟲ KizzieFK Support women inventors+entrepreneurs this holiday season. @mominventors shares some great mom-invented gifts http://is.gd/5ifaQ #giftguide
11:19 AM Dec 10th from Seesmic
Retweeted by MomInventors and 1 other

Here are some of my tweets. I support my friends and fans, start conversations, link to my blog posts, and retweet interesting stories and positive comments about my business.

Figure 10.9: Sample tweets.
Source: Twitter.

Susan Reynolds was diagnosed with breast cancer, she reached out to the Twitter community for support, and they responded big time—by setting up donation sites; adding frozen peas (which she used as ice packs on her sore chest) to their avatars (profile images) in support; and creating a huge phenomenon that garnered a good deal of press on blogs and news sites.

You can also provide great, instant customer support via Twitter. Comcast helps people out with their cable woes with their ComcastCares account (twitter.com/comcastcares), making direct connections with consumers, and there are many other companies that are in on the "customer service for complainers" trend.

There's also a great mom community on Twitter; they even throw girls' night out parties on the site, complete with giveaways for participants. These parties are a place to show off a product or new site, learn a little something, connect with other moms, find more followers, and just have fun. The organizer of these parties, Amy Bair, has actually made the service part of her marketing business.

PAY CLOSE ATTENTION TO YOUR TWITTER PROFILE OR IT MAY CREATE HEADACHES

Twitter is powerful because it can facilitate a movement. However, that power can also be a headache for businesses. Recently, when a company selling pain medication released a new ad about "baby wearing" and the pain it causes, Twitter moms revolted, posting negative comments about the ads, writing negative blog posts, and joining together to let the manufacturer know they were offended. The company pulled the ads and issued some apologies, but since the company wasn't on Twitter—and the backlash started over a weekend—it took them a while to hear about it and respond.

Finally, Twitter opens doors. Since Twitter is a relatively even play-ing field, you can expect responses from just about anyone you DM (direct message) or @reply (see below). Whereas you might not expect Guy Kawasaki or a celebrity like Stephen Fry to respond to an e-mail, they may well respond to you on Twitter. Twitter helps bring people together and helps you make connections with people you never thought you could reach.

CASE STUDY: AUCTION DIRECT USA

One company that's had great success on Twitter is used car retailer Auction Direct USA (twitter.com/AuctionDirect). They started using Twitter as a communications and marketing channel to inform cus-tomers about car news and to get feedback on their site. They had such success with people responding to their tweets, they started a blog, www.tweetandgreet.com, which showcases Twitter interviews with their followers about cars. They have found that their guests tend to put a link to their interview on their own Web sites and social sites, which creates significant new traffic back to the Auction Direct USA site.

TWITTER TIPS AND TOOLS

Here are some tips to help get you tweeting like an old pro.

A SOLUTION FOR LIMITED MESSAGE SPACE

One effective way to leverage Twitter is by including links in your tweets. Due to the 140-character limitation, you need to use space efficiently. There are some free tools that enable you to do this. Just copy the URL link you want to share, then paste it into one of these tools, and a shorter version of the URL will be generated. From there, copy your new abbre-viated URL and paste it into your Twitter message. Free tools that do this can be found at www.tinyurl.com, www.snipurl.com, and www.snurl.com.

TWITTER LINGO

It may seem like the tweets you're reading are in another language—and in some cases, they are! Try www.urbandictionary.com to translate

Web terms, and try pistachioconsulting.com/top-15-twitter-acronyms to look up Twitter acronyms. Laura (@Pistachio) is a great Twitter resource. Follow her!

"UNFOLLOW" SOMEONE

On *rare* occasions someone will send you content you find offensive. You may choose to confront them, ignore them, or go a step further and "unfollow" them. This can be done by going to their Twitter page and clicking on the "Following" check mark under their profile picture.

Unless you notify them that you have done so, they will not automatically know that you have "unfollowed" them, but if they try to send you a direct message (DM), they'll find that they no longer can. If you want to be notified when someone "unfollows" you, you can subscribe to useqwitter.com.

Another option is to "block" someone from following you. I have done this myself, but only when I had been sent inappropriate material or realized that the user was a spammer. When blocked, a user can't follow your updates.

SET UP YOUR MOBILE DEVICE

One of Twitter's best features is how mobile it is. This comes in especially handy if you're traveling or want to connect with people at conferences. You should set up Twitter on your phone even if you don't plan to use the SMS function immediately. Go to Settings > Devices and enter your phone number. When you receive the verification code, text it back to 40404 (in the U.S.) and you're ready to go. Once it's set up (which is instant), just send an SMS text message from your phone to 40404, and the message will appear on your Twitter page instantaneously.

What is an SMS text, you ask? If you have a phone or mobile device with texting capabilities, you can tweet on the go. I have a BlackBerry, and to send a message to Twitter, I type in the Twitter number 40404 and it gives me the choice to compose an e-mail or compose an SMS text message. Click on "SMS" and then type in your message. When you hit "send," your text message will show up as a tweet on your Twitter profile for everyone to read instantly.

You can also use various Twitter apps such as Dabr, Tweetie, TwitterFon, and TwitterBerry to send and receive updates on your mobile.

DESKTOP APPLICATIONS

You don't want to be stuck checking your Twitter site constantly, and getting messages via phone can become disruptive while you're working. I recommend downloading a third-party desktop application. There are many to choose from, but some popular ones include TweetDeck (www.tweetdeck.com/beta), Seesmic Desktop (desktop .seesmic.com), Nambu (www.nambu.com), Tweetie (www.atebits .com/tweetie-mac), and twhirl (www.twhirl.org).

These third-party applications sit on your desktop, sort of like an instant messaging client, and give you a running stream of updates that you can choose to read immediately or at your leisure. They will also give you alerts for @replies and DMs. Plus you can make updates

SPOT TWITTER SPAMMERS AND MAKE SURE YOU DON'T LOOK LIKE ONE

What constitutes a Twitter spammer?

- They follow a lot of people but have few followers of their own.
- They have a very new account with very few posts and no name or photo.
- They post mostly or only links.
- If you follow them, they immediately follow up with a DM with a link for a free offer, like an e-book.

To deal with spammers, ignore their follows, unfollow them if you're already a follower, or block them.

directly in the application, search users, view people's profiles and individual streams, follow and unfollow users, shorten URLs, filter your messages, retweet, and search terms. Many of the desktop clients also allow you to save custom searches and segment the people you follow into groups. They also give you quick links on users' images to send DMs and @replies, and some let you manage multiple Twitter accounts. Using an application like this will change how you connect and make it much easier to participate and to follow along.

FOLLOW TWITTER ETIQUETTE AND BEST PRACTICES

The topic of etiquette is important because when you misstep on a social network, everyone hears about it! For the most part, novice mistakes or etiquette breaches are quickly forgiven. However, you won't want to be seen as a novice for long. There is a full section dedicated to social network etiquette in a later chapter, but these pointers are specific to Twitter:

- Try to keep your following:followers ratio close to even.
- Be patient and add new followers gradually.
- Respond in kind—to an @reply with an @reply, to a DM with a DM.
- Have a mix of @replies, plain text posts, and posts with links.
- Don't post too many links or be too repetitive.
- Keep your messages in line with your business's culture; everything you say is public.
- Have your name, company name, and picture on your profile along with a link to your site.
- Link to Twitter from your site or blog so people can be sure it's really you.
- Don't set up an account and forget about it because people will forget about you if you're not active. This is a community where you really get out of it what you put in. If you don't @reply anyone,

don't expect anyone to @reply back. It's OK to take breaks—even for days at a time—but you must participate to see an impact.

CONCLUSION

Hopefully, you've gotten a flavor for what Twitter can offer—and you feel more comfortable about using the network if you haven't already. Next stop: YouTube, LinkedIn, and MySpace—and how to tie them all together. We'll explore how to use these social networks in the next chapter and how the proper etiquette while using any of these tools is absolutely essential to your success.

YouTube, LinkedIn, MySpace, and Etiquette

Your social calendar isn't quite full yet—at least not when it comes to your business. That's because YouTube, LinkedIn, and MySpace offer even more opportunities to get the word out and make connections with your target markets. In this chapter, you'll learn the ins and outs of all three of these sites, and how to link all your social networks together to create efficiencies that save time. You'll also find out about some essential etiquette you should know when using any social network so that you avoid making costly or embarrassing mistakes.

PUTTING THE "YOU" IN YOUTUBE

YouTube is a video-sharing Web site platform and network that allows users to post and watch videos and leave comments either in the form of text or video.

The site is very popular among younger users, but its videos can be embedded anywhere, so they get exposure to people of all ages. The most popular videos tend to be focused on comedy or music, but people post everything from speeches to commercials to conversations between them and their friends. YouTube also has social elements to which you can subscribe.

WHY YOU SHOULD USE IT

YouTube is just one way to publish video about your business, but since it's so portable (you can embed YouTube videos in other sites) and so many people are on the site, it's a premier destination for publishing video content. By having video content about your business—which you could embed in your Web site, blog, Facebook page, MySpace page, etc.—you are letting people see another dimension of you and your product. People love to watch videos because they feel more personal than reading text, and they give a better perspective on what your business does and what you stand for.

YouTube also functions like a social network. You can subscribe to people's video updates and receive notifications when they post new videos, and you can add members as mutual friends. You can also create a profile on your "channel" with links to your sites. You can then build a social network, much as you do on Facebook and Twitter, by "subscribing" to other people's channels and allowing them to subscribe to yours.

YouTube is a great place to have a presence for very little work. You don't have to upload videos frequently to get mileage out of those you already have, and you don't have to interact with the community to continue to see a benefit. If you have video or want to have video in the future, it's a good idea to start a YouTube channel to reach the maximum audience and create more links back to your sites.

Also, don't stress about your video "going viral." You can receive a moderate number of hits and still generate page views and new business. You don't have to be a YouTube sensation for YouTube to work for you. That said, it can also make a phenomenal impact if you do create a hit video.

HOW TO EXTEND YOUR REACH WITH YOUTUBE

There are many different ways you can use YouTube to find new business:

- Create a product demonstration video.
- Post videos of speeches you give at conferences.
- Create video tutorials to teach something related to your business.

- Show a typical day at the office with you and your employees (edited down to only a few minutes, of course).
- Leave helpful and nice comments on other YouTube videos. If you really want to get attention, create a video response. This can help drive traffic back to your page and can help you form connections with other YouTube posters.
- Create a video blog that you post on YouTube.
- Create a commercial for your business.
- Create video holiday greetings.
- Create a video from an event you have hosted, and be sure to feature some of your guests. If they're savvy about their online presence, they'll post the video on their sites too.

HOW TO LEVERAGE YOUTUBE FOR BUSINESS

Here are some strategies for using YouTube to further your business goals:

- Communicate with other business owners or potential customers by sending them messages. You can write to them about collaborating on projects or using their videos on your site, but sending promotional messages is generally frowned upon (though you might want to include a link to your site as part of your e-mail signature).
- Once you create a video, post it everywhere your customers may be looking—on your blog, your Web site, your Facebook and MySpace pages, etc. Encourage others to post it on their sites as well.
- You don't need to post videos frequently—even having a few can give you some reach if they get posted elsewhere. If you do post regularly, though, you'll likely get some more attention and attract more followers.
- Customize your video channel so that it's aligned with your brand image. You can change the colors and look of your channel (via your YouTube profile), and you can add some information about yourself, such as where you're from, with links to your other sites. You can also organize your videos into playlists and choose featured videos if you have many of them.

- Link back to your YouTube page from your site and your social site profiles.
- Buy sponsored video links or search results (ads.youtube.com/ index) to make sure your videos get in front of as many people as possible, and invite viewers to "become a fan," which takes them to your Facebook fan page.
- Enter a video contest to increase visibility—and possibly win something! See www.youtube.com/contests_main.

GETTING STARTED ON YOUTUBE

You can sign in to YouTube via your Google account (if you have one), or you can create your own user name and password. When you sign up, you automatically get a channel, whether you have posted videos or not. This is like your profile page on Facebook—a place to put all your con-tact and bio information.

From there, you should customize your channel by clicking "Edit Profile." You can set your channel info and channel design and organize your videos (i.e., choose videos to highlight as your favorites). To change your personal information, go to "My Account." Under "Profile Setup," you can change the information displayed on your channel about you, including your geographic location, Web site, and interests. You should display your business information, including your address (if you have a brick-and-mortar business), your Web site, and a little about what you do.

Under "Customize Homepage," you can select which boxes to show on your channel. You can also set your privacy settings under "Privacy." And you can set up your blog to publish to YouTube under "Blog Setup." It's good to display your blog in as many places as possible. The videos you upload to YouTube must be fewer than 10 minutes long and smaller than one gigabyte (1 GB). It's easy to post a video—just go to "Upload" and select the file from your computer.

Recording Video

Creating videos is easier than ever. You can record video on all sorts of devices, from your webcam to cell phones to digital cameras to digital video cameras. Once you record your video, you'll probably want to edit it with a program like iMovie (www.imovie.com), Final Cut Pro (www.finalcutpro.com), or other video editing software. If you use a PC, you likely already have Windows Movie Maker (another editing program) loaded on your PC, as it was included with Windows XP Service Pack 2 and updated for Windows Vista.

If you want a really high quality video, you should hire a professional to help you with light, sound, shooting, and editing. You'll want your video in MP4 or AAC format to upload it to YouTube. Programs like iMovie have a special setting for export to YouTube that will create a file that meets YouTube's specifications.

Once your video is ready to post, click first on the yellow "Upload" button in the top right corner of YouTube and then click on the yellow "Upload Video" button. When you click on this second button, it will prompt you to browse your computer to find the file you saved (see Figure 11.1).

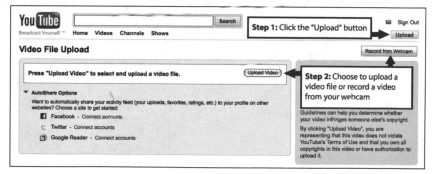

Figure 11.1: How to upload videos to YouTube.
Source: YouTube.

You can also record directly to YouTube with your webcam by going to upload and choosing "Record from Webcam." You will record your message and then be prompted to upload it as a video (it will not be posted as a live stream). Here's a direct link: www.youtube.com/my_webcam.

CHANNELS TO CHECK OUT

Though there is no dedicated business category on YouTube, you can still find plenty of business advice and other business-related information. One channel to check out for ideas on how to use YouTube for business is HarvardBusiness, the channel of Harvard Business Publishing (www.youtube.com/user/HarvardBusiness), shown in Figure 11.2.

Figure 11.2: Harvard Business Publishing channel on YouTube.
Source: YouTube.

You can actually create your own YouTube TV channel. Talk about power!

Here are some other YouTube channels that may inspire you:

• Tenori-On shows how to maximize video for product demonstrations: www.youtube.com/user/tenorion1.

- Zappos highlights customer feedback and customer service: www.youtube.com/user/ZapposExperience.
- Tony Alessandra offers clips from keynote speeches: www.youtube.com/user/TonyAlessandra.
- EepyBird shows innovative online marketing videos: www.youtube.com/user/EepyBird.

CHECK OUT USTREAM FOR CREATING LIVE BROADCASTS

I just learned about a new resource—Ustream (www.ustream .com)—and I can't wait to use it. Ustream is a powerful, interactive platform that enables anyone with a camera and an Internet connection to broadcast to an online global audience of unlimited size quickly and easily. In less than two minutes, you can become a broadcaster by creating your own channel on Ustream or by broadcasting through your own Web site.

Ustream enables a live dialogue among participants, allowing for a new way to experience online media. The site has integrated with Twitter and Facebook so that you have the ability to interact via chat while your live event is occurring.

While not a social network, per se, Ustream is an awesome platform that can complement your use of social networks. Whereas YouTube hosts recorded videos, Ustream lets you stream live video. If that feels intimidating, there is the option to record footage streamed live—then download it afterward. Best of all, it's free! See Figure 11.3 to get started.

How to Use Ustream for Business

Use Ustream as a tool that will help build you up as an expert— or help build your brand. Here are just a few ideas:

- If you are in the service business—say, rug cleaning or landscaping—you could offer your followers video tips.
- If you are an expert, you can discuss different topics (e.g., a patent lawyer could share information on the latest legislation, or an artist could share tips on drawing).
- If you give speeches, conduct workshops, or offer seminars, you can stream them live.
- If you make and/or sell products, you can give product demonstrations or show fun uses for them.

Step 1 - Sign up for a Ustream account and create your channel
Step 2 - Plug in your camera
Step 3 - Click "Broadcast Now"
Step 4 - When asked, "allow" the broadcast console to access your video or webcam
Step 5 - Click "start broadcast" in the console. You are now live!

Figure 11.3: Getting started on Ustream.
Source: Ustream.

BUILD BUSINESS CONNECTIONS WITH LINKEDIN

Where Twitter, Facebook, and YouTube facilitate connections, they are best used to generate buzz and interaction. LinkedIn is more like an online, supercharged Rolodex—a social network for professionals that lets you build an online résumé, send and receive testimonials, join business-focused discussion groups, and ask and answer business questions. LinkedIn is used by people at all stages of their careers as a professional landing page and résumé, a place to connect with other professionals, and a place to find and post jobs. From its inception, LinkedIn was geared more to fostering network connections within the business community, and it's common for entrepreneurs and corporate managers alike to seek out partnership opportunities for their business through this site.

WHY YOU SHOULD USE IT

You don't have to devote much time to LinkedIn. You can create your profile (which includes work history, information about what you do now, and some other basic information), build your network a bit among friends and contacts, and write testimonials for others' work. You'll also want to ask them to write testimonials to recommend you, which looks good to potential customers you may refer to your LinkedIn page or those who search for you online.

LinkedIn can also help you get in touch with former colleagues and keep them updated on your projects. It also lets you highlight your Web sites and social sites and post your blog.

The most compelling thing about LinkedIn is probably the "six degrees of separation"—the concept that we are never more than six connections away from anyone in the world. With LinkedIn, you can start to see this concept come to life. For example, when you create a link with someone, you can then see who they are linked to. The power of this information is obvious. If you need to find a way to connect with someone in particular, you can search your own connections until you find a connection to that specific person, even if you must go through several levels (or "degrees"). For example, say you're a marketing consultant who's wanted to connect with a particular advertising agency in town to offer your services. Chances are, as you build your LinkedIn network, one of your current contacts is already linked to someone at that agency. With this knowledge, you can get in touch with your current contact and ask for a referral.

If you want to devote more time to the site, you can answer questions posed by other members in the "Answers" section and establish yourself as an expert in your field on the site to get more profile views and potentially more work. You can also send and receive private messages, which is a nice way to make business introductions, and become active in various industry and topical groups, whose messages are e-mailed out to users.

HOW TO LEVERAGE LINKEDIN FOR BUSINESS

Here are some strategies for using LinkedIn to further your business goals:

- Access key contacts you have identified via your own connections.
- Use it as a professional, public résumé so people can see your credentials and what you do.

- Recommend other businesses or individuals to work with, and have others recommend you.
- Answer user questions and establish yourself as an expert.
- Ask questions of the community to start discussions, do market research, and gain information on subjects you're curious about.
- Find employees by posting jobs.
- Find jobs by searching the job boards (some jobs are even exclusive to LinkedIn).
- Promote your sites and your blog.
- Let people know what you're working on.
- Connect with old colleagues, coworkers, and friends in a professional capacity—you never know when they can help.
- Send private messages to connect with people in your industry or other people you're interested in meeting.
- Join groups to ask and answer directed questions and receive updates for your industry, your university, etc.
- Manage business contacts.
- Find professional events to attend.
- Search company networks and see the employees who work there.
- Search for people to connect with based on their background, credentials, or location.
- Upgrade to a paid professional account if you want to do any serious recruiting. Otherwise, stick with the free account.

Maximizing Your LinkedIn Profile

Figure 11.4 offers an excellent example of how one social media expert, Mari Smith, has made great use of LinkedIn.

GETTING STARTED ON LINKEDIN

First, sign up for an account at www.linkedin.com. From there, LinkedIn makes filling in your profile really simple. It lets you know which areas you need to complete—including a photo, basic information, work history, and descriptions of your previous jobs. You can also create a direct link to your profile, which should be

Mari Smith ②

Social Media Speaker, Trainer & Consultant | President, International Social Media Association

Greater San Diego Area | Internet

Mari Smith "Everything has beauty, but not everyone sees it." Confucius (via @tonyrobbins) [SO true!! ❀] 3 hours ago from Twitter

Current	• President at International Social Media Association ⎘ • Social Media Speaker | Social Media Trainer at Mari Smith | Social Media Keynote Speaker | Social Media Consultant | Facebook & Twitter Trainer ⎘ • Social Media Consultant, Speaker & Trainer at MariSmith.com
Past	• SuccessTracs Results Coach at Peak Potentials Training
Education	• B\Coach Systems, LLC - Coach2 • Elementary = BC, Canada; High School = Edinburgh, Scotland
Recommendations	16 people have recommended Mari
Connections	500+ connections
Websites	• Join Me on Facebook • 7-Day Facebook Marketing Tips • Social Marketing Quick Start!
Twitter *NEW*	• MariSmith
Public Profile	http://www.linkedin.com/in/marismith

Figure 11.4: Mari Smith's LinkedIn profile.
Source: LinkedIn.

linkedin.com/yourname (or some variation on your name if your name isn't available).

Linking to Contacts

Once you have your profile complete (or at least partway complete—you can always go back to it), start looking for friends. Go to "Add Connections," and you can import your address book, search people by name, or search people who are in your networks (previous employer, same school, etc.). LinkedIn will provide much more value if you build a nice-sized network. You should focus on people you actually know and trust. If you send an invitation to someone and they tell LinkedIn that they don't know you, your account can be penalized. If you receive invitations from people you don't know or don't want to connect with, it's best to just ignore them instead of saying you don't know them so the person doesn't get penalized.

If you do want to connect with someone who may not know or remember you, send a personal note. I have often accepted connections from people I didn't actually know who sent a personal note telling me why they wanted to connect—be it that we're in the same industry, have a mutual friend, etc. LinkedIn will also recommend friends you may know in the top right corner of your home page.

ESTABLISH YOURSELF AS AN EXPERT

The best way to establish yourself as an expert on LinkedIn is by answering a lot of questions in the "Answers" section. If your responses are chosen as "best answers," you will be featured on the "Answers" home page. This can drive more traffic to your profile.

Also, if a person is looking for a consultant or a journalist is looking for someone to interview—and your answers are stellar—you may get some work or press by actively answering questions.

JOINING GROUPS

Participating in LinkedIn groups is another way to find contacts, interact, and ask and answer questions within a more limited community. There are groups for alumni from different universities, professional organizations, local organizations, and various industry-related groups. It's a good idea to sign up for a few groups so you can stay up to date on what's happening in your business community and foster connections with other members. Group discussions are also e-mailed out to group members, so your questions and answers can get quite a good reach among group members.

UPDATING YOUR CONTACTS

Aside from asking questions that can help you research a new project, you can also tell your network what you're working on by updating your "What are you working on?" status on your home page. Similar to your Facebook status, though more specific, this lets you tell your professional network what you're doing and what you need—and keeps you at the top of their minds. These status updates are e-mailed on a regular basis to LinkedIn members.

WRITE RECOMMENDATIONS

One of the best ways to build a positive personal brand—and your business—is by getting referrals from customers, associates, and other people with whom you do business. LinkedIn gives you the option of asking people for referrals, but this can seem tacky. It's a much better idea to start writing referrals and hope that those people write referrals for you in return. Plus, you don't want to get into an awkward situation of asking someone to write you a referral when they might not want to. By writing nice referrals for other people, you'll also build your profile on the site and make people feel good and supported.

DO MORE WITH APPLICATIONS

You can add even more value to your LinkedIn profile with applications. For example, you can conduct polls for market research, add your blog feed to your profile, and share presentations. One free application is Google Presentations, which enables you to showcase a recent talk or presentation, display a visual portfolio of your work, and introduce yourself to recruiters and professional contacts who see your profile. Go to docs.google.com to get started.

MAKING THE MOST OF MYSPACE

MySpace was a pioneer among large social sites. Like Facebook, it lets you create a profile, add friends, send public and private messages, and join groups. It also has a classified section and can be used to send event invitations. Its users skew a bit younger—in their teens, twenties, and thirties.

For business, MySpace is best used for bands, comedians, filmmakers, and consumer businesses. Its profiles offer a lot of flexibility in terms of customization—you choose the colors and images, you can adjust the layout, and you can really make it look like part of your brand.

WHY YOU SHOULD USE IT

Because of its younger demographic, MySpace reaches an entirely different market than LinkedIn. MySpace profiles can range from the simple, standard template the system provides you, to a completely customized one that's in line with your brand and gives lots of links back to your site. With an audience of more than 200 million, there are a lot of people to reach and a lot of other business owners trying to connect. If your products or services target young adults, then this is where you should be. If your business is more traditional and skews to a more affluent or older audience, however, this platform may not convey the level of professionalism that you may be seeking.

While MySpace has fallen out of favor recently, it has created many Internet celebrities—and it's also helped smaller businesses. By networking with your target market on the site, you will build trust, establish referral relationships, and have a new venue to promote your goods and services. MySpace acts as another Web site for your business, pointing potential customers in the right direction and letting them know more about you and your business. As with other social networks, having a MySpace page can also help increase purchase intent since you've made a connection with your customer, and its cost is so low that it really outshines other modes of advertising.

HOW TO LEVERAGE MYSPACE FOR BUSINESS

Here are some strategies for using MySpace to further your business goals:

- Create a free, Google-searchable Web site with lots of information about your business.
- Send bulletin messages to update all your friends about new products, events, new content on your page, and more.
- Join groups and post to their forums to connect with other business owners and potential customers.
- Create events for big sales, openings, and other events—and invite your MySpace friends.
- Leave public comments for your friends that include a small tag

promoting your site/product at the end so all their friends see it and can click on it. Remember not to send a straight ad, though. Leave a personal comment first, then just include a small, one-line promo, perhaps in your e-mail signature.

- Create blog posts about your business or industry that everyone can see. You can also copy and paste your blog posts from other sites.
- Add a calendar of events to your page to let people know about different promotions, conferences you're going to, etc.
- Add video and audio clips to your profile that can highlight your business or your expertise.
- Update your status to let people know what you're doing and stay top of mind.
- Create a personal connection with potential customers to increase purchase intent.
- Post and find items on the "Classifieds" board for free—the "Classifieds" cover jobs, real estate, products and services, and more.
- Start and add to discussions in the forums to meet other entrepreneurs and potential customers.

GETTING STARTED

First, register at MySpace.com and fill in your e-mail address, choose a password, and provide some basic information like your name, location, and date of birth. From there, you start creating your profile. The site will lead you through the areas you can fill out, starting with Personal Info > About Me.

Your headline is one of the first things that people will see about you, so make it good and catchy. For me, it would be something like, "Helping moms bring products to market since 2002." Alternatively, I could add a more personal element by saying something like, "Hi, I'm Tamara, and I've helped 1,000 moms turn their inventions into real-life products." Regardless of your approach, you want to have something catchy, pithy, and informational about you and/or your business.

The next most important section to fill out is "About Me." You can add HTML in this area, so feel free to include photos and videos.

This is the main area of your profile, where you can really show what you do. The "Who I'd Like to Meet" section is also important, because here you can define your target market. Talk about whom you want to connect with, why, and why they should want to connect with you. The other sections lie within Personal Info > Interests. These include topics like music, movies, and more, and can be filled out to display your interests. You don't have to fill these out, though, or you can provide other information you'd rather have people know.

Under Personal Info > Basic Info, you can control what name people see when they view your profile, when you leave a comment, or when you send a message. You can also show your site's URL. Think carefully when choosing a URL since you can't change it. Preferably, use your business name (for me, that would be www.myspace.com/mominventors). If your name isn't available, you can modify it slightly or include your name in some way. This is the direct link to your page.

Now, there are multiple options for how your name will be seen. You can change your first and last name (used for search purposes) and your display name—the name that shows up on your profile. You can put your first and last name in the name fields and your business name in the display name area so that all the names are searchable. If you are the focus of your business (e.g., if you run a consulting business or another type of business where you're giving a lot of personal advice), consider using your real name as your display name instead of using your business name.

MYSPACE ASKS FOR A LOT MORE PERSONAL INFO
Under Personal Info > Basic Info, you also set your gender, age, and location. For some reason, this is mandatory for MySpace, and you have to be over 13 years of age for your profile to be public, so you can't necessarily go with your business's age. You can hide this when customizing your profile (see "Look and Feel" below). In Personal Info > Details, MySpace wants to know your marital status, zodiac sign, and other personal information like sexual orientation. Thankfully, you can leave most of this blank. And you can turn sections off or hide the entire box completely with the Profile 2.0 tools (again, see "Look and Feel" below).

Under Personal Info > Networking, you can clearly define whom you want to network with and what field you're in. Select a category, subcategory, and field, and write a little about your networking goals. You can add music and video to your profile without code as well. Music is popular but can be annoying because it usually starts up without the user clicking on it, so I'd advise you not to use it for a business site. You can add a profile song, if you'd like, that will play for anyone viewing your page in Personal Info > Music & Video.

CUSTOMIZING YOUR PROFILE

MySpace has made some big changes to its profile page, so you can more easily hide content areas, benefit from complex privacy settings, and add themes without coding. If you go to Edit Profile > Customize Profile, you can switch your layout, add custom themes, and change colors to be in line with your brand.

As with Facebook, you can edit directly on the page and turn items on and off with checkboxes when you click the pencil/edit tool on that area. And you can remove an area by clicking the X in the upper right-hand corner of the module-editing box. If you need to add it back in, click on "Modules" in the upper left and select the module you want to add back in.

You can also add one of MySpace's stock themes from the "Appearance" box at the top of the page, or you can set your own custom colors, layout, and CSS. You can paste code into your content areas to further add to the experience your visitors will have. Finally, you can put in YouTube and other embeddable videos, create your own widgets on sites like Widgetbox (www.widgetbox.com), and use online tools to create slideshows of your photos. You can even add shopping cart widgets to sell items right on your page.

MySpace applications are also available for further customization. Get started by searching the "Jobs, Business, Money" applications listings under More > Apps Gallery. You'll find apps like Lending Club, Shopit Store, and Spare Change.

With these new tools, it's easier than ever to create a good-looking page, but if you want something truly custom, you can contact a Web designer who can help you. It's a good idea to include lots of pictures on your page because that helps draw people in. When you're finished editing the look and feel of your profile, don't forget to click "Publish" at the top of the page to save your changes.

Privacy Settings

MySpace also enables you to customize your privacy settings. For instance, you can request that people trying to add you as a friend either know your e-mail or last name to help combat friend spam. But remember that it's a good idea to have at least some part of your page public so it's searchable. And if you have a consumer business, you shouldn't create any barriers to someone adding you as a friend.

FINDING FRIENDS

As with other social networks, you can find friends through searches for names, schools, and interests. You can also browse friends who meet certain criteria, like gender, age, reason they're on the site, and geographic location. When you're adding someone you don't know or haven't talked to in a long time, it's a good idea to add a personal message with your friend request. You can also search your e-mail accounts for matches to friends under Friends > Invite Friends and send them invitations to join the site from that tool as well. MySpace will also recommend friends you may know on your home page, so watch that space once you start growing your network.

You should accept all friend requests you get as long as you believe the requester is a real person and not a spammer or bot. (A bot is a computer program that performs automatic tasks.) You don't want to risk offending any potential customers. MySpace differs from Facebook in that it doesn't have quite the same feeling of privacy, and it seems more people are "friends" with total strangers on the site.

LINKING YOUR NEW ONLINE IDENTITIES TOGETHER

If your first question was "What is a social network?" or "How do I get started?" eventually you will ask, "How do I manage them?" After all, it can seem like a lot of time and work, especially if you're creating a presence on multiple social networks. Plus you have a business to run!

Here are some good tips:

- Sign up for FriendFeed (friendfeed.com) and import information from LinkedIn, MySpace, Twitter, YouTube, Facebook, your blog, Yelp, and more into one central feed that friends can follow—and that you can use to repurpose on your blog or Web site to let people know what you're doing all over the Web.
- Turn on e-mail alerts for the sites. You don't want to have to check all these sites daily to see recent activity. Set each network to alert you when there are new comments on your page, new messages in your inbox, and new friend requests waiting for you. You can even set up a filter to put these all into a folder, which you can check once a day to avoid getting overwhelmed by a constant barrage of alerts.
- Look into programs that can help you manage multiple social sites from a single location. Flock (flock.com) is a Web browser, similar to Firefox, that lets you manage many of your social profiles from sidebars in the browser. Minggl (www.minggl.com) is a Firefox add-on that also lets you consolidate accounts and do things like update your status on multiple sites from one central location. Other social media aggregation tools to explore are www.ping.fm, www.digsby.com, www.profilactic.com, and www.meebo.com. I use www.hootsuite.com.

Wherever you decide to set up a social profile page, make sure to link directly to your Web site and blog. The more links you have, the more cross-platform friends you'll have.

VIRTUAL MANNERS: SOCIAL NETWORK ETIQUETTE

For most people, trying to navigate social networks can be extremely difficult when they're uncharted territory. But there are some definite rules of etiquette you should follow to make the most of your presence on these sites—and to avoid making costly mistakes. If you're creating personal *and* professional pages on these sites—or mixing the two into a single profile or page—extra caution and consideration must be used!

Each network is different, and each person you deal with may have different expectations. In general, though, the best rule is still the "golden rule"—treat people like you'd like to be treated, and never say anything online you wouldn't say in front of your advisory board, your most important client, or your mom! Some other rules to follow:

Don't send an e-mail invite to everyone you know. When starting out on Facebook, LinkedIn, and other sites, you will be asked to share your current e-mail addresses (and password) with the site so it can check if your contacts are already on the site and so you can invite those who aren't. Use this feature with caution. Facebook, LinkedIn, and Twitter are safe sites that will not send out an e-mail to your contacts without your explicit consent. You can safely give them your e-mail information to find people on the site, and it will be obvious if you're sending an invitation to people to join. There is no spam issue here, though you still want to be cautious about inviting people to join who are not close contacts. Some less reputable networks may take your address book information to invite your whole contact list without your knowledge. This may annoy your friends. So when joining newer or smaller social networks, you should exercise caution before giving up your e-mail password and first ensure that they will not send out any e-mails without your consent. Also, instead of giving up your password, you can export your contacts and just paste in the e-mail addresses, which is a much more secure way of finding out if your friends are on a network. If you do e-mail your whole address book by mistake, issue a quick mea culpa and promise your contacts it will never happen again.

Do keep your profile in line with your company culture. If you have an informal company culture or work in an informal industry, go ahead and post goofy jokes, party pictures, and anything else you don't mind sharing with the world. If your business is a bit more formal, though, retain a more professional manner and keep any private or personal profiles set to private and share with only friends. Basically, don't post anything publicly that you wouldn't want your biggest client or your oldest board member to see, and steer clear of talking politics, religion, and other taboo topics (unless you're OK with possibly offending potential clients or customers). And if you think there could be a conflict of interest between your personal and professional side, create separate profiles, and allow only close friends to see your personal page.

Other good tips: don't post to your sites if you're "under the influence," and don't post if you're angry (unless it's really important and relatable and can drum up support). Also, even if you can "erase" an update, someone's likely to have seen it, and if you're popular enough, they may have even screen-grabbed it so they could post it elsewhere. Once it's out there, you may not ever be able to delete it.

Do respond! If you establish a presence on a social site, you will be expected to be social. Respond to any messages or posts in kind (a private message for a private message, a public comment for a public comment).

Don't be a hype machine. There is a thin line between "spam" and "information." Some sites are meant for self-promotion (like LinkedIn), while other sites are meant for communication and collaboration (like Twitter). Don't annoy your contacts by constantly posting links to your site, especially if you don't have new information to share. And don't post the same thing over and over again. You don't want to abuse your friendships, and you don't want your contacts to feel like your communication is only one-way. Plus, they can "unfriend" you if you get too annoying, which would be counterproductive to your goals.

Do aim for a sense of parity. Some social networks force you to accept contacts mutually (such as LinkedIn, Facebook, and MySpace), but others let you follow at will (such as Twitter or FriendFeed). If you don't have a ratio of friends-to-followers that is close to 1:1, you can look like you're a spammer, especially if you're following far more people than are following you. Don't follow people just to pump up your numbers or drive one-time site visits when you don't say anything of interest and don't have some people following you. If you have tons of people following you but you don't follow anyone, you may be seen as uninterested in your community, though this isn't as bad as following tons of people without any follows in return. Some sites (mostly news sites) just post their RSS feed or other updates that don't require responses, and they can be quite popular.

Don't try to grow your network too quickly. If you start adding many people right off the bat, people you don't know probably won't follow you back (since you'll look like a spammer), and you may actually get flagged as a spammer by the network (Facebook, Twitter, and many other sites suspend the accounts of suspected spammers). It's best to start your network by adding people you know, then as you add more information, you can start adding people you don't know, or people who you may just be interested in connecting with. Though it may seem that the more friends you have the better you'll be doing, by creating a network that has value to you and by growing organically, you'll ultimately gain more followers and wield far more influence.

Do use a name people will know. This seems obvious, but people don't always follow this rule. If you're newly married and have changed your name, make sure to include your maiden name; otherwise people may not recognize you, especially if you don't have a photo up yet. Also, make sure to include both your business name and your full name, as opposed to an obscure screen name, so the widest number of people can see who you are and remember that they know you.

Do send a short personal note when asking to connect. You don't want to be rejected because someone doesn't remember you, so send long-lost contacts a quick note reminding them of how you know each other when requesting their friendship. If you're asking a stranger or friend of a friend to be a contact, let them know why you want to connect (mutual friend, in your industry, in a group you belong to, etc.). It will greatly improve your chances of being followed back. Note that on Twitter, it's common to befriend strangers, but if you want to increase your chances of being followed back, send an @reply to the person to get their attention.

On a business professional profile, accept anyone you believe to be a real person. Don't run the risk of offending someone by not accepting them as a friend if you have a business or professional profile. As long as it's not a spammer, let them in.

Do feel free to delete inappropriate comments from your profile. If someone says something unprofessional that you don't think should be part of your public persona, hit the delete key. Be careful about deleting any constructive criticism, though. Still, you don't have to tolerate spam or lewd comments on your page.

If someone posts a photo of you that you don't like, remove the tag. On Facebook or MySpace, anyone can post and tag (i.e., label) any photo of you, and that photo will appear on your profile. If you don't want it to, go to the photo and remove the tag. If the photo is on a site where you can't remove the tag yourself, politely ask the publisher to remove the tag.

Do have two-way links to your site and from your site. Let your clients and social networking friends know that you're really who you say you are by linking to your Web site from your social networks and vice versa. It lets them verify that the profile is official—and it can drive traffic back to your site.

Do choose your apps wisely. An app is a software application that allows you to add a new feature to your blog, Web site, or social network page. Facebook has a lot of apps that can enhance your profile page, like Blogcast. It also has apps that can cause clutter and essentially spam your friends. Don't use the latter; you will know these because they don't offer any business value, are gimmicky, and require your friends to register to interact with them. If you value your friends, you don't want to waste their time.

Don't immediately e-mail new friends or followers with a "special offer to download your e-book" or other similar marketing stunt. This will make new friends and followers feel like you're just trying to sell to them, and they'll likely drop you. You can, however, send a short welcome note.

Do be supportive. If friends create a group or business page, support their endeavor as you'd like them to support yours. If you leave positive comments, even better. And also consider promoting—or at least commenting on—friends' blog posts and sites when appropriate.

Don't ask for referrals or recommendations. On LinkedIn, it looks great if you have recommendations from people you've done business with, but you shouldn't have to ask for referrals to get them. The best way to go about getting referrals is to write referrals for others and hope they return the favor. They won't always do it, but it certainly puts the idea at the top of their mind. If you must ask for a referral, ask only your closest and most trusted colleagues or friends. And don't write a referral for someone who asks for one if you don't truly believe in his work.

As a general rule, don't drop friends. It's seriously awkward if people confront you about unfriending them, so in most cases, don't do it, especially to people you know or may run into. If you have a spammer or someone you really don't know who doesn't add value to your network, drop the person. Otherwise, change your settings to see less about that person, and you'll likely forget about him without causing any offense.

Do listen for problems, then do something. Use a social search engine to monitor mentions of your name, your company's name, and your product's name. You can also listen for terms in your industry. If you can help resolve a problem you see, you'll be held in high regard for providing quick customer service, even when no one asked for it. But just because you respond doesn't mean you have to add the person as a friend. Let that be up to the person. Just be helpful. People will remember that and know where to go for help if they need it again.

Do join conversations. If you want to improve your visibility, don't just post about your own endeavors, but also join others' conversations. Respond to their updates and posts, and offer construc-

MISS MANNERS ADDS HER TWO CENTS REGARDING SOCIAL NETWORKS

Dear Miss Manners: What is the appropriate way to let someone know that you don't want to be their friend on Facebook? Especially if it is someone you do know and perhaps know very well but haven't seen or spoken to in, let's say, 20 years, what is the proper tact with that one?

Gentle Reader: Send your long-lost friend a postcard—an actual postcard, with a stamp and a handwritten message, saying it was nice to hear from him. On Facebook, nothing. Oh, and no return address on the card. Miss Manners trusts that this will be profoundly confusing to the recipient. You have not snubbed him, but you seem to have taken his offer of friendship literally when he only wanted to rack up numbers, make you peek at his life, and perhaps peek at yours. Why (he will wonder) have you answered in such an archaic way, instead of just clicking? Surely you do expect him to make a similar effort? You may leave him with that mystery and make no further effort.

Source: Judith Martin, "Miss Manners," August 16, 2009, Bay Area News Group.

tive or at least supportive advice. It will make people want to be friends with you.

Don't underestimate the power of images and videos. Your social networking sites are places to build your personal brand, and by having a friendly looking headshot, or at least a professional-looking logo, you'll be doing yourself a big favor when it comes to being recognized and seeming approachable. It is best to use the same photo across networks (and even in your e-mail signature) so that people begin to recognize you in the same way that we recognize brands in the grocery story without even reading the label. Add video and other multimedia elements to your page, and you'll be doing even better.

Design is an important aspect of your social networking profiles. Many social networking sites let you alter the design of your page, which can aid in aligning your presence on the site to your brand. If you're not design-savvy, ask your designer or someone more skilled to put together a look for your Twitter profile, your MySpace page, and your YouTube channel. Having a professional and customized look will help establish you as a pro.

Don't leave special offers, promotional flyers, or other marketing materials on friends' profile pages, and *never* send your newsletter or e-blasts to your contacts unless they request them or proactively sign up themselves (called opting in). The proper place for promotional material is your status updates, posted items, bulletins, or other more passive content area that your contacts will see but won't have to host on their profiles. Facebook and other sites give you access to users' e-mail addresses. Under no circumstances is it appropriate to sign a person up for your e-newsletter without his or her expressed consent. Use their e-mail addresses only for personal communication. You can, however, put a sign-up link for your e-newsletter on your profile page if you'd like.

CONCLUSION

When it comes to social networks, the party is just getting started. The conventional wisdom is that they will become as powerful as the telephone, radio, or TV were when they became mainstream—only it will happen infinitely more quickly. Today, literally within the next 24 hours, you have the ability to dive into any or all of these social networks. Creating a powerful presence on those networks can strongly reinforce your brand—or, in fact, even create it.

While you have gotten a lot of information in these last three chapters, you may not be sure which network(s) to select. Just choose what "feels" right—and, if you join a network I am participating in, I hope you will drop me a note!

PART 3

◆

Putting Your Dream
into Action

Twenty-First-Century Business Responsibilities and Efficiency

While all of the previous chapters have involved the most modern business practices, this chapter focuses on two very specific trends in the business world: innovation and efficiency, including socially conscious approaches to running your business. Why are these traits important? It's vital for today's entrepreneurs to incorporate both humanity and innovation deliberately into everything they do. Not only does it benefit your business from a marketing and financial point of view, but having a sense of corporate responsibility is simply the right thing to do.

In this chapter, you will find many resources that will help you with setting up the basics for running and managing your business. In this chapter, we'll also discuss the importance of being a good corporate citizen—and how, in the end, that will also help your business thrive and grow in the twenty-first century.

DEVELOPING A SOCIALLY CONSCIOUS BUSINESS
IT ALL BEGINS WITH YOU

Social awareness is critical to today's businesses—and being socially aware starts with being conscious of yourself. It makes no sense to embark on a path of making money your way if "you" are not taken care of along the way. If you succeed in creating a business but suffer anxiety, gain unwanted weight, or operate on a diet of junk food, what have you really accomplished?

It may seem strange to include advice about health, nutrition, and exercise in a business book, but I can't overemphasize the need to be at your physical best if you plan to sustain a business. When you launch a business, no matter how excited and energized you are, there are simply not enough hours in the day to accomplish everything you wish. And things never get better "later." There is always more work to fill any "free" time that becomes available. But the healthier you are, the more energy you will have, which provides a necessary foundation for success.

As a business owner, I have struggled with this myself. But I have found these strategies to be essential for staying focused, and that's why I'd like to share them here. Here are some tips for ensuring you are in the best mental and physical shape possible; everything else is built from your own solid foundation:

- Create and include personal care objectives in your business plan, a topic that is covered in Chapter 13.
- Schedule regular exercise or walks—preferably with someone else—and treat them with the same priority you'd give to an important customer meeting.
- Take a few minutes each morning just to breathe and center yourself before your feet hit the floor and you start running.
- Get rid of the office "candy jar," and replace it with a fruit or trail mix bowl.
- Be the boss of you, and accept no excuse not to do this for yourself.

SUPPORT A CAUSE
Another critical piece of being a socially aware business owner is taking into account the world around you. As an entrepreneur, you have the freedom to adopt important causes and help improve the world

around you. Take advantage of this opportunity. Years ago this was a novel idea. Today it is almost a requirement. If income is tight, just promote a charity on your Web site; volunteer your time, staff, or facility; donate products; or help in any way you can. If you are able, dedicate some of your profits or proceeds to your cause. Then talk about it. While this will positively benefit your business image, more importantly, it sets a good example for others. It will also help establish a company culture that you can sustain as you grow and flourish.

CASE STUDY: CLIF BAR & CO.

One-time start-up Clif Bar & Co., a maker of energy bars based in Berkeley, California, donates more than 2,000 hours of volunteer work and as much as $1 million per year in grants to social and environmental causes. Its employees have access to, and are encouraged to use, an on-site health and fitness facility and earn time for a two-month sabbatical for every seven years of employment. While Clif Bar is a large company today, it started out with a company culture that promoted similar values and practices.

GO GREEN

Another cause that can and should be woven into your business (and every area of your life) is environmental consciousness. But lest you think this is just a "feel good" measure, it's also smart business. That's because, at its core, being green is about wasting less, and that is the ultimate measure of efficiency. At the time of this writing, there is no consensus on a national accreditation process by which any business can become officially "green." However, there are initiatives being implemented on a local and regional basis to achieve this. In California, for instance, the program can be found at www.greenbiz.ca.gov. Check with your own local power, water, and waste disposal companies as well as local county or city offices and your chamber of commerce to learn of similar initiatives in your own community.

Based on how your business is set up (home versus commercial office, product versus service company), there are different ways you can become more "green," but there are some universal strategies most businesses can adopt to help conserve. Encourage your employees to think and act "green"—and if you are a sole proprietor, feel good about doing your part. And feel free to share on your blog or Web site what you are doing to make a difference, and invite others to share their tips too.

Here are some basic ways to "go green":

Energy Conservation

- Take the time to figure out what your monthly energy consumption is by looking at past bills. Then set a goal to reduce this over time.
- Replace facility light bulbs with energy efficient bulbs.
- Replace CRT computer monitors with LCD monitors, as they use much less energy.
- Set computer monitors to go off after a set period of inactivity.
- Turn all computers and lights off at night.
- Set office thermostats so they don't overly cool or heat the office, and encourage employees to wear warmer clothing to work if necessary.
- Make sure doors and windows are sealed, and keep them shut, or open, depending on the heating or cooling benefit.

Facility Conservation

- Use window blinds and/or coat windows with film to reduce the need for heating and air-conditioning.
- In most homes, the largest summertime consumer of energy is the air conditioner. If you have an older model, look into replacing it with a new energy-efficient model. Look for the Energy Star seal, which indicates that the model meets government efficiency standards.
- Have the existing heating and air-conditioning system cleaned, and replace filters regularly.

- If you own the facility, look into alternate power supply options such as solar energy.
- Install low-flow toilets and motion-operated faucets.
- Encourage employees to walk to work, carpool, or take public transportation. Provide shower facilities so employees who walk or bicycle to work can shower when they arrive.
- If your company uses vehicles, consider using biodiesel fuels or hybrid cars or trucks.

Supply Conservation

- Have recycling bins placed in multiple locations. It's estimated that wastepaper that could be recycled represents 70 percent of office garbage.
- Buy recycled office paper and other products when possible.
- Use shredding companies that recycle when possible.
- Use real cups, mugs, and plates rather than disposable ones.
- Use double-sided copies and printing whenever possible.
- Use recycled printer ink.
- Recycle used batteries.
- Use nontoxic cleaning supplies.
- If you have a retail store, encourage customers to reuse bags and consider shifting to paper bags only, rather than plastic.
- Eliminate wasteful catalogs and junk mail you receive by removing yourself from those mailing lists at www.catalogchoice.org, www.dmachoice.org, and www.optoutprescreen.com.
- When you get rid of old computer equipment, recycle it rather than throw it away. Search in your area for electronics recycling programs. Remember to wipe hard drives clean first.
- Most importantly, discuss the impact of each of your activities on the environment, and create an office and business culture that seeks new ways to conserve. Also, make it a habit to ask each vendor you hire about their own business practices and to explain their sustainable practices and attributes to you. Then try to choose vendors whose values correspond with yours.

CONSERVING GOODWILL

While business success is our focus and our vehicle for achieving the lifestyle to which we aspire, at the end of the day most people want to show other contributions they have made to society beyond just making profits. Twenty-first-century businesses place their impact on people as a high priority. In Chapter 5, I talked a good deal about how important it is to create value for customers. It is also important to create the sense that you and your business represent value to other people with whom you interact. That will include your vendors, peers, and employees. Many companies "talk" about the importance of their employees, but twenty-first-century businesses "show" their employees that they are important to them. I recommend doing both.

VALUING EMPLOYEES

Anna's Linens was founded in 1988 by Alan Gladstone, who named the business after his mother. The first point in the mission statement on their Web site states, "Treat all Anna's family members, customers, and business partners with respect and dignity every day." This sounds nice, and I have seen other companies say similar things. However, recently I had the opportunity to witness how Alan truly puts this into practice. After meeting him in person and talking about his company, I was touched by how much he seemed genuinely to care about the people who work for him and run his stores, which have already grown in number from 1 in 1988 to nearly 300 today. In the same conversation, I found out that at one point a few years back, he learned of a store associate who was facing an unusual personal financial crisis. At that time, he chose to loan that employee the money she needed. From that incident, a company employee loan program was created, and Anna's has since loaned more than $3 million to its employees.

Another twenty-first-century business practice is to recognize that employees also want to have a life that is supported by their work rather than the other way around. You have the ability to make this happen. Many companies offer their employees flexibility in their schedules or the ability to work from home. This can be challenging, but I highly recommend that you include your employees in helping construct a solution that works for all parties involved. Recognizing that your employees want to give back to society in their own way is also important. While you should never let your business be harmed by outside projects—and employees should, of course, be held accountable for their company work—you can also encourage them to volunteer by offering them the leave or flexibility they need to contribute to outside causes, or by rolling "volunteer time" in some way into your company culture.

EFFICIENCY IS THE KEY TO TWENTY-FIRST-CENTURY BUSINESS

In previous chapters, we've covered the concept of creating and delivering "value" as it relates to your customer. The other side of that coin is to create value in the form of reduced costs and to increase profits by running your business in an efficient manner. Today more than ever, companies are forced to accomplish more work of higher quality with fewer staff, less cost, and in less time.

Just 10 years ago, it was the exceptional entrepreneur who deliberately and successfully found technology that he or she could leverage to make significant improvements in the efficiency of the business. For the twenty-first-century entrepreneur, this is not an opportunity but a requirement.

Fortunately, a boom of innovation to respond to these needs has equipped small businesses and entrepreneurs to become more productive. In many cases, what used to take hours, if not days, can often be done in minutes. Previous chapters have mentioned many tools to maximize this efficiency (e.g., using the Internet for marketing and sales efficiency), but let's focus on some new ones here—specifically, those tools that relate to how you operate your office and how they can make you more productive. In fact, many of the tools and services I use today did not even exist when I wrote my first book in 2005.

This section will focus on outlining the operational areas of your businesses that can benefit most from greater efficiencies and offering you some helpful resources. Due to the almost daily proliferation of new tools, Web sites, and companies, it is not possible to present all of them here, or necessarily even the best. Some of the "nuts and bolts" of setting up and running your business are not the most exciting material. However, it's exciting to come across new ways to do familiar things.

In the next section, I will break these up into distinct operational areas of your business.

GET LEGALLY EFFICIENT

You will need to give careful thought to how you want your company structured. Some people will operate simply as a sole proprietorship or via a partnership, while others will want to set up a corporation. The main benefits of setting up a corporation have to do with creating personal protections. For example, if for some reason your business is subject to a lawsuit, the corporation will be sued—not you personally. This provides a layer of protection to your personal assets. In addition, there can be tax benefits associated with a corporation for certain businesses. Many small businesses have found that setting up a limited liability corporation (LLC) is a good solution for their needs. However, if you plan to seek outside investment dollars, you will probably want to have either a Subchapter S corporation or a C corporation. When selecting between these two, be sure to understand the differences as they relate to how taxes are handled and the restrictions on the number and types of investors you are allowed. (An S corporation is more investor-restrictive, for instance, than a C corporation.) A good description of each structure can be found at www.sba.gov.

LegalZoom (www.legalzoom.com) also provides a good description of each and can actually get your company structure set up very inexpensively. If you prefer to work directly with a local attorney, you can get a referral through your local bar association, chamber of commerce, or www.lawyers.com. Note that these resources will also be useful for other future legal needs. West Patent Law (www.westpatentlaw.com) is a good resource for intellectual property (e.g., patents, trademarks, copyrights).

When you set up your business, you will also need to register your business and your trade name with your state's secretary of state. The required information and procedures can be found on their Web sites. Find each state's listing at www.e-secretaryofstate.com.

A MORE RESOURCEFUL OFFICE

If you are just launching your business, you will need a place to run it. Many twenty-first-century businesses are launched to construct a business around one's life—instead of the other way around. Commuting to an office consumes time and fossil fuel and is generally something people seek to reduce or eliminate. I launched my company from a spare bedroom and then moved into our refinished garage—and it's worked out very well.

The extraordinary technological and other resources available to small businesses today enable you to conveniently and cost-effectively maintain a high level of professionalism, even if your office is at home. Virtual receptionist services employ live operators to answer your calls and can be found online (see the resources section at the end of this book). Or, if you need more space and resources away from home, you don't necessarily have to start from scratch. "Executive suites" enable you to maintain an office with a professional receptionist and access to meeting rooms in a corporate setting. These are like co-op office spaces, set up with shared facilities that provide you with a receptionist, copy machine, and shared conference rooms. It's a professional-looking office environment that you can have almost instantly. In the online resources section, you'll find some suggestions on where to look for such executive suites.

SAVE ON YOUR COMMUNICATIONS TOOLS

The key to leveraging many of the opportunities for today's efficient business models is the ability to be connected—and connectible. That connectivity begins with your phone. Fortunately, it's easier than ever today to have a cost-effective connection and still provide the image you wish to portray. While it is certainly possible to get by with just a cell phone, especially for certain types of businesses, it may be necessary to establish a dedicated business phone service. But if you thought choosing a cell phone plan was complicated, land line plans can be equally mind-boggling. Here are some options:

- Contact your local phone carrier and have them establish a phone line and provide long distance services as well.
- Search on Google or another search engine for "discount long distance" to find long distance services that can cost quite a bit less than your local phone carrier's plans. I have used www.unitel group.com, which provided me all of my long distance at a cost that was less than my local company was charging just for my monthly 800 number fee.
- Take advantage of bundled opportunities. If you are setting up your business at home, you may be able to bundle your phone services with your cable and Internet connection. Whichever you select, be sure you can add voice mail services that include multiple mail boxes.
- Look into Google Voice (www.google.com/voice). This is currently a free service from Google that provides you with a phone number that you give out to others. Each person who calls is routed exactly where you want them routed. For example, you can have your spouse's call go through to all your phones, whereas you can route people you don't know to go into your business line or voice mail.
- Look into Voice over Internet Protocol (VoIP) service. It bypasses the regular phone system and uses the Internet for voice calls. This is how companies such as Vonage (www.vonage.com) provide your

phone service. Typically these services can save you substantial money as they eliminate the need for your local and long distance carriers. Furthermore, they may provide more value-added services such as virtual assistants, call transferring, and multiple voice mail box capabilities—perfect for a small business with big aspirations!

As the telecommunications, cable, and Internet services are all converging, you can secure connectivity from any number of providers. It's perhaps best to set up a secure wireless router so you have the ability to connect to the Internet anywhere in your home or office without having to have hardwired connections for each computer or other device.

When shopping for your Internet provider, consider these questions:

- Does the provider have a 24 hour customer service department? If your e-mail suddenly fails or your connection goes down, you will not want to wait until the next day for support.
- Does the provider offer high-speed connectivity (i.e., DSL or cable speeds)? This is critical to using your time efficiently. The days of using dial-up access for a professional business are gone.
- Does the provider offer bundling opportunities and discounts? If not, the competitor across the street may, so do your research to find the best package.

As we discussed in Chapter 7, you will also want to set up a Web site or blog for your business. If you plan to hire help, I recommend using local referrals to find a qualified Web designer. Another option is to use one of the many simple Web site template options online (discussed at length in Chapters 7 and 8).

I also recommend establishing an e-mail address that is based on your domain name. For example, my domain name is www.mom inventors.com, and each of our staff's e-mail address uses the company name (e.g., lindasmith@mominventors.com). This creates consistency and legitimacy. As a short-term solution, there are numerous free e-mail services (e.g., Google's Gmail and Yahoo! Mail) you can set up through the same portals that offer many other services. It's important to emphasize "short term." When a businessperson begins to communicate using a free e-mail address, such as those mentioned above, the immediate perception is that this is a one-person, nonprofessional, or not well-established company. Even if you eventually establish paid e-mail and domain names, you can still set up your free account to receive newsletters and other noncritical e-mail you want to review at your discretion.

Finally, fairly early on—preferably after you have established your phone numbers, address, and Web site—you will need a logo and business cards. Both of these services can be handled online, and there are several options listed in the online resources section. In addition, these can be designed and printed with a local printer or at a local office supply store.

BE EFFICIENT ABOUT EQUIPMENT AND SUPPLIES

While there are some businesses that will be less dependent on information technology (IT) infrastructure—a professional masseuse comes to mind—most twenty-first-century businesses cannot function without an adequate computer system.

You might want to hire an IT consultant if you are not technically advanced and don't have a teenager or relative who is able to help you get set up. Some consultants will procure your computers and other equipment for you, or you may prefer to buy the equipment yourself. Consider your specific needs, including travel, graphics and video editing capabilities, storage capacity, and the need to create a network. While not always the case, in my personal experience, when machines have the same core features such as memory, hard drives, etc., I have seen a strong correlation between quality and price. In other words, cheaper machines seem to have more problems and need more consulting repair hours—ultimately, at a higher cost. Therefore, price is not necessarily the only important indication of value when it comes to your computer.

Mac versus PC

Also consider the operating system and software you install. PCs (Windows) and Macs each have their own operating systems, although you can actually install a whole software version of Windows onto new Macs if you need to. Macs have a reputation for having fewer problems than Windows-based machines and have historically been the platform of choice for people working with graphics and video while most companies use PCs. Viruses are a huge problem in the PC world but almost nonexistent in the Mac world. On the other hand, Windows machines tend to be less expensive than Macs, and there are far more programs created for Windows machines. There is currently a lively debate on the value/cost comparison as power and features are added to create comparable functionality. If your business requires specialized software (e.g., the software Realtors use to connect to the multiple listing services), you should first check to make sure that it will run on either platform before you make your choice. I found numerous comparisons by searching "Mac PC comparison" using search engines such as Google and Yahoo.

Supplies

You will also find that you need a reliable source for your office products—supplies ranging from file cabinets, folders, and envelopes to Post-its, labels, and paper. One good source is eBay (www.ebay.com). In addition, the large office chains, such as Office Max, Office Depot, and Staples, have everything you need. One suggestion is to choose a single store so that you build up rewards points. In addition, most of them now offer free delivery for online orders. The best place I have found for shipping supplies such as boxes has been www.uline.com.

One supply that I am forever running out of is printer ink, which happens to be very expensive. Most printer manufacturers follow the razor blade business model: charge very little for the razor (printer) and make money by selling the continuously needed blades (ink). I have saved money by purchasing refilled cartridges at www.cartridge world.com and also by getting credits for recycling used cartridges at

Staples or Office Max. Not only does this save money, but it is less tax-
ing on the environment. It doesn't get much more efficient than that!

Laser printers tend to be much cheaper to operate than inkjet
printers. You might also check out the specific manufacturer's esti-
mates on print cartridge life and do your own calculation of what it's
going to cost you on a per-page basis. Kodak, for example, has put out
a line of printers that it advertises as much less expensive to operate.
Of course, if your business involves photography or graphics, you may
need a printer optimized for those purposes.

If you intend to buy a fax machine, and your printing needs are
modest, it is probably best to simply get an all-in-one printer that
includes faxing, scanning, and copying capabilities. However, before
you order a dedicated fax line, which will probably cost you about $20
per month minimum, consider a service such as eFax (www.efax.com).
For about that same cost, you can get a free fax number plus the ability to handle most faxing needs completely electronically. This service
enables you to virtually eliminate the use—and waste—of paper and
ink, not to mention the cost of a fax machine and maintenance. It
allows you to access your faxes by e-mail, which can be a tremendous
convenience if you are traveling. The downside of a service like eFax
is that you can't take a physical document and simply fax it to someone. You can fax only documents in digital form. The document has to
be a file you have in your computer or one that you can turn into a
computer file with your scanner. The service also offers other value-
added features that would not be available with a standard fax
machine.

MAIL SAVINGS

Even with electronic invoicing and bill pay, "snail mail" still has its
place in your company. For some businesses it's more critical than others, especially if you do any online sales and have to ship your products.
If you have a home office, a post office (PO) box is also an option. How
you ship your wares is another story. I have found the U.S. Postal
Service's Priority Mail to be the most economical for packages that

weigh under a pound or that will fit into the smallest flat rate boxes or flat rate envelopes. The packages arrive faster as well. The downside is that the tracking feature is not as specific as with, say, UPS. On the other hand, I have found UPS ground (www.ups.com) and FedEx ground (www.fedex.com) to be a better value when you get into shipping parcels over a pound except for international shipments up to a certain size. If you have a small box—say, under a few pounds—you may find USPS to be less expensive for international mailings. You can print USPS labels on regular paper and tape them to your packages. Since we ship to many customers and want to present a polished image, we order self-adhesive labels for USPS shipping (www.label universe.com).

All three services have relatively simple online systems and provide free boxes and envelopes, which is a great value, since the costs of buying your own packaging can add up. I especially appreciate UPS's free labels and simple Web site. If you belong to, or join, any industry associations, ask if they have any programs that offer members discounts with either FedEx or UPS. If you do a lot of regional shipping, you may also look for regional delivery providers, as they often offer lower pricing.

Perhaps the greatest time saver I've discovered is having a Pitney Bowes postage machine and scale in our office. I just weigh packages and pay for postage without leaving the office, which has virtually eliminated the need to stand in a post office line or ever buy stamps. The machine prints your postage directly onto your envelopes, and it reloads itself over a telephone line.

BACKING UP YOUR DATA: THE MOST EFFICIENT THING YOU MAY EVER DO

Some people think that their products, facility, or infrastructure are their most valuable assets. But imagine showing up for work and all of your customers' phone numbers, e-mail addresses, and invoicing history were gone. For most businesses, it's actually data that is the company's most valuable asset. And because of that, companies must ensure they protect this data through two must-have resources: virus protection software (for PCs) and regular computer backups.

There are a number of virus software companies, each with different strengths. Those I am most familiar with are www.norton.com, www.mcafee.com, www.trendmicro.com, and www.avg.com (which have a basic version for free). In Google, search "virus software reviews" for specific information on each one. Once you install your virus protection software, set it to look for virus updates automatically, and be sure to renew your subscription before it expires. You will receive automatic update requests.

Every computer stores data, including your precious business data. For most computers, the primary storage device is called a hard drive. Hard drives are pieces of equipment, and like any piece of equipment, they will eventually break down (called a "crash") or will be corrupted by a computer virus. If you're lucky, you'll have some warning, but oftentimes that breakdown happens suddenly and unexpectedly.

If your hard drive does crash, it can be *very* expensive to hire a service to try to retrieve your data from the drive, and even if they are able to do so, it can take them weeks or longer. It's also very possible that they won't be able to retrieve your data. The way to cope with this very real danger is to back up your hard drive—i.e., make sure that all the critical information on your hard drive is also saved someplace else. Fortunately, there are a number of easy ways to back up your drive.

The most rudimentary but often relied on method is to e-mail your critical files to another computer. This may work when you have only a few files but becomes a very cumbersome and difficult method to maintain as your business grows. The next evolutionary step is to copy important files manually (or automatically via special backup software programs) to a CD, tape, or external hard drive attached to your computer. This will help if a virus hits or the hard drive dies. However, neither of these methods protects your data in the event of a fire or other physical disaster, unless you've had the foresight to remove the backup drive to another location—a tedious process and one that few people can keep up regularly.

Therefore, I recommend using an online backup service. These services use your Internet connection to create duplicates of your files on the backup service's own hard drives (called "servers"). Not only does this ensure that your data gets backed up continually and automatically, it creates a current copy of all specified data on servers in another secure location. There are inexpensive services available—such as www.carbonite.com or www.mozy.com, at about $60 per computer per year—that allow you to restore all your files directly over an Internet connection. (If you have a Mac, the .mac feature is equally inexpensive.) Not only will this service save you money, but it could save your business.

Finally, it's also important to dispose of documents with confidential or sensitive information. For most small businesses, an inexpensive shredder will suffice. If you produce significant amounts of documentation that requires shredding, create a process for depositing sensitive materials somewhere and contracting with a qualified outside shredding service. Similarly, when you discard used computers, take the time to wipe clean your hard drive. Note that simply deleting a file from your computer's hard drive doesn't actually remove the file. It's still there until it has been overwritten by other data. So be sure to protect the privacy of your data if you are going to dispose of the hard drive or the whole computer. It's best to store your old hard drive in a safe location until you know you have more recent backups. When you are ready to dispose of it entirely, find a professional you can trust to clean it for you.

ADMINISTRATIVE SAVINGS

When you think of the word "administrative," you might think of internal processes like handling data files, money, and personnel. Because a twenty-first-century business must be nimble and lean—meaning every person on staff is doing the job of several people—being disorganized is not an option. And it's extremely helpful to be well-organized right from the start. Need an example? I recently experienced the joy of needing to find a document that had been filed a few years back. I found it only after spending the better part of a day digging through old files,

260 ◆ YOUR MILLION DOLLAR DREAM

because my filing system was less than stellar in the beginning. Assume that the cost in terms of my time was at least a few hundred dollars. Now, multiply this cost across a company, and, over time, you can see the value of organizing intelligently from the start.

Organization must be an ongoing, regular process, not a once-a-week or once-a-month "project." In the past, all businesses dealt with physical documents and had a great need for file storage. You might think from the start about how using computers can minimize the physical documents you will have to organize and store. Even so, almost every business will have paper documentation created by others and sent to your company, or created by you, and these must be stored somehow. Start with more file cabinets than you think you will need and plenty of hanging files and a label machine. Create a system with categories for each aspect of your business. Every time you have a new document to move from your desk, take one of three actions: act on the document in some way (e.g., send it somewhere or respond to it); file it in an existing or new file; or recycle or shred it.

The same process should be followed with electronic documents. Your e-mail program or random desktop is not a twenty-first-century business filing methodology. Instead, when you start your business, create a folder structure on your computer that you think will accommodate your business, and begin placing documents there. Folders on a computer are analogous to the file drawers, dividers, and folders in your file cabinet. The one big advantage of filing on a computer is that the software in your computer can search every folder, every document, and every word in most documents, which can make retrieving information much simpler than in the paper world. The other advantage is that on the computer, the same document can be "filed" in more than one place. For example, your invoices for the month of June can be filed in a folder called "Invoices," and a link to that same file can also be put in the folder for all "June" documents if that makes sense for your business. In the same way you file physical documents, each time you have a document that doesn't correspond to existing folders, create a new folder.

BOOKKEEPING BASICS

Bookkeeping and accounting tend to be closely connected to how organized you are. The first point I wish to make is the importance of your bank. Not only do I believe you should develop relationships with local branch staff members, but you will want to make sure your account has a robust online banking functionality. This is a huge time saving feature when paying bills, transferring money between accounts, or accessing information.

There are a number of ways to approach bookkeeping, many of which will be dependent on the nature of your business and the number of transactions you conduct on a regular basis. You can do it yourself, outsource, or hire staff to oversee your bookkeeping. One bookkeeping program commonly used by small businesspeople is called QuickBooks. This is a software program that resides on your computer and enables you to handle all your daily accounting and bookkeeping transactions, invoicing, and payments. Another thing to consider is how you will manage payroll. Because of payroll taxes and other complicated regulations and laws governing payroll, it's necessary to use a payroll module with a program such as QuickBooks or a third-party system. In addition, your business bank may offer payroll services. To find professional bookkeepers and accountants, ask friends and other local businesspeople for referrals. Your banker or attorney or other advisors undoubtedly have someone they use, so ask them as well.

Finally, insurance is often the big and unpleasant "surprise" for new businesses. Depending on the nature of your business, you may need an umbrella policy, product liability insurance, E&O (errors and omissions) insurance, workers compensation insurance, "key man" insurance, or others (there are dozens of different kinds of insurance policies). Since each business will have its own risks, the best advice is to develop a relationship with a good insurance brokerage firm, and make sure that you have appropriate coverage within your financial means.

Then there is health insurance. As this book is written, a heated national debate is under way about expanding health care. Small busi-

nesses are currently at a substantial disadvantage in providing this benefit to their employees, but it is nonetheless a critical offering. If your
business consists of just you, relying on the company health benefits of
a spouse or enrolling in a family plan, if possible, is probably the best
route. However, the addition of employees raises the importance of
offering company health insurance and other possible benefits such as
401(k) and other savings and benefit programs. Currently, in order to
be eligible for a company-based health insurance plan, your company
must have at least two employees on payroll. Note that the per-person
premium for a company-based health insurance plan will likely be
quite high, and individual family plans, if both employees are eligible
(i.e., have no preexisting conditions) may be more economical.
Insurance brokers can help review and select the best option.

If you have employees, you will need information about best personnel management practices, including forms, regulations, and actions. The
most comprehensive source for these issues is at www.hr.com. Another
option for companies with 10 employees or more is to use a company like
Administaff (www.administaff.com). This company provides outsourced
HR services and can generally provide advantageous benefits by aggre-
gating their customers. That way, when they negotiate rates with, say, a
health insurance company, they have significant bargaining power.

EFFICIENCY THROUGH COMMUNICATION AND COLLABORATION TOOLS

Nothing is more relevant or important for a twenty-first-century company than the willingness to embrace and leverage new time- and
money-saving tools. I have special appreciation for these tools given
the nature of my own business and infrastructure. Almost daily from
my home office, I work with contractors and consultants in New York,
Pennsylvania, Los Angeles, Phoenix, and San Francisco, and I have
held online seminars for people from all over the country.

Solutions I have used include GoToMeeting (www.gotomeeting
.com) and Zoho (www.zoho.com). These services provide terrific
online meeting platforms from which users can log in and view

PowerPoint presentations and any other files while on a telephone conference bridge. Similar platforms that are currently free include DimDim (www.dimdim.com) and Vyew (www.vyew.com). A more expensive but excellent service is WebEx (www.webex.com). To post PowerPoint slides to be shared and viewed by the general public, check out www.slideshare.com. For simple voice conference calling, I use www.freeconferencecall.com.

When creating presentations, you will also find certain tools beneficial. One in particular, called SnagIt (www.snagit.com), enables you to take screen grabs of any document or Web site, and then paste it into documents or presentations you are creating. It even allows you to overlay comments and highlights you wish to add—as I have done for some of the figures in this book. Microsoft offers a similar "snipping tool" as part of the Vista operating system. You may already have it without realizing it! And if you need to e-mail a file that is too large for your Internet service provider (ISP), you can send it via www.sendthisfile.com or www.yousendit.com for free.

PERSONAL PRODUCTIVITY SAVINGS

There are also many tools that can be used to help with getting yourself organized, including customer relationship management systems such as Salesforce (www.salesforce.com), TaskAnyone (www.taskanyone.com), your Outlook Business Manager, and other free tools such as your Google Calendar. This technology can only work if it is put to use; however, no amount of technology can overcome a lack of organization and focus. Here are some tips on personal productivity and time management:

- Plan each work day the night before.
- Check e-mail and voice mail at set times throughout the day, such as in the morning, before lunch, and when you are shutting down. Don't check all day long.
- Set appointments you have out of the office on the same days each week, and, if possible, geographically coordinate each in back-to-back time slots.

- When you ask for appointments, especially sales appointments, avoid offering 10 a.m. and 3 p.m. first. Those are the easiest slots to fill. Try to book 9 a.m., 1 p.m., and 4 p.m. first. That leaves you the ability to book additional meetings at 11 a.m. and 3 p.m.
- When you agree to meet current or prospective vendors at your office, meet them only when you are free, and protect your core work hours.
- Send your most important e-mails in the evening, Monday through Thursday, so busy people receive them first thing in the morning. Avoid sending important e-mails on Saturday and Sunday, because Monday morning the recipients are likely to have too many messages in their inboxes.
- No matter how small your staff is, schedule a management meeting every week.
- Whenever you plan a meeting, prepare an agenda to keep you focused.
- Read articles relevant to your business. Subscribe to relevant newsletters, and sign up for relevant RSS feeds. Print the articles and keep them in your briefcase or purse so you have them with you when you find unanticipated free time.

Lastly, remember to thank people. Even if you are paying for a service, express your gratitude sincerely and often. It will make them feel good—and it makes you feel good.

The importance, and attendant pressure, of delivering value through efficiency in a socially conscious manner is higher than at any time in the past. And given today's pace of business and competition, there is little room for error. However, there has also never been a better time to be an entrepreneur. The tools and information available to you today are better than at any time in history, and due to the growth and enthusiasm of the entrepreneurial market space, it will only continue getting better. Also, the personal rewards of incorporating social consciousness into your business are instant and substantial. Your business will be stronger, and it will benefit from the positive impression this creates with your customers, clients, and community members.

If you find tools you think should be shared with others, please visit my Web site (www.yourmilliondollardream.com) and let me know.

In the meantime, read ahead to the next and final chapter on creating your business plan.

Your Plan: Turning Your Ideas into Actionable Steps

Few terms in business conjure a greater emotional reaction than "business planning." For many people, including myself when I first started out, just hearing those two words causes a sudden rise in blood pressure and a flood of self-doubt.

It's kind of like visiting the dentist; there's a tendency to anticipate the worst and put it off, which can cause issues to get out of hand. But as with visiting the dentist, when you face business planning head-on, you'll prevent complications and lay the groundwork for your future business health. And it's rarely as painful as you anticipated!

> *Think you can, think you can't; either way, you'll be right!*
> —Henry Ford

Business planning is not a new idea. There are numerous models, templates, and guides available both online and in the bookstore. While the process and language may vary, the core elements of most decent systems will be similar. So the tool you choose doesn't matter as long as you are able to organize your thoughts and plans effectively. One approach particularly well suited to entrepreneurs is a system called "The One Page Business Plan," developed by my friend, Jim Horan, founder of the One Page Business Plan Company.

In fact, I find this method to be so effective that in 2009, Jim and I coauthored a special edition called *The One Page Business Plan for Women in Business*. While this chapter will not replicate the detail and impact of that workbook, it will provide a foundation from which to develop a simple yet strong plan in the space of a single page by focusing on the core aspects of the system and providing some brief exercises.

Creating a business plan helps you make purposeful choices, avoid pitfalls, and direct your company down a well-constructed path. There's a reason I've saved this chapter for last—it's so you can incorporate many of the strategies, ideas, and tactics presented in the past 12 chapters into your thought process as you develop your plan. You might find that your current notions about what a business plan entails—and what it takes to get there—have been exaggerated. The process can actually be straightforward, relatively simple, and even pleasurable. In this chapter, you'll learn exactly how to make it that way.

WHAT'S IN IT FOR YOU?
BENEFITS OF A BUSINESS PLAN

Before you even begin to create your business plan, it's good to know how it will help you. First, realize that it's a concrete stepping-stone to help you realize your million dollar dream—giving you the framework to think about your business in a top-to-bottom way. It enables you to put all your best ideas and thinking that you have generated so far into a single plan, and turn those thoughts into clear, actionable, and measurable steps. It also sharpens how you'll communicate about your product or service because it forces you to articulate clearly your thinking with meaningful words. Writing a plan also becomes an effective tool because it can facilitate input from others—including bankers, investors, shareholders, vendors, and customers—as you consult people about your plan. And perhaps the most significant benefit is that it provides you with an incredible sense of accomplishment.

Generally speaking, loan and investor applications will have extensive requirements. However, your One Page Business Plan will enable you to succinctly describe your business. You may be surprised by the impact it makes. One woman recently reported to me that within two weeks of finishing her one page business plan, she applied for and received a business grant—*free cash*!

By creating a workable, actionable plan, you will also find clarity of purpose and measurable benefits. In fact, as you embrace this process, you will be amazed how any sense of confusion, doubt, or feeling "stuck" falls away.

In this chapter, you will gain insight into the process of planning, get a clear sense of direction, begin articulating your goals, and create the basics for a plan that will help launch or take your business to the next level. Best of all, you'll do it all on one (nonintimidating) page—by far the best method I've discovered to develop a first business plan.

In launching a business, though, some of the strongest resistance you encounter will be internal, so before we get into the business plan, let's address, head on, some of the stories we tell ourselves about this process. We'll explore these "hang-ups" in depth and dispel the validity of any excuses you may have for *not* creating a business plan.

SIX EXCUSES FOR NOT MAKING A BUSINESS PLAN

Over the years, I've met hundreds of people in business—or about to launch businesses—and I've been privy to countless excuses and reasons why they've opted out of creating a business plan. Rarely, if ever, are they sound. In fact, even some businesspeople I've encountered who've become very successful in the long term have expressed regret, wishing they had developed a solid business plan from the start. They say that a business plan would have helped them avoid costly mistakes, hiccups, and delays in the growth of their businesses.

Here are some of the more common excuses I've heard.

EXCUSE 1: "I DON'T NEED A PLAN"

Whenever a person says this to me, it makes me think of being invited to go on a cruise ship and then, just after boarding, hearing the captain greet the passengers by announcing, "Welcome aboard! I've decided that we don't need to follow a map this time. I thought we could see where the currents take us. Sound good?" My reaction would be, "Get me off this ship!" Others will react in a similar manner as you begin seeking their support for your business without being able to show them a clear plan. Business cannot be created in a void. You need other people. Friends, family, colleagues, and prospective investors are more likely to support you if your goals are clear and you can explain in simple, straightforward terms the direction in which you plan to take your business.

EXCUSE 2: "I KNOW WHAT I'M DOING"

This can be one of the most difficult and dangerous mindsets to overcome, because it leaves little room for creativity. In fact, it feels like the unspoken end of that sentence is, ". . . so don't get in my way." On one hand, it's good to feel confident. However, if you already "know" everything, then many opportunities will be lost. It's impossible to know everything you need to know. Also, when you come from a place of inquiry and are open to different ideas and ways of doing things, doors open in unexpected and surprising ways.

EXCUSE 3: "I DON'T KNOW WHAT I'M DOING"

Most people have never written a business plan, so you are not alone. Even if you've worked in the business world for years, it's likely you were never asked to write such a document. It's always challenging to do something you've never done before, and it can feel overwhelming and uncomfortable. It's common to want to spend time, instead, on the things you excel at and avoid the things that make you feel uneasy. But once you get into the process—especially the one outlined for you here—you'll be surprised at how quickly you'll get it and how helpful the results will be.

EXCUSE 4: "IT'S TOO INTIMIDATING, I CAN DO WITHOUT"

Feeling fear about creating a business plan for the first time is to be expected, especially if you have preconceived notions about what the experience will be like (although these usually end up being inaccurate). The reality is that most things rarely, if ever, materialize exactly how we imagine them. The anticipation stories we create in advance about how things will turn out are often completely different from the actual experiences. Without our realizing it, these stories can create self-constructed roadblocks before we know it.

EXCUSE 5: "I'VE HAD A BAD EXPERIENCE WITH BUSINESS PLANS IN THE PAST"

Perhaps you have tried to write business plans in the past without success. Many of us learn early on to give up when things aren't working or say negative things about ourselves like, "I can't do this; I don't have any business experience; I'm not good at figuring things out." We say, "*I want to do a business plan but I don't know how to start*" or "*I've failed in the past.*" Disconnect these two ideas. They are only connected because you choose to connect them! It's only fiction that you've accepted about yourself.

Unlink them and say, "I choose *to do a business plan* because I choose *to do a business plan.*" There it is. Once you've made this statement, you've created a new truth for yourself.

EXCUSE 6: "I'M TOO BUSY TO PLAN"

I have used this excuse myself. I'd say, "How can I plan? I'm too busy running my business." But these feelings often have more to do with the fear of not knowing how to start. What I have learned from the seven years of running my business is that time and money are wasted by not planning. Free time doesn't exist, and it does not ever volunteer itself. It must be created for priorities. Planning needs to be scheduled into your routine just like any other essential task. And planning time needs to be considered sacred and nonnegotiable. It needs to be a

AIMLESS ACTION CAN BE COSTLY

Sometimes taking action (for example, making sales calls, sending press releases, or ordering inventory) feels satisfying—even if it's not action that's going in the right direction. I can relate to this feeling. Pure action can provide a feeling of accomplishment. You feel a sense of relief that you are "doing" something to move things forward. However, action in the wrong direction can have a more negative effect on your business than inaction. For example, you could spend endless hours generating media or traffic to your Web site, but if you don't have a viable product or service to sell, your effort has been wasted. Over time your business will change and evolve, and these changes are costly. A business plan will help you minimize these mistakes and provide a better framework from which to adapt to change.

choice, a declaration: "I am taking this time to work on my plan." As you will see in this chapter, the people who overcame their fear and put a stake in the ground and embraced the planning process came out feeling energized, grounded, and confident.

Before starting her plan, a participant in one of my business planning workshops wrote,

> I had absolutely no idea where to start. I felt I was at a crossroads in my business, knowing I needed to ramp things up or go in another direction. So, in that confusion, I didn't know how I would write a business plan. I felt frustrated. I had no idea where I was going, so how could I put that in writing?

After starting the planning process, she wrote,

> If you really want to get clear on the direction you are heading, planning is definitely the place to start. It's a simple and

concise way to get your focus back! I have a new and exciting direction that I am going to take my business.

If you've been procrastinating in developing your own business plan, I hope confronting some of these common excuses has helped to dispel some of your reasons "why not." In the next section, you'll learn how business planning is really a lot simpler than you probably anticipated.

THE BUSINESS PLAN DEFINED

Many people think of a business plan as a tool they need to pitch to an investor or banker, so they disregard it in the early stages as something they don't need. In addition, business schools have developed elaborate business planning methodologies, and countless venture capitalists, corporate managers, business gurus, and pundits have weighed in. As a result, there is a flood of business planning books, systems, and approaches from which to choose.

So what exactly should your plan entail? The idea of writing a business plan might conjure up images of a financial spreadsheet that includes numbers, forecasting, elaborate and specific projections, and other often mind-numbing and difficult to digest details—something separate from the nuts and bolts of actual day-to-day business activities. This type of plan is actually something you may develop later. But for now, your business plan should be written as strictly operational— to give you focus and clarity on your own vision, mission, objectives, strategies, and action plans.

WHICH ROUTE DO YOU TAKE?

Early on I struggled with creating my own business plan, until one day I stumbled on a process developed by Jim Horan called "The One Page Business Plan." Immediately, this method spoke to me, and I began using it to focus and grow my business. Over time, I felt Horan's approach had so much merit that, as mentioned previously, I ended up teaming with him to coauthor *The One Page Business Plan for Women in Business*, a workbook with sample plans, step-by-step instructions, and a CD with templates. In this chapter, I'll share this approach—and what I've observed about the many entrepreneurs who've adopted this method for their own businesses.

Here are a few points on what your business plan is *not*.

A Business Plan Is Not *Financial Spreadsheets*

As your company evolves and you start presenting to investors, you most likely will need financial spreadsheets and projections. Many people mistakenly believe that financial spreadsheets are the plan. Financial spreadsheets are there to support your plan, and the numbers are intended to support your intentions—they tell a story about your business and illustrate how you plan to accomplish your goals. But financial spreadsheets alone have no meaning.

For your operational plan, it's not necessary to create extensive financials. However, you will want to use measurable objectives in your business plan. For instance, are you planning to make an extra $20,000, $150,000, or hit the million dollar mark? It can be as broad a goal as that at this point.

A Business Plan Is Not *Lengthy*

Another myth is that a business plan is only worthwhile if it's a long, "bookish" document. Actually, the opposite is true! If you are able to describe your plan in one page, then every word matters, and clarity comes when describing things succinctly. When volumes are written, one tends to wander off on tangents and get lost in the minutiae, and the focus and interest vanishes.

A Business Plan Is Not *Business Jargon*

Nothing frustrates me more than business jargon. First of all, entrepreneurs are people from every background imaginable, some with extensive business experience and others with none. Technical jargon and clichés such as "best of breed" create a barrier, lack inspiration, and, frankly, are boring. In my experience, those with formal business school training seem to be more likely to use jargon than those without that training. Of course jargon can be a powerful shortcut that gets across a lot of shared knowledge quickly, but only if you're speaking to someone who shares that particular language. Since many of the people you'll be communicating with may be unfamiliar with those terms, it's best to stick with plain, concise English wherever possible.

Jargon not only can be intimidating and debilitating for you and other people who are perfectly capable of launching a business, but it can put off those whose help you would like.

WRITING A BUSINESS PLAN

Okay, now it's down to the nitty-gritty—actually creating the plan. If you have not yet identified the specific business you want to create, that is OK. I would encourage you to still go through this process. If you have several ideas, just choose one and use it for this exercise. If you end up going that route, you will have the foundation for your plan. If not, you will have some experience with the process that you will be able to apply to the route you eventually do choose. (Actually, this process can be used for virtually any area of one's life that requires planning to achieve goals. Keep that in mind!)

There are five essential elements in your One Page Business Plan. Instead of using complex, confusing definitions, Horan uses simple questions to help us craft our plan.

Vision. What are you building?
Mission. Why does this business exist?
Objectives. What results will you measure?
Strategies. What will make this business successful over time?
Action plans. What are your business-building projects?

Remember not to approach this task as a big, complicated process. As you fill in the information in the next few sections, don't critique yourself or spend much time perfecting what you write. You will have plenty of opportunities to edit later.

I would recommend you block out 45 to 60 minutes without interruption until you finish this exercise.

YOUR VISION STATEMENT

Your vision statement answers all the "whats" about your business-to-be. To write it, begin thinking about the following questions:

1. What type of company is this?
2. What markets does it serve?
3. What is the geographic scope?
4. What customers will it target?
5. What are the key products and services?
6. What size will the company be in three to five years?
7. What will revenues be?
8. What number of employees do you expect to have eventually?

Figure 13.1 offers an example of a vision statement from one of our *One Page Business Plan for Women in Business* workshop participants, jewelry designer Christina Ecklund (www.christinaecklund.com).

vision	Within the next three to five years, grow Chirstina Ecklund Design into a $500,000 national fashion jewerly business providing unique, trendy, and classic jewelry and fashion accessories to women ages 24 to 50 who want to be unique but don't want to spend a fortune (my pieces range from $60 to $145). Each piece is designed and handcrafted in the USA.

Figure 13.1: Jewelry designer Christina Ecklund's vision statement.

Here is your first task, right now, in just five minutes.

Step 1: Fill in the blanks to begin to develop a vision statement.

Company name:

_____

Geographical scope:

_____

Type of business:

_____

Core products/services:

_____

Description of ideal customer:

_____

Annual sales in three to five years:

_____

Number of employees:

_____

Step 2: Now incorporate all of these elements into a brief statement of one or two sentences.

_____
_____
_____
_____
_____

Common Mistakes

When it comes to your vision statement, the most common mistake is making it too broad, mentioning everything, including the kitchen sink! Ask yourself, "Is this describing precisely what I am building?" If not, keep working on it. A business plan is a fluid and flexible document that can be updated as often as you wish—even daily or weekly. Regardless, revisit your vision statement often to make sure that you are actually building the company you had envisioned.

Another common mistake is omitting revenue and size from your vision statement. It's important to know how much in annual sales you wish to make over a given period of time. Beware of putting sales figures in your vision statement that are too small—something that women in particular seem to do, as if apologizing for appearing greedy or dreaming too big. To avoid this line of thinking, imagine how making money will give you the opportunity to contribute to your family's income and help others in ways not yet imagined. You might also keep in mind that if you are looking for investors, most investors are much more likely to want to invest in your business if they think there's a possibility of making a substantial return. If you're too modest in your goals, they might think, "Why should I bother taking the risk?"

Now, taking the common mistakes above into consideration, take a second pass in just five minutes to revise your vision statement.

_____

_____

_____

_____

YOUR MISSION STATEMENT

While the vision statement creates a picture, with words, of the design and structure of your business and answers the question, "What are you building?" the mission statement is the "heart" of your business. In other words, it is a short, powerful statement of intent that expresses the commitments and promises behind starting or growing this business. It answers the question, "Why does the business exist?" It should contain a "wow" factor, letting your passion come across and inspire others. Business guru Guy Kawasaki explains that this statement should be your own "mantra." A mantra is defined as "a sacred verbal formula repeated in prayer, meditation, or incantations such as an invocation of god." Examples of business mantras include Disney's "Fun family entertainment" and Nike's "Authentic athletic performance."

In about 8 to 12 words, the mission statement should answer the following questions:

1. Why does this business exist?
2. Who are you in service of?
3. Why are you serving this customer?
4. Why is this important, needed, or beneficial?
5. What promise or commitment are you making to your customers?

Figures 13.2 and 13.3 present "before" and "after" mission statements from a participant in a recent workshop, Sarah Oliver of Sarah Oliver Handbags (www.saraholiverhandbags.com).

We create high-end and contemporary hand-knit handbags utilizing untapped and/or underutilized local human resources.

Figure 13.2: First draft of mission statement for Sarah Oliver Handbags.

We provide fashion conscious women with fabulously sophisticated handbags that have an inspiring and heartfelt story.

Figure 13.3: Later draft of mission statement for Sarah Oliver Handbags.

Which mission statement are you attracted to? For me, Sarah's mission statement went from being vague—without providing any hint as to who was being served or how—to being clear, fun, and inspiring. Your mission statement should evoke passion and move the reader. For me, the second one has a much more profound impact. Can you hear the difference?

Think of *your* "mantra" and in five minutes fill in the blanks below to begin creating your mission statement:

Who are you in service of?

_____

_____

_____

What does your product or service promise them?

_____

_____

Write a mission statement of 8 to 12 words based on your answers above.

_____

_____

_____

Common Mistakes

While you may be tempted to make your mission statement sound sophisticated, professional, and/or technical, this is, instead, where the heart of your company should come across in plain English.

Another common mistake is making your mission statement too long. Recognize that writing everything that you are offering can diminish its impact. The intention, instead, is to inspire others to want to learn more. Once you connect with people, then you will have ample time to share more details. Challenge yourself to keep it under 12 words. The shorter the mission statement, the more powerful it becomes.

Spend five minutes rewriting your mission statement, taking into consideration the common mistakes outlined above:

_____

_____

_____

_____

Once you have come up with your vision and mission statements, you have answered the big questions, "What are you building?" and "Why does this business exist?" The next three sections provide the "how."

YOUR OBJECTIVES

Objectives are graphable business results; they are intended to tell what will be measured. This section will include elements of your overall business model, including your achievable goals and specific targets.

Every objective must be measurable, because only by measuring can you see results. This helps monitor progress, which leads to understanding. Then you can determine what _is_ and what _isn't_ working in the business.

Figure 13.4 offers an excellent example of one of our workshop participant's objectives. Greta Olano launched an educational consulting company called Educate Advocate Now (www.educateadvocatenow.com), which specializes in advocacy services for children with attention-deficit hyperactivity disorder.

objectives
- Earn pre-tax profits of $30,000 in 2009
- Earn monthly pre-tax dollars of $6,000 in 2010
- Add 2 new school accounts in 2009, each having an est. value of $5,000
- Have a min. of 20 parents sign up for each pro bono workshop in 2009
- Increase client retention rate from 80% to 95% by Q3 2010
- Return new client interest inquiries within 24 hours from 48 hours
- Obtain AD/HD coaching certificate from ACO to better market myself as an expert in AD/HD
- Write 1 article per quarter in 2009 and 2010 for CHADD organization

Figure 13.4: Greta Olano's objectives for Educate Advocate Now.

When thinking about what to include in your objectives, you will want to include things like your sales in units and dollars, gross profit, profit before tax, number of clients or customers, cost per unit (payroll, materials, overhead), number of speaking engagements, etc. Don't forget to set goals for life balance, like the maximum hours per week you will work and the number of vacation days you'll take per year, etc.

Eventually you will have five to eight total objectives. Take five minutes and list five objectives:

Sales: Sell _____ ($ or # of clients) by _____ (date)

Profit: Earn _____ ($ or % profit) by _____ (date)

Number of clients: _____ by _____ (date)

Average sale: _____ by _____ (date)

Marketing: _____ by _____ (date)

Education: _____ by _____ (date)

Personal: _____ by _____ (date)

Attend: _____ (classes, events, mixers, etc.) by _____ (date)

Do _____ by _____ (date)

Do _____ by _____ (date)

Common Mistakes

The most common mistake I have witnessed here is creating objectives that are not measurable. Here are a few examples of how to improve objectives by making them more measurable:

- "Create a profitable business" becomes "Increase profit margin from 10 percent in 2009 to 15 percent in 2010."
- "Improve customer satisfaction" becomes "Achieve 80 percent 'above average' rating on an annual customer survey in 2009 and 90 percent rating in 2010."
- "Improve my industry knowledge" becomes "Attend two industry trade shows each year."
- "Gain balance in my life" becomes "Spend two weekends away with my partner this year."

Another common mistake is to include only those objectives that can be measured in dollars. Don't omit nonrevenue objectives that are measurable, such as marketing activities, personnel matters, educational and learning objectives, and your own personal objectives. You can and should include these as well!

Finally, be sure that there is a strategy in place to drive each objective. These strategies will be covered in the next section. In other words, if you have an objective to make sales in Europe, there must be a strategy that will enable you to achieve that objective.

Take another 5 or 10 minutes to revise your first five objectives. If you have other objectives that come easily to mind, feel free to write them all:

_____

_____

_____

_____

_____

_____

YOUR STRATEGIES

Strategies explain how you will build your business and what will make it successful over time. They also describe how you will achieve the goals listed in your objectives. They are the types of things you will do that will produce a desired outcome. They set the direction for your company and answer the question, "How will this business be built?" Sometimes, they consist of processes or programs you plan to implement, or ideas that provide a special "hook." They can even set limits on what a company will do or will not do.

Figure 13.5 provides an outstanding example of how Karen Horrigan, owner of Galaxy Group Promotional Products (www.galaxypromotionalproducts.com), another workshop participant, came up with specific strategies to support her business objectives.

strategies	• Target companies with in-house marketing departments • Attract customers who value service/product knowledge w/ professional print materials • Create new customer opportunities online by using Google AdWords and Constant Contact • Provide fair pricing and match competitors when needed • Strengthen marketing by implementing quarterly promotions • Enhance implementation by setting definite deadlines • Improve reorders by sending reorder notices and discount coupons

Figure 13.5: Karen Horrigan's business strategies for Galaxy Group.

In the next few minutes, craft a strategy that defines how your company is going to accomplish these critical business activities by filling in the blanks:

Focus on selling our products/services to _____, _____, and _____.

Make people aware of our products/services by _____, _____, and _____.

Make it easy for people to make their first purchase by _____, _____, and _____.

Make sure our products/services are high quality by _____, _____, and _____.

Common Mistakes

Be sure that you have a strategy that will enable you to achieve each of your objectives. Without a strategy backing it up, an objective will be difficult to achieve.

In five minutes, write three revised strategies. Again, feel free to write more as they come to mind:

_____

_____

_____

YOUR ACTION PLANS

Action plans define the business-building work to be done, the specific tasks the business must undertake to implement strategies and to achieve objectives. When devising your action plans, name each task and assign a specific date for completion to help you stay on target.

In Figure 13.6, Karen Horrigan shares a draft of her action plans. As you can see, they support her strategies.

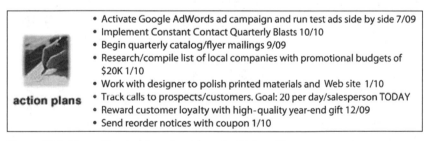

action plans
- Activate Google AdWords ad campaign and run test ads side by side 7/09
- Implement Constant Contact Quarterly Blasts 10/10
- Begin quarterly catalog/flyer mailings 9/09
- Research/compile list of local companies with promotional budgets of $20K 1/10
- Work with designer to polish printed materials and Web site 1/10
- Track calls to prospects/customers. Goal: 20 per day/salesperson TODAY
- Reward customer loyalty with high-quality year-end gift 12/09
- Send reorder notices with coupon 1/10

Figure 13.6: Karen Horrigan's action plans for Galaxy Group.

Eventually, you will have about eight action plans. Take five minutes to write five action plans now:

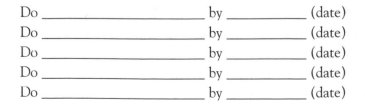

Do _____ by _____ (date)

Do _____ by _____ (date)

Do _____ by _____ (date)

Do _____ by _____ (date)

Do _____ by _____ (date)

Common Mistakes

Understand that you will do many tasks in your business. The action plans listed here should be the big things that will grow your business! Also, make sure that your action plans support your strategies and objectives.

Spend five more minutes revising your first five action plans. Again, if you have more in mind, feel free to write them.

_____

_____

_____

_____

ADDITIONAL TIPS TO KEEP IN MIND

As with any new venture, there are pitfalls to avoid, but knowing about specific potential pitfalls in advance may help. Here are some tips that can help you as you think about your plan.

VIEW IT AS AN EVOLVING DOCUMENT

Actually jotting down your thoughts in each of these sections above should help you "start" the process and help you quickly see that you can create a solid plan in your own words and in your own way.

Now, however, you will need to take what you have done and put it into the proper format. The One Page Business Plan in Figure 13.7 is an example of how it looks when it all comes together. To make yours similar, create section headings for "Vision," "Mission," "Objectives," "Strategies," and "Action Plans." Take what you have written so far in this chapter and retype it onto your newly formatted document. Go over it a few times, editing and adding thoughts as they arise.

Entrepreneurs tend to move fast. We expect things to be done yesterday, and we often aren't patient—myself included! But taking the time to go back and revise your business plan is essential. When you do so, be sure it ties together bottom up and top down. In other words, does each action support a strategy that supports an objective that supports the mission and vision? Also, check how you feel after reading the mis-

ONE
PAGE
PLAN

Galaxy Group, Karen Horrigan, Owner   Last Updated: 08/12/2009

vision

Within the next 1.5 years grow Galaxy Group into a $1.3 million promotional products company. We provide customized marketing products utilized for trade shows, sales incentives, and customer/employee gifts. Our ideal client is a growing company with an in-house marketing department who values brand consistency.

mission

THE source for promotional products that make you say WOW!

objectives

- Increase annual sales from $728K in 2008 to $1.3 million in 2010.
- Grow pre-tax profits from $96K in 2008 to $180K in 2010.
- Increase vendor product discounts by 10% with 5 key vendors by December of 2009.
- Add 25 new accounts for 2nd half of 2009; 100 in 2010 for a total of 375 accounts.
- Increase average sale from $1500 to $2500 by 2010.
- Win 95% of client proposals in 2010 from 80% in 2009.
- Increase repeat orders from current clients by 20% or $50K by 2010.
- Increase customer/prospect follow-up from 15/day/salesperson to 20/day/salesperson.
- Attend 4 industry trade shows in 2010; from 1 in 2008.

strategies

- Target companies with in-house marketing departments thru mailings/online marketing.
- Focus on customers who value product knowledge and professionally printed materials.
- Create new online customer opportunities by using Google AdWords/Constant Contact.
- Pricing strategy: to provide fair pricing and to match competitors when needed.
- Strengthen marketing by implementing quarterly promotions, both e-mail and mail.
- Enhance implementation by setting definite deadlines.
- Improve customer reorders by sending reorder notices and discount coupons.
- Narrow online products to 5 vendor lines so that discounts can be negotiated.

action plans

- Research/compile list of local companies with promotional budgets of $20K. Jan. 2009
- Send reorder notices with coupon by January, 31, 2009.
- Work with designer to polish printed materials and Web site. April 2010
- Activate Google AdWords advertising campaign and run test ads side by side. July 2009
- Track calls to prospects/customers. Goal 20 per day/salesperson. Start today.
- Implement Constant Contact Quarterly Blasts by September 30, 2010.
- Begin quarterly catalog/flyer mailings. Sept. 2009
- Reward customer loyalty with high-quality year-end gift. Dec. '09

Figure 13.7: Karen Horrigan's One Page Business Plan for Galaxy Group.

sion statement. Are you moved? Are you confused? Or are you smiling?

Most plans take five or six initial drafts—and then they need to be adapted as you develop your business. The plan is an evolving document that will be changed regularly so that you have a clear, updated map for your business. Last night I revisited my own One Page Business

Plan and felt a sense of excitement as I reviewed the things I had already accomplished. That prompted me to add new items, as this is a fluid, ongoing process.

DISCERNING BETWEEN "PLANS"

The most important type of plan—especially at this stage—is the type we've covered here in this chapter, which is intended to inject order, focus, and direction into your course of action.

Eventually, if you'll be presenting a "plan" to investors, you'll need to gather additional information and components. The "plan" used for these presentations is not so much a "plan" as it is a "story" about your plan, with words and numbers to support it, as opposed to the daily working document that is your One Page Business Plan.

GET INPUT FROM OTHERS

As you develop your plan and build your business, make it a point to get feedback from others. I've seen in our workshops that collective feedback will provide the impetus to help you move forward more rapidly. Even if you get one tiny kernel of an idea from someone you share your plan with, it's a victory—your business may have gone down an entirely different path without it. Sometimes it can be hard to hear feedback, especially if you've been mulling over your business idea by yourself for a while and your mind is set on your plans. However, it's important to realize that a fresh perspective can be absolutely invaluable, saving you from going down a wasteful path.

This chapter has all the guidance you need to create your operational business plan in earnest; it's sure to help you stay the course as your business grows and thrives! Because a concise business plan is such a critical element of your business success—one that requires initial energy and ongoing focus—we will be offering additional tools and courses in the future. Please visit and register at our Web site (www.your milliondollardream.com/bizplans) for new information and updates.

Conclusion

What a journey! In Part 1, we went through the process of identifying different business approaches and offered examples to help you choose the "right" fit for you. From there, you had the opportunity to make a commitment to your dream, get a handle on your personal finances, and identify the most likely options to fund your business. In Part 2, we went through the process of creating a brand with value, making sales, and then got started with leveraging the Internet to market your message to the masses. We then learned how to use social networks to pollinate thousands of flowering business relationships as does the brilliant and elegant hummingbird. In Part 3, you had a chance to think about creating an efficient business with meaningful awareness and purpose. And, in the last chapter, it all came together by taking everything that you learned and turning it into your own powerful plan of action.

You have seen evidence in the stories and experiences of other regular people from all walks of life, both in this book and in the business and popular media, that it is possible to realize your million dollar dream and make money *your* way. It has been my goal to provide you with the opportunity to make the life changes you desire by revealing the immense opportunities, choices, and tools available to each of us who wish to live our financial lives on our terms—terms that can include creativity, flexibility, control, and financial security.

I would like to leave you with a few last thoughts.

- First, this is a process that takes time.
- Second, it takes work. I did not create the tools in this book, but I know their power. If you reread, take notes, test out, and commit yourself to use the tools in this book and keep on learning, you will not fail.

- Third, entrepreneurs need the support of other entrepreneurs. There is a point where you will find that people who are not entrepreneurs will simply not be able to relate to some of the struggles you will face. So find a network that provides you with such support.
- Finally, every path takes unexpected turns, and they don't always lead straight to the pot of gold at the end of the rainbow. However, as long as you make the commitment every day that "today" is the first day of your someday life, you will find immense abundance in every respect.

More than any other book of mine, this project has been very personal. Perhaps it has to do with the economic challenges of our time, or perhaps it is because of the mindset I had going into this book. For it has been my sincere intention to help as many people as I can by sharing both what I know and what I have been able to find out and explain. If you have reached this sentence, there is a chance I have had an impact. In this respect, we share the experience of each having been through this material, although at different times. I invite you to join me directly by becoming a part of my online community at www.yourmilliondollardream.com.

I wish you much success as you forge your own path, and I leave you with these words from Earl Nightingale: "We can let circumstances rule us, or we can take charge and rule our lives from within."

Appendix

Money-Related Business Terms You Need to Know— Even If You'd Rather Pull Your Hair Out!

As your business begins to grow, whether you like it or not, at some point you may be speaking to banks and investors. Perhaps you're saying to yourself right now that you don't need to read this section because you're starting a fitness camp, doggy day care, or educational consulting business, and you won't need a bank loan or investors. Well, even if you are starting a business from your kitchen table, there are certain business terms you'll need to eventually understand, concepts like revenue projections, cost of goods sold (COGS), gross margins (GMs), and profit margins. Frankly, I wish I had known and understood these terms earlier and that they had been explained to me in a way that made sense.

Recently, I unexpectedly had to give an investor presentation in front of a live audience that was also broadcast live via Web telecast, with a panel of investors asking me questions. If you had told me when I first started my business from my daughter's bedroom that I would be broadcasting investor presentations one day, I would have laughed out loud. In fact, I would have emphatically told you that it wouldn't be possible because I don't "get" the numbers side of the business. My advice to you is to buckle down if you feel the impulse to throw this book across the room! If you are not inclined to understand "the numbers," it might help to think of it as a story where your "words" are just "numbers." I will explain the most important concepts here and detail how margins and markups work in practical terms.

DEFINITIONS

Cost of Goods Sold (COGS)—direct costs attributable to the production of the goods sold by a company. This amount includes the cost of the materials used in creating the good along with the direct labor costs used to produce the good. It excludes indirect expenses such as distribution costs and sales force costs. COGS appears on the income statement and can be deducted from revenue to calculate a company's gross margin.

Gross Margin (GM)—a company's total sales revenue minus its cost of goods sold, divided by the total sales revenue, expressed as a percentage. The gross margin represents the percent of total sales revenue that the company retains after incurring the direct costs associated with producing the goods and services sold by a company. The higher the percentage, the more the company retains on each dollar of sales to service its other costs and obligations.

Profit Margin—a ratio of profitability calculated as net income divided by revenues, or net profits divided by sales. It measures how much out of every dollar of sales a company actually keeps in earnings.

Profit margin is very useful when comparing companies in similar industries. A higher profit margin indicates a more profitable company that has better control over its costs compared to its competitors. Profit margin is displayed as a percentage; a 20 percent profit margin, for example, means the company has a net income of $0.20 for each dollar of sales. It is also known as the "net profit margin."

Source: Investopedia.com.

REVENUE PROJECTIONS

Revenue projections tell a story about where your company is headed financially in the future. Once you do a 12-month budget (see Chapter 3), that data will create a baseline of information (or the company's history) that will allow you to project growth into the future. The Web site Investopedia (www.investopedia.com) offers these guidelines:

> A good basis for the current year's revenue projection is the immediate historic trend . . . If a company has been growing revenue at a 10% annual rate in the past few quarters[1] it might be a stretch to assume revenue can grow at a 20% annual rate in the current year unless some fundamental change in the business has occurred that will drive this faster growth . . . like the company recently launched a new product line . . .

MARGINS AND MARKUPS IN PRACTICAL TERMS

Many entrepreneurs get started because they want an outlet for their creativity or are seeking more freedom in their careers. Rarely do they approach entrepreneurship or inventing from a number-crunching background. It seems that many people just aren't that comfortable with "the numbers." However, if you create a viable product, you've got to sell it, and pricing and profit margins are a critical part of that process.

Whether you sell directly to end users or to a retailer or distributor who sells to customers, you need to know how to price your product to ensure everyone in the process will make their required profits. In fact, this holds true for any business, including pure service businesses. As you probably suspect, this involves a bit of art—and a lot of science.

Common sense dictates that the price you choose should be neither too high nor too low to attract the most customers and generate the greatest amount of profit. Your price also needs to cover the cost of

---

[1] The 12-month calendar year is divided into four quarters of three months each: Q1 = January, February, and March; Q2 = April, May, and June; Q3 = July, August, and September; and Q4 = October, November, and December.

doing business. This is where understanding the basics of "markups" and "gross margins" can help.

Before we get into these concepts, I'd like to define a few terms that people often confuse:

> **Retail direct sales:** Sales of a product or service to an end user (e.g., the price you'll pay for cookies at a grocery store).
>
> **Wholesale sales:** Sales by a manufacturer or distributor to a retailer (e.g., the price Nabisco charges grocery stores for its cookies).
>
> **Markup:** The difference (reflected as both dollars and percentage) between what a retailer will pay for a product and its retail price (what the end user will pay). For example, XYZ Cookie Company sells a bag of cookies to the grocery store for $2, and the grocery store charges customers $5. The markup is $3 per bag.
>
> **Gross margin:** The percentage of profit derived from a transaction. (Both the manufacturer and the retailer will calculate their own gross margins.)

HOW MARKUPS WORK

The best way to illustrate the concept of markups is with a simple example. Assume you, the manufacturer, make a product we'll call Gizmo for $1. You then sell it wholesale to a retail store for $3. Thus, your markup is $2 ($3 − $1 = $2), or 200 percent. (Remember, percentages are determined by moving the decimal point two spaces to the right and adding the percentage sign, hence 2/1 = 2.00 = 200 percent). If the retail store then sells Gizmo for $8, its markup is $5 ($8 − $3 = $5) or 166 percent (5/3 = 1.66).

FIGURING OUT YOUR GROSS MARGIN

Now that you know your markup, you can figure out your gross margin. (These two terms are often mistakenly used as though they're synonyms. They are related, but they're not the same.) This number is calculated by dividing the markup by the price to acquire it.

Using the above example, we'll first figure out your gross margin as the manufacturer. Divide your markup ($2) by the price the retailer paid for Gizmo ($3). Thus, your gross margin as the manufacturer is 67 percent (2/3 = .67). So in this case, a 200 percent markup resulted in a gross margin of 67 percent.

You should also figure out your retailer's gross margin. (I'll explain why this is important in the next section.) Calculate it the same way, only using the retailer's markup ($5) and price ($8): 5/8 = .625, or 62.5 percent. Thus, the retailer's 166 percent markup resulted in a 62.5 percent gross margin.

RETAILER MARKUP AND GROSS MARGIN

So why is it important to know your retailer's gross margin? Well, retailers often have minimum margin requirements, so this will help determine what price you'll set. Although minimum requirements will vary widely depending on the type of retailer, it's not uncommon for a retailer to expect a minimum gross margin of 50 percent. This is often referred to as a "keystone" markup.

An easy way to figure out this number is to double your wholesale price. For example, if you sell your product wholesale to the retailer for $5, the retailer will need to charge the consumer $10 to achieve a keystone markup. When you need to work backward to figure out a price that gives your retailer the desired margin, it's helpful to use the 50 percent "keystone" expectation as a starting point.

Another good thing to know is that high-end specialty retailers will often require an even higher gross margin. So don't be shy about asking your retailers what their margin requirements are—it's how retailers think. Most of the more experienced buyers you'll deal with will offer either a specific number or at least a pretty narrow range.

Now that this is clear, or at least a bit less murky, I'll throw in a new wrinkle: distributors.

DISTRIBUTOR GROSS MARGIN

Distributors are companies that typically buy products (and warehouse inventory) from manufacturers and sell to retailers. They're commonly used by larger retailers that handle a large volume of products, such as grocery stores.

Distributor margin requirements vary by product price point, industry, segment, country, and size, but they're typically lower than retailers—20 to 40 percent is not uncommon. That's because, as the middleman, there are two markups required, the distributor's and the retailer's.

For example, the margins and markups for a product sold through a distributor might look something like this (assuming a 50 percent gross margin for the retailer and a 30 percent gross margin for the distributor):

$10 retail price—sold by retailer to consumer (retailer GM = 50 percent)

$5 wholesale price—sold by distributor to retailer (distributor GM = 30 percent)

$3.50 distribution price—sold by you to distributor (manufacturer GM = 43 percent)

$2—your cost to produce product

HOW MUCH IS ENOUGH GROSS MARGIN?

There is no one "magic" gross margin to strive for—they vary dramatically by industry and product type. Even within a single industry, they fluctuate. A large, mass-oriented manufacturer may be satisfied with 20 to 30 percent or less. At a massive sales volume, they can be profitable at this rate. However, many smaller businesses strive for a 50 to 70 percent gross margin. Here are some strategies to figure out where yours should fall.

On the high end, your gross margin should be as much as you can get. The factors influencing this are your own production costs, your retailer's margin expectations, and the market price at which your product will sell (this last number is the most important). So if your production cost is extremely low and your product is in such demand that you can sell it for a 1,000 percent gross margin, go for it!

What about the low end? When is your gross margin too low to sustain the cost of doing business? The answer lies in your goals and expenses. Remember that all your company costs, including salaries, rent, marketing, and other operating costs, must be covered by the gross margin earned on your sales. There's a term for this, too—"net profit margin," or the percentage of money left after paying for all these expenses plus production costs. So what's a decent net profit margin?

Let's use the following as an example: Assume you can make an 8 to 10 percent return in the stocks and bonds market without much risk or effort. You may conclude that you need to outperform this return on any output of capital (i.e., investment in your business). In other words, if you can make 8 percent relatively easily in stocks, you'll definitely want to make a higher net margin on a business venture in which you're putting so much more time, effort, and risk.

Back to gross margin. You'll know it's too low if you find you're unable to meet the costs you regularly incur to operate your business. In this case, you have two options: find a way to lower your production and operating costs, or raise your price.

A final factor to keep in mind: your gross margin may grow over time. In the early stages, manufacturing runs are often smaller, thus more expensive per unit. Plus, you need to create demand for your product, so you don't want to set your price too high. Therefore, you may need to forgo large profits in the beginning to get a sense of your market and create sales traction. Then, once your demand begins to grow, your production costs will decrease and your gross margin will grow.

Want to calculate your profit margin? Try using the free online margin calculator shown in Figure A.1.

Figure A.1: Free online margin calculator.
Source: Free Online Calculator (freeonlinecalculator.net).

Additional Online Resources

CHAPTER 3

Other personal financial management and community sites to check out are:

www.mymoney.gov   www.wesabe.com

www.gezeo.com

CHAPTER 4

Information on the Los Angeles Jewish Free Loan Association (JFLA) business loans can be found at www.jfla.org/loans/lp-smallbusiness.php.

For more factoring choices, visit www.business.com/directory.

CHAPTER 5

Other great places to join group discussions are:

www.makemineamillion.org   www.startupnation.com

www.workitmom.com   www.ladieswholaunch.com

Here are a few recognition opportunities:

www.athenafoundation.org

www.entrepreneur.com (Entrepreneur of the Year)

www.eileenfisher.com/ourcompany/cons/women_owned_bus_prog
.asp

www.entrepreneur.com/womanoftheyear

www.stevieawards.com/women

nawbo.org/section_28.cfm (Trailblazers Awards in conjunction
with Wells Fargo Bank)

As mentioned earlier, StartupNation is not only packed with resources and forums but often runs contests as well.

Other award opportunities include:

- Industry awards and honors relating to your particular product or industry, such as Dr. Toy (www.drtoy.com/main/index.html)
- Ernst and Young Entrepreneur of the Year (www.ey.com/us/eoy)
- Minority business awards such as www.gaminoritybusiness awards.com, www.marketplace.wi.gov/minority-business-awards .html, and www.nmbc.org/home.html

There is an abundance of free press release distribution services. The public relations blog Naked PR (nakedpr.com/2007/07/29/big-list-of-free-press-release-distribution-sites) provides this list:

1888PressRelease.com	24-7pressrelease.com
AddPR.com	BizEurope.com
eCommWire.com	Express-Press-Release.com
Free-News-Release.com	Free-Press-Release.com
Free-Press-Release-Center.info	FreePressIndex.com
FreePressRelease.co.cc	FreePressReleases.co.uk
i-Newswire.com	IndiaPRWire.com
MediaSyndicate.com	MyFreePR.com
NewswireToday.com	PageRelease.com
PR.com	PR9.net
PR-Inside.com	PRCompass.com
PRlog.com	PRurgent.com
PRzoom.com	PressAbout.com
PressBox.co.uk	PressFlow.co.uk
PressMethod.com	PressRelease.com
PressReleasePoint.com	TechPRSpider.com
TheOpenPress.com	

Naked PR also suggests sending releases to the Associated Press (www.associatedpress.com), but be sure to find the appropriate editor first!

CHAPTER 6
A few resources to investigate for sales leads include:

www.referenceusa.com	www.csig.com
www.salesmansguide.com	www.infomat.com
www.hoovers.com	www.zoominfo.com

CHAPTER 7
Here are some more examples of e-commerce:

www.froogle.com	www.etsy.com
www.shopit.com	www.theknot.com
www.zazzle.com	www.cafepress.com

CHAPTER 8
Other resources to know about for earning affiliate commissions are:

www.clickbank.com	www.e-junkie.com
www.paydotcom.com	

If you sell e-books or software, these Web sites match you with affiliates to help sell your digital download products.

CHAPTER 10
Here are some links to find the most popular Twitterers:

twitterholic.com	twitterank.com
twitter.grader.com	shortyawards.com

CHAPTER 12

Here are some resources for green business:

www.greenbiz.com   www.sustainlane.com
www.lamprecycle.org   www.earth911.org
www.greendisk.com   www.greenofficesupply.com
www.thegreenoffice.com   www.ecopreneuring.biz

Here are some more legal resources for intellectual property needs:

www.uspto.gov   www.westpatentlaw.com
www.simplepatents.com (for patent searches)

For legal documents, www.docstoc.com is an incredible resource to find documents of almost any kind.

Virtual receptionist services are available at:

www.callruby.com   www.avirtualreceptionist.com

Electronic virtual receptionists include:

www.angel.com   www.onebox.com
www.ringcentral.com

If you're looking for an "executive suite," try the following:

www.intelligentoffice.com   www.abcn.com
www.regus.com/officesolutions   www.esuite.com
www.offices.org   www.pbcenters.com

There are many business card and logo design service options, such as:

www.printresponsibly.com (which offers green business cards)
www.vistaprint.com   www.overnightprints.com
www.123print.com

The following are a number of IT-related resources.
Free or inexpensive software bundles are available at:

www.openoffice.org   www.google.com/apps

For information and technology reviews, visit:

www.pcworld.com www.cnet.com

Inexpensive or used equipment can be found at:

www.ebay.com www.craigslist.com

Popular computer brands include:

www.dell.com www.hp.com
www.ibm.com www.sony.com
www.toshiba.com www.frys.com
www.apple.com

Additional information and providers can be found at www.online-backupreviews.com.

New online services for small businesses that provide simple book-keeping tools for free are:

www.freshbooks.com www.outright.com

Companies that provide payroll services are:

www.perquest.com www.smallbusinessadp.com
www.paychecks.com www.surepayroll.com

If you need payroll or accounting services immediately, try a temporary staffing firm, such as www.westaff.com or www.accountemps.com.

A qualified online broker is www.ehealthinsurance.com.

Additional HR information can be found by searching "human resources" at www.inc.com, www.entrepreneur.com, and www.allbusiness.com.

Here are some more helpful tools:

- For collaborative project management, see www.basecamphq.com, www.goplanapp.com, and www.liquidplanner.com.
- For enhancing productivity, see Google Documents (www.google.com/apps) and Zoho (www.zoho.com).
- For storing documents remotely for collaboration (and updating), see www.getdropbox.com.

These platforms provide a place where anyone can post documents and collaborate with others. They have free templates and numerous features that support collaboration among people in different locations. Such platforms also address storage issues and eliminate backup concerns.

Index

ABOUT THE AUTHOR

Tamara Monosoff is the author of the bestselling books *The Mom Inventors Handbook*, *Secrets of Millionaire Moms*, and coauthor of *The One Page Business Plan for Women in Business*. She has appeared on *Today*, *Good Morning America*, *NBC Nightly News*, *The View*, CNN, and the front page of the *Wall Street Journal* and is a columnist for Entrepreneur.com. Monosoff lives in the San Francisco Bay Area.

Visit www.YourMillionDollarDream.com and www.mominventors.com.